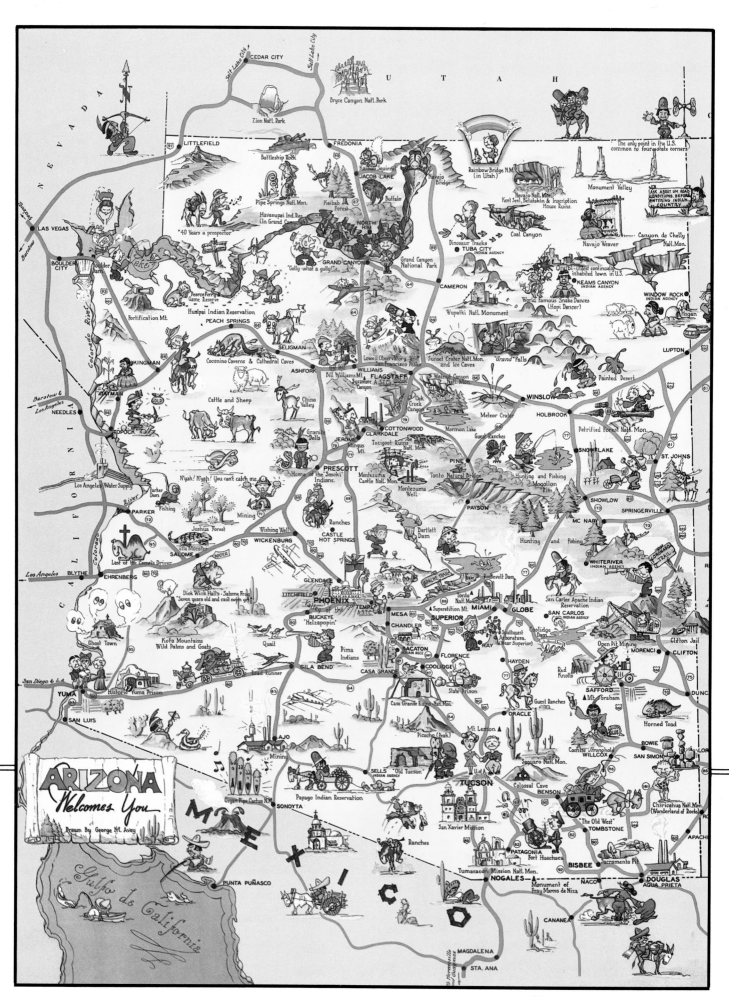

Map from Arizona Highways, *1940*

Diamond
in the Rough
An Illustrated
History of Arizona

by Marshall Trimble

♦

design by
Patrick S. Smith

THE
DONNING COMPANY
PUBLISHERS
NORFOLK/VIRGINIA BEACH

A prickly pear cactus bloom hosts a visiting honey bee. Photo by Gary M. Johnson

The Donning Company/Publishers
5659 Virginia Beach Boulevard
Norfolk, Virginia 23502

Edited by Diana L. Bailey and Richard A. Horwege

Library of Congress Cataloging-in-Publication Data

Trimble, Marshall.
  Diamond in the rough.

  Includes index.
  1. Arizona—History. I. Title.
F811.T745   1988   979.1   87-36412
ISBN 0-89865-585-4

Printed in the United States of America

*To My
Beautiful Wife Gena—
the Wind in My Sails.*

Table of Contents

The Grand Canyon. Photo by
Gary M. Johnson

*This view of the Verde River as it winds
through the Mazatzal Wilderness is representative of the Sonoran Desert.* Photo
by Gary M. Johnson

"King" cotton thrives in Arizona's climate.
Photo by Gary M. Johnson

An eagle watches the sun set near Mormon Lake. Photo by Gary M. Johnson

Acknowledgments

◆

A special *muchas gracias* to Joan Metzger of the Arizona Heritage Center for the countless hours spent researching and gathering photographs and photographer Gary Johnson, who provided much of the color photography for this book, along with chasing all over the state taking pictures to satisfy my whimsical notions. Last but not least, Shirley Shoemaker, a very dear friend and long-time word processor with the patience of Job. ◆

Horses graze at dawn in a lush Arizona pasture. Photo by Gary M. Johnson

This springtime photo depicts the San Francisco Peaks, the state's highest point, near Flagstaff in northern Arizona. Photo by Gary M. Johnson

The sun sets at Tovrea Castle. This "house in the design of a wedding cake" was the home of cattle baron Ed Tovrea. South of the "castle" were Tovrea's feed lots where some fifty thousand cattle were fattened up for market in what was one of the world's largest feed lot operations. Photo by Gary M. Johnson

The high country near Flagstaff lies in a blanket of snow after a blizzard. Photo by Gary M. Johnson

A rustic barn speaks of another time in Pleasant Valley near Young, Arizona. Photo by Gary M. Johnson

Sheep's Crossing in the White Mountains on the west fork of the Little Colorado River. During the summer months sheep are moved into the high country for grazing purposes. The

8

The Little Colorado Gorge near Cameron.
Photo by Gary M. Johnson

Introduction

◆

I've always had a great appreciation for old photographs. Why waste thousands of words describing the way things used to be when a few photographs can say it all. A photograph is instantaneous. All other forms of description must evolve over time. A photograph has the unique ability to freeze the moment. Thus, we can grasp the complex relationships of that instant. All other descriptions must, by their very nature, be serialized. Human perception simply is not as quick nor as complete as the camera's ability to record. In addition, a photograph has a sense of validity that no other graphic form possesses.

Photography gives fresh new perspective on a variety of traditional western subject matter, providing us with a visual documentary that's both historic and visionary. Through it we are transported into the continuum of history that carries us back to yesterday.

Let us return now, to those halcyon days when the pace of life was slower and just getting from one place to another was half the fun. ◆

Marshall Trimble

journey from the Salt River Valley to the White Mountains took about three months. This is one of the old established sheep trails in the region. Photo by the author

The mittens in Monument Valley. Photo by the author

9

Chapter 1

Diamond in the Rough

In the fall of 1736, a Yaqui miner named Antonio Siraumea, discovered a rich outcropping of native silver near the tiny Papago village of *Arissona*. Large chunks of native silver, "soft as wax," were uncovered. Some of these large balls and slabs weighed hundreds of pounds each. "A miracle," someone said, "placed here by the Almighty so that Spaniards might come to this place to settle," as if to offer justification for the seizure of Indian lands.

News of the fabulous strike spread like wildfire, bringing a stampede of Spanish prospectors to the area. Spanish law decreed that if a "miracle" had, in fact, occurred, His Royal Highness, God's partner in these matters, received a whopping 95 percent. On the other hand, if it was just another mortal mineral discovery, the king collected his customary *quinto* or 20 percent. Naturally, the decision was made by the king—and he naturally determined that a miracle had indeed taken place. The original discoverer, Siraumea, received a bonus of thirty-six pesos for his efforts. Not surprisingly, the industrious miners made off with most of the silver, some ten thousand pounds, before the royal exchequers arrived. Out of these events rose the legend of the Miracle of the *Planchas de Plata* (sheets of silver) and the fame of little *Arissona* spread far and wide.

Arissona was located about twenty-five miles southwest of present-day Nogales. The name was a Spanish corruption of the Papago word *ali-shonak*, meaning "place of small springs." Much like their American counterparts more than a century later, a boisterous boom town sprang up near the site and for a brief time attracted *gambusinos* (miners) from all over New Spain. But like most of these rollickin' places, when the silver ran out so did the miners, and *Arissona* soon returned to ob-scurity. This land that would someday be called Arizona had a name, in fact several names. During Spanish times New Mexico claimed the lands west of Santa Fe all the way to California. The *terra incognita* that reached as far north as the Gila river was called *Pimeria Alta* or "land of the upper Pima." North of the Gila was a dangerous, forbidding place where few white men dared venture. It was called *Apacheria*.

During the 1850s, when the American occupation began, this *despoblado* (wilderness) was a remote western part of the New Mexico territory, still pretty much unmapped and unsettled. Early on, the new residents clamored for separate status from New Mexico and sought a name that would give a separate identity. *Pimeria Alta,* and *Apacheria* didn't roll off the Anglo tongues easily. Neither did *Arissona* for that matter. During the early 1860s, Charles Poston, a mining entrepreneur, was using the name *Arizona,* a corruption of *Arissona.* In 1863 the new territory was admitted into the Union and officially named Arizona.

The fabulous lodes of gold and silver in the 1860s focused national attention on the new territory; however, ol' Ma Nature had designed this land with a rough hand, holding back settlement except by the most hardy pioneer men and women. The arrival of the railroads in the 1880s was man's most dramatic nineteenth-century achievement. Still, the elements—incessant wind, long droughts and searing heat, not to mention intractable Apaches, gunslingers and an immoral majority of un-churched, unmarried, and unwashed citizens—gave Arizona a notorious reputation that spread far and wide. Eastern journalists and writers of pulp westerns fed wide-eyed readers a steady diet of wild-and-wooly Arizona, contributing to its reputation as a forbidding place inhabited by rattlesnakes, scorpions, cactus,

This painting, by Bill Ahrendt, illustrates Cardenas Finding the Grand Canyon. *Garcia Lopez de Cardenas, an officer in Coronado's Expedition, 1540-42, was sent to investigate a great river beyond the Hopi villages. The Spaniards had hoped to discover and claim the mythical Strait of Anian or Northwest Passage, an east-west waterway across North America. The formidable cliffs of the Grand Canyon kept the* conquistadores *from reaching their objective and this great chasm would remain a barrier to western travel for centuries.* Photo by Gary M. Johnson, courtesy of John Augustine

desperados and Apaches. Negative first impressions by visiting dignitaries added to its reputation as the devil's playground. When Gen. William Tecumseh Sherman paid a summertime visit in 1880, one of Phoenix's early-day promoters made the mistake of asking the straight-talking general what he thought of the place. "Too damn hot and dry," Sherman declared. "All she needs," the promoter said soothingly, "is less heat, more water and a few good citizens." "Huh," Sherman replied gruffly, "that's all hell needs."

The old general's unsavory remarks about Arizona were far less devastating than his infamous swath across Georgia but they smarted nonetheless. When Geronimo and a few of his warriors were using Arizona's treacherous and hostile terrain to their advantage, eluding frustrated thousands of army troops, Sherman bellowed, "We went to war once with Mexico to get Arizona, now I think we ought to go to war again and make her take it back."

Kit Carson, that legendary mountain man who lived in and loved the outdoors, once testified before Congress that Arizona was so poor that a wolf would starve to death. Few people had reason to seriously doubt the satirical words of Mark Twain when he said, "the temperature remains at a constant 120 degrees in the shade—except when it varies and goes higher."

During the tumultuous second half of the nineteenth century, Arizona's magnetic lure attracted people from the wide gamut of frontier society. In 1862, Mike Goldwater opened a mercantile store in the gold-rush town of La Paz. By the turn of the century, Goldwater's was one of the Southwest's largest department store chains.

Joe Walker, a tireless explorer, climaxed a brilliant career in the "Winning of the West" when he found gold in the Bradshaw Mountains in 1863 where Prescott would be founded. Good-hearted Nellie Cashman immigrated from Ireland and came to Tombstone hoping to find the rainbow's end, finding instead legendary fame as the "Miner's Angel." Wyatt Earp, another restless adventurer, gained immortality as a notorious gunfighter as a result of a gunfight at the O.K. Corral in Tombstone. The entrepreneurial young Babbitt brothers arrived in pristine Flagstaff in 1886 with a few thousand hard-saved dollars and created a dynasty the likes of which will never be seen again in the high plateau country.

Henry Clay Day pioneered a cattle ranch along the Arizona-New Mexico line in the 1880s. He instilled in his family those frontier virtues: hard work, honest determination and self-reliance. One of his granddaughters, Sandra Day O'Connor, dreamed of growing up to be a cowgirl, but destiny had a more important role for her: the first woman to sit on the U.S. Supreme Court.

George W. P. Hunt rode in to Globe penniless on the hurricane deck of a jackass. A few years later he was mayor and president of a bank. In 1912 Hunt became Arizona's first governor. Not all displayed those honored virtues of frontier society: James Addison Reavis, a former St. Louis streetcar conductor with a talent for duplicity, forged documents that gave him a claim to some twelve million acres of prime Arizona real estate and earned him everlasting fame as the "Baron of Arizona." All, for better or worse, saw Arizona as a land of opportunity.

The colorful litany of picturesquely whimsical names is a reflection of the character of the early arrivals. A card game inspired the name of Showlow. When two ranchers decided the ranges were too crowded, they played cards to see who would move. Low card was the winner. "If you can show low, you win," said one. "Show low it is," replied the other as he drew the deuce of clubs, and Showlow it was. Showlow's main street, incidentally, is called Deuce of Clubs. When the entire populace in a Mogollon Rim settlement got lice, they just naturally decided to name the place Lousy Gulch. A treacherous-looking

outcropping of rock hovering above a southern Arizona mining camp compelled the locals to proudly proclaim the name of their town, Total Wreck. When folks started a community in a forlorn area in the desert east of Ajo, travelers kept asking, "Why would you want to live here?" Residents shortened it to Why.

One day back in 1876, Charlie McMillen went on a wild binge in Globe. His partner, Dorey Harris, didn't indulge, so the next day he gathered up Charlie and loaded him on his trusty mule and they rode out prospecting. They hadn't traveled far when Charlie climbed down, claiming he was too hungover to go any farther. So, while Charlie slumbered, Dorey took his pick and started hacking away at a nearby outcropping. Sure enough, he uncovered a rich vein of silver. Overnight a boom town materialized which was called, appropriately enough, McMillenville, and before the mine played out, over a million dollars worth of silver was taken out. Charlie McMillen became known as the "man with the million dollar hangover." And there are more—Skull Valley, Wikieup, Dos Cabezas, Bullhead City, Sombrero Butte, Bumble Bee, Tombstone and Gunsight, to name a few. Each has a story to tell.

Arizona's people constitute a definite plural society. For hundreds of years the Navajo have occupied the steep-sided canyons, sandstone buttes and pillars that rise above the high desert plain in the vast Four Corners country. Nearby, the ancient Hopi cluster in their villages which cling precariously to the wind-swept mesas. They claim ancestry to the cliff-dwelling

The Wupatki ruins lie between Flagstaff and the Painted Desert. Photo by Gary M. Johnson

Anasazi, a prehistoric culture that dates back some two thousand years. The rugged mountains of east-central Arizona are the ancestral home of the Apaches. These determined peoples fought a long and successful war with the Spanish and Mexicans before the last elements surrendered to the U.S. Army just a century ago.

The Havasupai have the distinction of being the only native peoples living in the Grand Canyon. The only way in to their remote village, except by helicopter, is on foot or horseback. The river valleys are still home to the Quechan, Mojave, and Pima peoples, while the Tohono O'Odham (Papago) reside in the arid desert country near the Mexican border. Blessed with land others considered undesirable, they are perhaps the least influenced by the dramatic changes in Arizona during the twentieth century.

Arizona's Indians, more than any other, have been able to maintain close ties to their cultural heritage. The further removed from urban areas, the easier it has been. Tribes like the Hopi, Navajo, Apache and Papago have had better luck than, for example, the Pima, whose reservations butt up against Interstate 10 and the greater Phoenix area. Many of these reservations are located amidst incredible scenic beauty, atop valuable natural resources, or have vast claims to the state's most precious commodity—water. Others occupy real estate worth millions of dollars. A perplexing problem facing tribal leaders today is finding proper solutions that would allow their people to partake of the advantages and amenities non-Indians enjoy without sacrificing their rich cultural heritage in the process.

Another important minority from a historical perspective, the Hispanic peoples, have problems of a different nature. Although some trade their ancestry back to early to mid-nineteenth century, most arrived from Mexico in this century. Large numbers emigrated to the mining towns during the copper boom of World War I. A large number of these still retain close cultural ties with Mexico. Unlike other emigrants who left Europe and settled in America, Hispanics have no oceans or other barriers keeping them from visiting their homeland. Thus, many keep their language and, like the Indian, steadfastly refuse to become part of a melting pot.

Arizona's people are better described as a mulligan stew. Rather than a melting pot, and that is how it should be, for this is a definite region, with its own distinctive peculiarities much the same as Deep South, Appalachia or New England.

Arizona's land, like its people, is one of startling contrasts. All climactic life zones, from dry-tropical to arctic-alpine are found within its borders. A twenty-minute drive from Tucson, up the Mount Lemmon highway, passes from Sonoran desert to Canadian-Alpine. It has been determined that a change of one thousand feet in elevation has the same effect on plant life as three hundred to five hundred miles in north-south latitude. Annual rainfall amounts vary from 3.4 inches at Yuma to nearly 25 inches at McNary in the White Mountains. It's not unusual for two Arizona communities to record the nation's high and low temperatures on the same day.

Geographers have divided the state into three main physical areas: the high plateau, mountain, and desert. The plateau is the most scenic, characterized by the spectacular sandstone spires and buttes of Monument Valley; the Petrified Forest; the many-hued sands of the Painted Desert; the lofty tall timbers in the Kaibab National Forest; the lovely reaches of the Strip; the state's highest mountains, the San Francisco Peaks; and nature's grandest architectural masterpiece, the Grand Canyon.

The mountain zone makes a hefty diagonal slash across the center of the state and includes some thirty different mountain ranges. Most of these are twenty-five to seventy-five miles long and five to fifteen miles wide. They usually range from 4,000 to 6,000 feet in elevation. Some go much higher. Mount Graham, in the Pinalenos, is the tallest, topping out at 10,713 feet. The Chricahuas, Santa Ritas, Santa Catalinas and Virgin Mountains all have peaks ranging over eight thousand feet. Several peaks in the Bradshaw Mountains, north of Phoenix, are in excess of 7,000 feet. The drainage in these mountains is southwesterly flowing into the Salt, Gila and Colorado river watersheds.

The desert zone includes part of the Sonoran, the world's most prolific when it comes to flora and fauna. The mountains usually range no higher than four thousand feet and are separated by broad, flat valleys that do not exceed two thousand feet elevation. Irrigation has transformed some of these valleys into some of the world's most productive farmlands.

Arizona's nearly 114,000 square miles of land ranks it as the nation's sixth largest. The population, about 3.5 million, places it twenty-sixth largest. About 85 percent of the people live in either Tucson or the greater Phoenix area. Flagstaff, Yuma, Prescott, Kingman, and Sierra Vista claim most of the rest. Dozens of other communities dot the state but the majority are settled in the above-mentioned areas, leaving vast reaches of wide open spaces that belong to everybody and nobody.

Arizona is the only state in the Union that claims large numbers of settlers from all four directions. Back in 1629, the Franciscans from Santa Fe founded missions among the ancient Hopi Indians. In 1692, the Jesuit padre, Eusebio Kino, came in from Sonora and established missions along the Santa Cruz river. Later Spanish settlers built adobe communities at Tubac and Tucson. In the 1860s, the lure of riches brought a backwash of devil-may-care jackass prospectors from the gold fields of California. At the same time emigrants from the "States" began a migration that continues to this day. During the 1870s, Mormons from Utah "took up their mission" and established colonies in the wilderness of Arizona. During World War I, a manpower shortage in the mines attracted Mexicans who came north in search of work. And the years following World War II, coupled with the advent of that wondrous wonder of wonders, air conditioning, brought about the greatest mass migration of greenhorns since the children of Israel set out in search of Canaan.

In 1864, a year after Arizona became a separate territory, a census declared some forty-five hundred non-Indian residents, more than a third of them living in Tucson. When statehood arrived in 1912, more than two hundred thousand called Arizona home. In 1987, on Arizona's seventy-fifth birthday, the state claims more than 3.5 million residents and still counting.

A journey across Arizona by wagon a century ago might take weeks, and every day could seem like a lifetime. Roads were nothing more than cattle trails and the forbidding heat of the southern desert or the bone-chilling cold on the northern plateau left dog-tired travelers with memories they'd not soon forget. "The trails were not only impassable," one traveler noted, "they weren't even jackassable." Today, sleek automobiles cruise along Interstates 40, 10, 17 and 8, crossing these once forbidden barriers in a few short hours.

Arizona's history is marked by five milestones, all of which played a major part in the state's unprecedented growth and prosperity. The first was the vast mineral riches—gold, silver and copper. From the day that first prospector's pick turned over pay dirt during the 1860s to the present, mining is still an integral part of the state's economy. The second was the arrival of the railroads in the 1880s. The steel rails opened up the heart of Arizona for commerce and transportation. Earlier the main link with the outside world was by steamboat. Freight, ore and travelers arrived by way of the Colorado River. From river ports like Yuma, Ehrenberg and Hardyville, goods and passengers were transported by wagon, afoot or on horseback to remote communities like Tucson and Prescott. By 1895 every major community was linked by rail. The third milestone was the completion of Roosevelt Dam in 1911. With the guarantee of a water supply from the 13,000-square-mile watershed above the Salt River Valley, the future growth and prosperity of the area was assured. The fourth was the advent of the evaporative cooler, followed a few years later by air conditioning. And finally, came World War II and the high technology that resulted from that war. During the early 1940s, thousands of soldiers trained under the clear Arizona skies and afterwards came back to live.

Industry saw advantages in relocating: a large labor supply, mild climate and an opportunity to grow with the state. More people came, citing the lifestyle. Tourism blossomed into a multi-billion dollar industry, second only to manufacturing in dollars and number one in jobs. Phoenix grew from a city of sixty thousand in 1940 to nearly a million in the mid-1980s. Sleepy little Scottsdale had some 400 residents at the outset of World War II. By 1987 its population had risen to some 120,000.

The population boom has created prosperity but the price has been high. Like most major metropolitan areas, Phoenix has serious transportation and air pollution problems. More subtle, however, is the threat to Arizona's unique history and culture. Since man first walked upon this earth, migrations by larger, more dominant groups have enveloped other cultures. And the danger of that happening in Arizona is real. Much of what was old Arizona has already been "plowed under."

Arizona Republic publisher Pat Murphy pretty well summed it up recently when he noted:

> One of the greatest weaknesses in a state such as Arizona, where the growing population increasingly is made up of people with roots elsewhere, is that it tends to be a gathering place for strangers with not much sense of tradition or historic perspective on their new home.

> Without those values, newcomers tend to lack the spirit to preserve, to protect and to perpetuate qualities that attracted them here in the first place. ♦

The bobcat or Lynx rufus *is the most common of the wild cat family found in Arizona.* Photo by Gary M. Johnson

The red-tailed hawk is a soaring bird of prey characterized by its heavy body with short, wide tail and broad wings. Photo by Gary M. Johnson

In recent years, the majestic but seldom seen desert bighorn sheep has been re-established in several rugged mountain ranges, including the North Rim of the Grand Canyon. Photo by Gary M. Johnson

The wild turkey is one of Arizona's ten major game species and is found mostly in the forest lands of the high country. Other members of the "big ten" are the pronghorn antelope, bear, whitetail deer, mule deer, javelina, mountain lion, elk, desert bighorn sheep, and bison. Photo by Gary M. Johnson

The western diamondback or Crotalus atrox, *is the most common of the sixteen species of rattlesnakes found in Arizona. This reptile is the most aggressive and accounts for more deaths in North America than any other rattlesnake.* Photo by the author

Javelina are found in the most rugged areas of central and southern Arizona. Adults usually weight about forty pounds and can be ferocious when cornered. Photo by Gary M. Johnson

15

The Window Rock at the capital city of the Navajo Nation. The American name is a translation of the Navajo word for a large natural rock window. Elected representatives from the sprawling Navajo reservation meet here as the Tribal Council. Window Rock is a new community, dating back to the mid-1930s. Photo by the author

Red Rock Crossing, Sedona. Photo by the author

The Clan Rocks in Moenave Wash. Traditionally various Hopi clans visit this sacred place and leave their clan symbols etched on the sandstone rocks. Nearby Mormon colonists passing through in the 1870s left their names carved in stone. Unfortunately modern day vandals have obliterated some of these markings. Photo by the author

White House ruins, Canyon de Chelly. The ruins, plastered with white clay, were called Casa Blanca *or "white house" by early travelers. In 1873 army surveyor Captain George M. Wheeler translated a Navajo word meaning "horizontal white streak in the middle of the house" to White House on his maps. Canyon de Chelly, pronounced "D'Shay" is a Navajo word meaning "among the cliffs." These cliff dwellings date back to about A.D. 1050.*

Montezuma's Well is a limestone-lined sink formed after the collapse of an underground cavern. both the well and the Sinagua Indian ruins nearby were mistakenly named after the Aztec ruler Montezuma by early settlers who thought the "castle" was of Aztec origin.
Photos by Gary M. Johnson

The Tuzigoot Ruins, as seen here from the top, are all that remains of a Sinaguan village built between 1125 and 1400. Tuzigoot is Apache for "crooked water." Photo by Gary M. Johnson

The San Xavier del Bac Mission is a landmark on the Papago Indian Reservation south of Tucson. Photo by Gary M. Johnson

The Tumacacori Mission was built near the old Spanish presidio of Tubac, between Tucson and Nogales. Photo by Gary M. Johnson

This painting by noted cowboy artist George Phippen depicts The Walker Party. *Joe Walker was a western explorer who found gold where Prescott would be established.* Photo by Gary M. Johnson courtesy of the Prescott Public Library

The Golden Reef Mine still stands north of Cave Creek. Photo by the author

The Vulture Mine near Wickenburg. Henry Wickenburg discovered gold here in 1863. Since there was no water, the ore was hauled to the Hassayampa River, eleven miles away, for reduction. The Vulture was nineteenth-century Arizona's greatest producing gold mine. Photo by Gary M. Johnson

Lee's Ferry at the entrance to the Grand Canyon. John D. Lee ran a ferry boat here until his execution by firing squad in 1877. Lee was tried and convicted for his part in the Mountain Meadows Massacre in Utah. He was accused of leading a party of Mormons and Paiute Indians in an attack on a wagon train in 1857. Lee hid from federal marshals in this remote country for twenty years. The ferry boat remained in operation until the 1920s when a bridge was constructed nearby. Photo by the author

Planchas de Plata. In 1736 a rich lode of native silver was found here. Described as "soft as wax" the discovery touched off a silver rush to the area. A nearby Papago Indian village named Ali-shonak *or "place of the small spring" provided the basis for the name Arizona. Ali-shonak was corrupted into* Arissona *by the Spanish, then altered once again to Arizona when the Anglo-Americans arrived in the 1850s.* Photo by the author

Tyin' Knots in the Devil's Tail, a painting by George Phippen. The story about the two drunken cowboys who tamed the devil is a classic old tale in Arizona. Back around the turn of the century two cowboys, Bob Heckle and Gail Gardner rode into Prescott and went on a wild binge on famed Whiskey Row. On the way back to their outfit, old Lucifer jumped out and tried to "gather in their souls." The irrepressible pair roped ol' devil, "cropped and swallar-forked his ears," and branded his hide. To add insult to the humiliation, they tied knots in his tail and tied him up to an oak tree. Years later, Gail wrote a cowboy poem called "Sierry Petes" or "Tyin' Knots in the Devil's Tail." The popularity of the poem inspired famed cowboy artist George Phippen to recreate the event on canvas. Photo by Bill Kiviat

Zane Grey, the famous western writer, painted a picture of the Old West that captured its beauty as well as its barren, harsh elements and fostered the stream of emigrants into the state that continues to this day. The cabin, pictured (at left) where he lived and worked still stands nestled under the Tonto or Mogollon Rim (below). It is also near the site of Mogollon Rim tunnel, a promotional scheme in the 1890s to build a railroad from Flagstaff to Globe. Promoters raised a bundle of money to bore a hole in the Mogollon Rim. The project fizzled after tunneling a few feet into the rim. Promoters took the money and left the area. Photo by Gary M. Johnson

These paintings, by Tombstone artist Marjorie Reed, depict the legendary Butterfield Overland Mail that operated in Arizona from 1858 to 1861. *(A)* Picacho Pass, *(B)* Arrival at Tucson, *(C)* Changing Horses and Coach at Gila Bend, *(D)* Colorado River Crossing. Photos by Gary M. Johnson

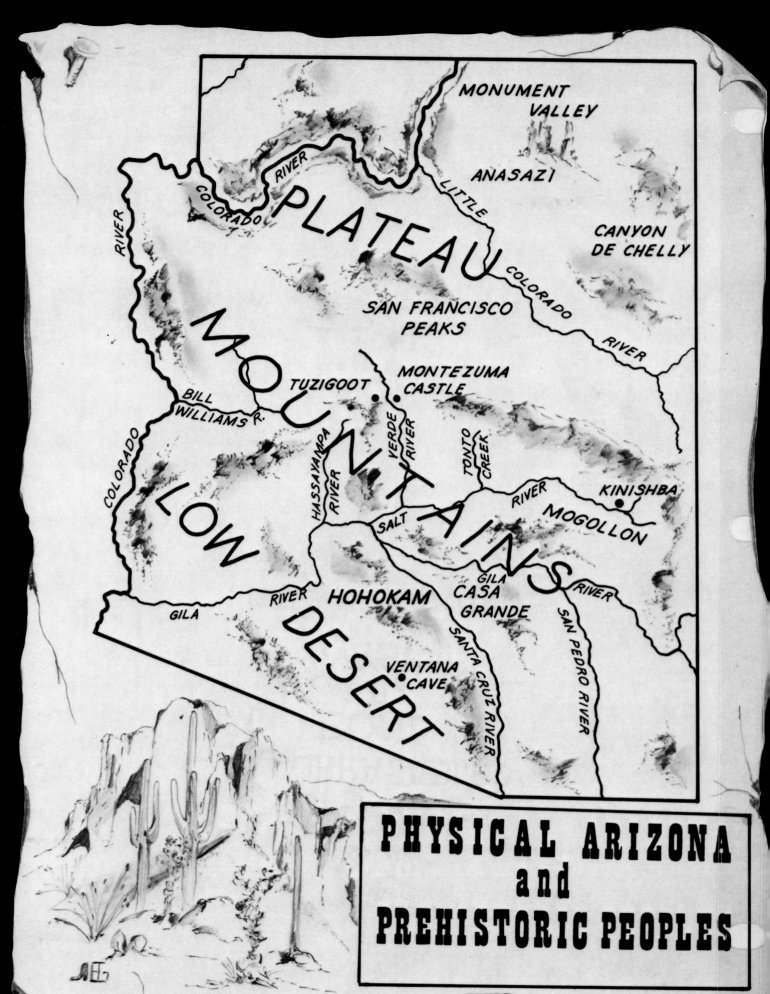

PHYSICAL ARIZONA
and
PREHISTORIC PEOPLES

© M. TRIMBLE

Chapter 2

Prehistoric Arizona to A.D. 1540

The summer monsoons struck with a vengeance during the late summer months of 1951. The rains that fell in the Huachuca Mountains of southern Arizona sent water cascading down the usually-dry arroyos toward the tiny San Pedro River sweeping everything in its path. After the waters subsided, Ed Lehner, a local rancher and amateur archaeologist, made an incredible discovery. In an arroyo behind his house, the rushing waters had washed away the banks, exposing the long-buried bones of prehistoric animals dating back thousands of years.

Lehner called in the experts from the Arizona State Museum, in Tucson, who uncovered the remains of nine elephants. Along with these beasts the archaeologists dug up the bones of a small, primitive horse, a bison and a pig-like animal called a tapir. Ashes from remains of a cookfire dated the site to eleven thousands years ago.

Other remains located at nearby Naco included a large mammoth with eight stone spear points in its head and rib cage.

The so-called paleo-Indians that hunted the large animals probably arrived in Arizona after a long journey that began in Asia about eleven thousand years ago. After the last great glacier began to recede, hunters crossed a land bridge in the Bering Strait and eventually drifted into what was then a cooler and wetter Arizona. Huge mammoths and *mastadons* standing thirteen feet high at the shoulders inhabited the lush, green valleys of southern Arizona. Prehistoric elephant hunters set up kill sites near watering holes. Using stone knives, they charged the beast and cut the tendons on the legs so the animal couldn't escape, then killed it with spears.

Scientists still debate the reasons for demise of these great animals. The likely reason is a change in the climate. As the region became more arid, these animals simply didn't adjust and became extinct.

Some four thousand years ago, people called Cochise who likely descended from the paleo-Indian elephant hunters, learned to cultivate a primitive corn. The corn was ground into meal using a hollowed-out stone, called a *metate* and a hand-held *mano* or grinder. Thus, these early farmers had learned, in a small way, to control their environment. They also hunted small animals such as rabbits and gathered fruits and berries to supplement their diet. The Cochise people were the link between the ancient elephant hunters and the prehistoric Anasazi, Patayan, Mogollon, Salado, Sinagua and Hohokam.

The Hohokam, Anasazi, and Mogollon are considered the major prehistoric cultures in Arizona The origin of the first two are uncertain but the Mogollon are believed to have descended from the Cochise culture. The Hohokam lived in the deserts and river valleys of southern Arizona where they skillfully engineered irrigation canals and ditches. They are recognized today as the master farmers of the Southwest. The Anasazi occupied the sandstone canyons of the Four Corners area. Although they didn't move into the cliffs until the later stage, around A.D. 1100, they are best remembered as the cliff dwellers. Both Hohokam and Anasazi are names applied by modern man.

The so-called paleo-Indians that peopled prehistoric Arizona probably arrived after a long journey that began in Asia about eleven thousand years ago. After the last great glacier began to recede, hunters crossed a land bridge in the Bering Strait and eventually drifted into what was then a cooler and wetter Arizona.
Map drawn by Dean Lyon; art by Jack Graham; courtesy of the author

Hohokam is a Pima word meaning "all used up" or "the vanished ones" and *Anasazi* is a Navajo word for "ancient ones." The Mogollons lived in the rugged central mountains of eastern Arizona. Their name and that of the giant escarpment that slashes across the plateau is named for Juan Ignacio Mogollon, an early Spanish colonial governor of New Mexico.

The Hohokam, Anasazi, and Mogollon, along with the lesser-known Salado, Sinagua, and Patayan, adapted well to their respective environments. Despite many differences and great distances, there was a great deal of intermingling, sharing and trading. During their heyday, the Hohokam and Anasazi had a culture that was in advance of Europe, which was then emerging from the Dark Ages. All these cultural groups went into decline about A.D. 1250. By the time of the Spanish entrada in the sixteenth century, they had mysteriously vanished, and modern man has been able to piece together only a fragment of these once-great civilizations. Many believe the Hohokam evolved into today's Pima and Tohono O'Odham (Papago). The Anasazi are thought to have become today's Pueblo Indians of Arizona and New Mexico. The Mogollons went south to the Casas Grandes region of Chihuahua. The Sinagua, who lived in the Flagstaff—Verde Valley area, probably immigrated to the Hopi mesas. Hopi legends tell of a people who came from the south to live among them. The Salado—cliff dwellers along the Salt River, distant cousins of the Anasazi and known for their beautiful polychrome pottery—were intermingled and perhaps assimilated by the larger Mogollon and Hohokam peoples.

The Patayan, who lived in the Flagstaff—Prescott areas and along the Colorado River, most likely evolved into the Yuma-language peoples of western Arizona.

The rise and decline of these ancient ones follows a pattern as old as man. Their time in the sun was brief. Their battles against the elements were epic. In this pristine wilderness they carved empires and built civilizations far superior to their contemporaries in Europe.

In the end, the elements won out. What finally drove them away? Was it drought? A long dry spell persisted between A.D. 1276 and 1299. Was it pestilence, famine or plague? Or did the arrival of warlike Apaches and Navajos cause them to depart? Since they left no written accounts and science has unearthed only a fractional account, the complete story may never be known. ◆

This diorama at Arizona State Museum on the University of Arizona Campus at Tucson depicts prehistoric Arizona life. Paleo-Indian elephant hunters waited for their prey at watering holes, then ganged up on the beast with stone spears and boulders. Photo by Helga Teiwes, courtesy of the Arizona State Museum, University of Arizona

This diorama of the Arizona State Museum depicts Arizona as it was some ten thousand years ago. The setting is around Ventana Cave about a hundred miles west of Tucson. During the 1940s, archaeologists sifted though fifteen feet of layered debris. The material gathered enabled scientists to learn how man evolved from hunter to food gatherer to farmer. Five layers of debris dated from 8000 B.C. Paleo-Indians; two layers from the Cochise Culture; the Hohokam from about A.D. 1 to A.D. 1400; and the modern day Tohono O'Odham (Papago). Photo by Helga Teiwes, courtesy of the Arizona State Museum, University of Arizona

Hohokam Indians, the "master farmers" of the Southwest, came into the Salt River Valley about A.D. 700 and farmed this area for about seven hundred years. The Hohokam, *a Pima Indian word for "all used up" or "departed," are considered the most advanced of all prehistoric peoples in what is now the continental United States. Brilliantly engineered canals and ditches enabled them to control their environment, a rarity among pre-Columbian peoples living in the desert. The Hohokam mysteriously abandoned their cities in the Salt River Valley by A.D. 1400. American settlers in the 1860s cleaned out the abandoned canals and ditches and farmed the Hohokam fields. Pueblo Grande is in the background of this painting by C. Kemper. The ruins of this structure can still be visited in east Phoenix.* Courtesy of the Salt River Project archives

This diorama depicts life in the Salt River valley, around A.D. 1000. Hohokam Indians are digging irrigation ditches with primitive stone tools. Camelback Mountain, a modern day Phoenix landmark, looms in the background. Courtesy of the Salt River Project archives

28

A detail of the diorama reveals a Hohokam corn planter. Courtesy of the Salt River Project archives

The Casa Grande ruins, a national
monument near Coolidge, remain a mystery.
They may have been a temple to some leader.
The eleven-room structure was built around
A.D. 1300 and abandoned a century and a half
later. Father Kino visited the site in 1694 and
American mountain men mentioned seeing it
in the 1820s. The first scientific excavation was
made in 1892 by the Smithsonian Institution.
It became a national monument in 1918.
Photo by Buehman Hartwell circa 1900,
courtesy of the Arizona Historical Society
Haynes Collection

This limestone sink, half-filled with water, is
Montezuma's Well as it appeared around
1880. Water from the reservoir flows at a rate
of 1.5 million gallons a day. Prehistoric
Indians constructed small cliff dwellings and
pueblos around the well. Water was diverted
into irrigation ditches and carried to farmlands
below. The limestone content in the water
coated the ditches and preserved them into
modern times. Photo by Leo Goldschmidt,
courtesy of the Arizona Historical Society

These are the Tonto cliff dwellings, near Theodore Roosevelt Dam. The Salado Indians built their dwellings inside this hollowed section of mudstone about seven hundred years ago. Salado, *a Spanish word meaning "salty," was* given to these people because they lived near the Salt River. They moved into the Tonto Basin about a thousand years ago, coming from the area around the Little Colorado River. Originally they lived on the floodplain but about A.D. 1200, they moved into the cliffs. Reasons for this move remain a mystery. By the early 1400s the Salado had moved on. The site became a national monument in 1907. Courtesy of the Arizona Historical Society

These Indian pictographs are in Canyon del Muerto, a branch of Canyon de Chelly, Arizona. The carvings were made by Navajos, circa 1540-42. Courtesy of the Arizona Historical Society

The Coronado
Expedition
1540~1542

Platte River

QUIVIRA

Arkansas

Green R.

River

Grand
Canyon

Hopi
Villages
TOVAR
1540

Rio Grande

CARDENAS
1540

Tiguex

CORONADO 1541

Hawikuh

Red River

[CALIFORNIA]

Colorado

Salt River

River

Rio

[TEXAS]

Gila

Rio Pecos

DIAZ-1540&1541

CORONADO
1540

Rio

CABEZA DE VACA
1528-1536

PACIFIC OCEAN

SEA

MARCOS DE NIZA 1539

Rio Conchos

GULF
OF
MEXICO

ALARCON

OF

Rio Grande

CORTEZ

1540

[MEXICO]

© M. TRIMBLE

In February 1540, Francisco Vasquez de
Coronado and his army of three hundred
horsemen and foot soldiers as well as one
thousand Indian allies, began their quest for
the fabled Indian village of Hawikuh where the
natives reportedly wore giant pearls, gold beads
and emeralds, ate their meals out of gold and
silver utensils and decorated their doors with
turquoise. Two years later, he returned to
Mexico City as a failure, never realizing that he
had opened vast new lands laden with riches for
future explorers. Map drawn by Dean Lyon;
art by Jack Graham; courtesy of the author

Chapter 3

Glory, God, and Gold

"Granted they did not find the gold, at least they found a place in which to search." So wrote Pedro de Castenada, of the famed Coronado expedition. One cannot find a more apt description of this *tierra nueva*. The hopes and dreams of getting rich without working were dashed in 1542, when Francisco Vasquez de Coronado returned from his unsuccessful search for the fabled Seven Cities of Gold. Two years earlier, the greatest expedition yet seen in the New World had embarked on the quest for *El Dorado*. They found instead, unconquerable natives, vast arid lands so poor "you couldn't even raise hell on them" twisting, impenetrable canyons and brawny, rough-hewn mountains—awesome barriers one and all. The inspiration for such a hazardous journey can be summed up in four words: Glory, God, and Gold.

In 1492 Spain emerged victorious from a long war with the Moors. Her fighting instincts were honed to a fine cutting edge. The new nation was ripe for overseas conquest. In the years following Columbus's successful landing in the New World, Spanish conquistadores like Cortez and Pizarro found unbelievable riches in Mexico and Peru. Overnight, Spain became the wealthiest nation in the world.

The success of Cortez and Pizarro inspired other conquistadores to seek fame and fortune in the New World. Legends began circulating throughout New Spain of other wondrous places far to the north, and these bold adventurers reasoned the vast hordes of gold and silver already located proved the existence of more in the unexplored north.

Along with this insatiable quest for conquering new lands and seeking treasure was Spain's penchant for saving all the lost souls in the New World. During these troubled times for the Catholic Church in Europe, Spain was determined to be the bastion for Catholicism. The thousands of natives in the New World provided a bountiful harvest for the zealous missionaries.

The stage was set for the great Coronado Expedition several years earlier, in 1528, when an expedition was shipwrecked off the west coast of Florida. Using makeshift rafts, the survivors tried to make their way back to New Spain by following the gulf shore of today's United States. They wrecked again, this time on the Texas coast. Taken captive by local Indians, four men, Cabeza de Vaca, Castillo, Dorantes and the latter's slave, Esteban, were the sole survivors. De Vaca's prowess as a healer eventually gained freedom and respectability for the four pilgrims. They spent the next eight years walking across the wilderness of today's Texas and northern Mexico.

In 1536, the four naked, half-starved stragglers were found near Culican, Sinaloa. Taken before viceroy Antonio Mendoza, de Vaca unraveled a tale of great cities. He hadn't seen them but had heard stories from the natives of the existence of seven cities of gold.

Mendoza attempted to suppress the rumors of gold to prevent a rush, while quietly organizing an expedition of his own. He recruited a handsome, dashing young hidalgo named Francisco Vasquez de Coronado to lead the quest. Meanwhile he sent a Franciscan padre, Fray Marcos de Niza, and Esteban, the Moorish slave, north on a reconnaissance mission to verify the existence of the golden cities.

In 1539, de Niza and Esteban ventured north, crossing into Arizona through the San Rafael Valley. Somewhere along the way they parted company and the Moor was sent ahead. A few days later Esteban arrived at the Pueblo Indian village of Hawikuh, near today's Zuni, New Mexico, and made his customary request for food and female companionship. The inhospitable natives cut his brash visit short—literally and figuratively—puncturing his body with arrows. His frightened escorts were sent scurrying back down the trail to de Niza's camp. The thirty-eight-year-old friar hurried back to Mexico City. The further he got from Hawikuh the more his imagination began conjuring tales of great wealth in the new lands. In his fertile mind the tiny, mud and wattle village of Hawikuh grew into a city larger than Mexico City with buildings ten stories high where natives wore giant pearls, gold beads and emeralds, ate their meals out of gold and silver utensils, and decorated their doors with turquoise. When de Niza finished his tale, all Mexico City went into a gold-crazed frenzy.

In February 1540, Francisco Vasquez de Coronado, dressed in gilded armor, rode out at the head of a resplendent army numbering nearly three hundred horsemen and foot soldiers. Behind them came one thousand Indian allies followed by native and black slaves. The intrepid explorers, with Fray Marcos as their guide, trudged through the wilderness for nearly six months before arriving at Hawikuh, bone weary and half starved.

The disappointment endured at the sight of the mud-walled village was the first of many on the journey. After a brief battle, the hungry Spaniards stormed the village and confiscated the native's food supplies. The battle, fought on July 7, 1540, marked the first between Indians and whites in what is now the United States.

The natives quickly learned that the best way to rid themselves of the pesky Spaniards was to tell them the treasures they sought could be found elsewhere. Seven cities existed, they said, some distance to the northwest. Coronado quickly sent an expedition off in that direction. Arriving at the Hopi villages, the horseback Spaniards once again had to fight and win before the stubborn Hopi admitted them into their ungilded villages. They had no gold but learned that further to the west a great river flowed. Hoping this might be the eagerly sought but mythical Northwest Passage, a fabled waterway across the continent, they hurried back to report the news to Coronado. Another expedition of twenty-five horsemen set out to find the river, which was at the bottom of the impenetrable Grand Canyon.

Frustrated at his failure to find gold or a passage to the Orient, Coronado turned his attention eastward towards the Rio Grande.

During the next several months, expeditions ventured east into the dreaded Llano Estacado (Staked Plains) and north into Kansas in a fruitless search for the golden cities. Finally, in 1542, the disappointed expedition returned to Mexico City.

Coronado was considered a failure for not finding cities with streets cobbled with the golden boulders of the *madre del oro*. He died a few years later, never realizing that he'd opened vast new lands laden with riches for future explorers.

Forty years after the Coronado Expedition, Antonio de Espéjo led a small group of prospectors to the Hopi villages. From there he dropped into the Verde Valley and found ore of an undetermined value. He also found warlike Indians. The only thing that held the Indians back was the fear of the four-legged critters ridden by the interlopers. Espejo returned with ore specimens and a wild tale about a lake of gold somewhere in northern Arizona.

In 1598, another explorer, miner Juan de Onate, traveled across much of Arizona after establishing the first colony in New Mexico. One of his officers, Captain Marcos Farfán, led a troop of eight men to the vicinity around Prescott where he found rich silver ore.

It wasn't until 1604-05 that Oñate was able to recruit an expedition and return to Arizona. He saw much of the country but didn't find a lake of gold or even an easy route to the Pacific Ocean. Local native yarnspinners did entertain him with tales of a rich island of bald-headed men ruled by a fat woman with big feet; a tribe of one-legged people; some Indians who slept in trees; others who slept under water; and a great lake where the natives decorated their bodies with gold jewelry.

Eventually, Oñate returned to New Mexico empty-handed. World events were causing Spain to re-evaluate its position in regard to control of its northern frontier. Henceforth, missionaries would be sent out to Christianize the vast lands. By bringing these natives under the Spanish umbrella, Spain believed it could thwart attempts by the Russians, French, and English to penetrate the Spanish empire's northern frontier.

Frederic Remington painted this view of the Coronado Expedition. Courtesy of the Arizona Historical Society/Tucson

Padres and Conquistadores, *by Jack Graham*

The Coronado National Monument stands at this mountain pass at the south end of the Huachuca Mountains in southern Arizona. The pass looks out upon the San Pedro Valley where it is believed Francisco Vasquez de Coronado entered Arizona through this valley in 1540. Photo by the author

A simple memorial commemorating Fray Marcos de Niza's entrance into Arizona in 1539 was erected at Lochiel, a small border community on the Santa Cruz River. Photo by the author

The diorama at Tumacacori National Monument depicts Father Kino in the Arizona desert, his parish. Photo courtesy of Tumacacori National Monument

This statue of Father Kino stands at the Arizona Heritage Center in Tucson. A duplicate is in Statuary Hall, Washington, D.C. Photo by the author

Tumacacori National Monument memorializes the site first visited by Father Kino in 1691. In 1701 a visita *("mission station") was established by Kino. It did not become a full-fledged mission until 1771.* Photo by the author

Pictured are the ruins of the Mission San Gabriel de Guevavi. Father Kino first set foot in Arizona in January 1691 after receiving an invitation from Pima Indians living along the Santa Cruz River. His first stop was at the village of Guevavi. In 1701 he returned and established a mission. Because of Apache raiding, the mission was abandoned in 1773 and relocated at the mission station at Tumacacori. Photo by the author

The San José de Cosmé Mission in Tucson, a two-story convento *built in the early 1880s by the Franciscans as a home for missionaries, was located near Sentinel Mountain, a site named by Father Kino. Today, the site is called "A" Mountain because University of Arizona students traditionally paint the letter A on its side.* Photo by Haynes, courtesy of the Arizona Historical Society/Tucson

Just below the Arizona-Mexico border is the old Kino Mission of Cocospera. Established in 1689, the original mission was destroyed by raiding Apaches nine years later. It was rebuilt in 1700 only to be destroyed again forty-two years later. Again the church was rebuilt, then abandoned. It is considered the most impressive mission ruin in northern Sonora. Photo by the author

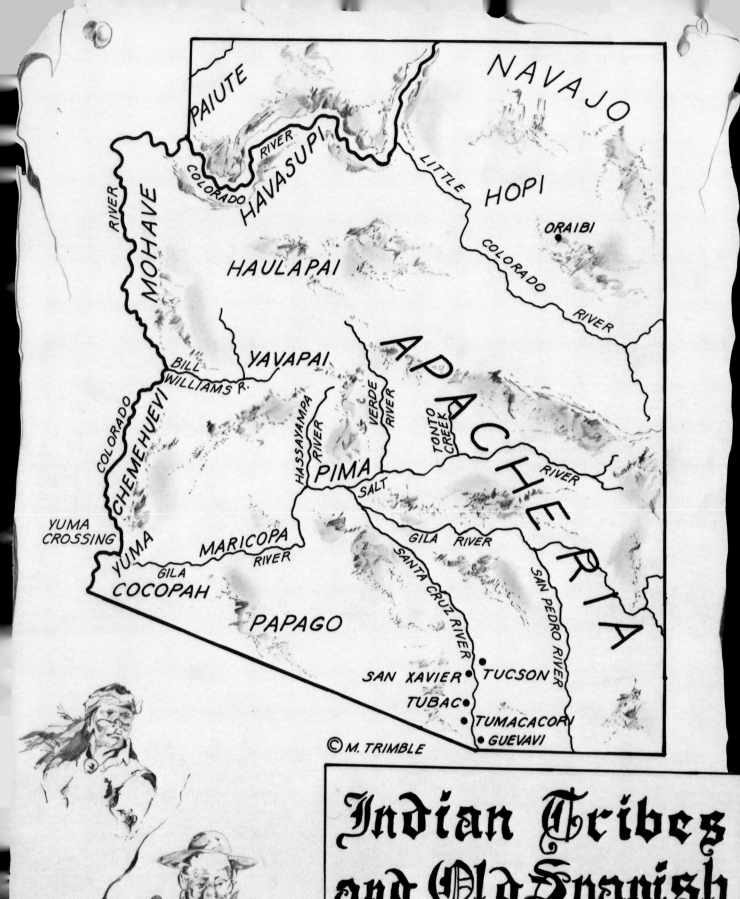

PAIUTE

NAVAJO

MOHAVE

HAVASUPI

COLORADO RIVER

RIVER

LITTLE

HOPI

ORAIBI

HAULAPAI

COLORADO RIVER

MOHAVE RIVER

BILL
WILLIAMS R.

YAVAPAI

APACHERIA

COLORADO

CHEMEHUEVI

HASSAYAMPA RIVER

VERDE RIVER

TONTO CREEK

RIVER

PIMA

SALT

YUMA CROSSING

YUMA

MARICOPA

GILA RIVER

GILA RIVER

SANTA CRUZ RIVER

SAN PEDRO RIVER

COCOPAH

PAPAGO

SAN XAVIER • • TUCSON

TUBAC •

• TUMACACORI

© M. TRIMBLE

• GUEVAVI

Indian Tribes and Old Spanish Missions

1629·1820

Chapter 4

The Rim of Christendom

The first missionaries to arrive in Arizona were Franciscans from New Mexico. Three friars arrived at the Hopi villages in 1629 and established the first permanent structures for use by non-Indians in Arizona. The peace-loving Hopi clustered in permanent villages atop three arid, limestone-colored mesas. Since they didn't move from place to place, the Spanish naturally figured it would be easy to establish missions in their villages. What they failed to consider or chose to overlook was the fact that these village people had a well-organized government and time-honored native religious practices and they didn't particularly cotton to these newcomers moving in and telling them how to live. Since the Hopi were the farthest removed from Spanish authorities at Santa Fe, they were the least influenced by Spanish customs and were able to maintain their own traditions. Other Pueblo peoples seeking to escape Spanish oppression often sought refuge among the Hopi.

Naturally, the deeply religious Hopi were openly hostile to the three Franciscan padres. Native spiritual leaders especially resented the competition. However, when Padre Francisco Porras healed a blind child, relations eased and the missionaries began to make a few conversions. However, in 1633 the medicine men poisoned Father Porras. The fate of the other two is unknown. In time, other priests arrived and zealous persistence paid off. By 1675 there were three missions and two *visitas* (mission stations) in Hopiland. After some eighty years of oppression the Pueblo Indians cast off the yoke of Spanish rule.

The great Pueblo Revolt in 1680 spelled an end to the missions in Hopiland. On August 9, all the Pueblo Indians in Arizona and New Mexico struck in unison and, when the dust had settled, some four hundred settlers, including twenty-two priests, had been brutally murdered. Arizona had no settlers

but three of the four priests were martyred and another enslaved. It wasn't until 1692 that Don Diego de Vargas led the reconquest of New Mexico. Vargas and his troops swept across the Hopi mesas and extracted a promise from all the villages except Oraibi to keep the peace. Only one village, Awatovi, allowed the padres to return. Soon after, the other villages organized a war party and destroyed Awatovi, killing the men and distributing the women and children to other villages.

The defiance of the Hopi ended attempts to establish a foothold from New Mexico. Settlement would come from the south under the gentle guidance of a Jesuit priest named Eusebio Kino.

Priest, explorer, cattleman, promoter, cartographer, and defender of the frontier, Father Kino was truly a man for all seasons. During the twenty-four years spent in the Pimeria Alta (Land of the Upper Pima), the tireless "padre on horseback" rode thousands of miles to ride herd on his loyal flock. Kino rightly believed the natives were more apt to accept Christianity on a full stomach. Putting these beliefs to practice, he introduced new crops and drove the first beef cattle into what would one day become Arizona. In 1692 he extended his "rim of Christendom" into the San Pedro and Santa Cruz valleys. By 1700 a small mission was located at the Papago village of Bac. Nearly a century later, on that site, the beautiful mission San Xavier del Bac was built. In 1701 he established Guevavi Mission near today's Nogales. A *visita* was located nearby at Tumacacori.

Kino rode the Pimeria Alta alone for nearly a quarter of a century. His dream of locating missions along the San Pedro, Gila and Colorado rivers was never realized. Spain was deeply involved in European wars and had neither the time nor money to spend on Kino's remote Christian outposts. The humble priest died in 1711. His deathbed consisted of the usual two calf skins for a mattress, Indian blankets for covers, and his old saddle for a pillow. He was buried in the chapel of his church at Magdalena, a few miles south of Nogales.

The Pimeria Alta fell into neglect during the twenty years following the death of Kino. During the 1730s, Spain was recovered enough from its wars to turn its attention to the frontier once again. Many of the Jesuits were recruited from German states, including Padres Grazhoffer, Middendorf, Pauer, Sedelmayr, Segesser, and Stiger. All were hardworking and demonstrated the zealousness characteristic of the Society of Jesus. None, however, had Kino's energy or ability to gain the love and respect of the natives enjoyed by the great Padre on Horseback. Native medicine men or shamans resented the competition and sought to undermine their efforts. The new padres were not as tolerant of native ceremonies as Kino and for Father Johann Grazhoffer it proved fatal. The padre criticized the polygamy and drinking orgies enjoyed by the natives and in 1733 someone put poison in his food.

The discovery of the rich Planchas de Plata silver strike in 1736 brought a mass migration of rough and tumble miners into the Pimeria Alta. The influx of populace upset the usually tranquil Pima. Near the silver town of Arissona lived a Pima headman named Luis. Earlier, Luis had helped the Spanish put down a rebellion and, as a reward, was given the lofty title "captain-general" and made a governor. His thirst for power grew and soon he was undermining the padres by spreading rumors of their cruelty to natives. At the same time, he was laying plans to drive the Spanish out and seize control of the ranches, mines and missions.

Luis set his plan in action on November 20, 1751. He lured some twenty Spaniards into his home under the guise of providing a refuge from an Apache war party, then set fire to the place. The victims either burned to death or were slaughtered while trying to escape. When word of the rebellion spread, other bands of Pima took up the cause. During the next few days more than a hundred Spaniards were killed.

Spanish soldiers were ordered to round up Luis and his followers. After a lengthy chase, the Pima warriors were cornered in the Santa Catalina mountains north of Tucson and defeated.

A year later the Spanish established a garrison or presidio at Tubac on the Santa Cruz river. Fifty soldiers and their families settled along the east bank of the river in 1752. For the first time in the history of Arizona, white women had taken up residence. Five years after its founding, the population had grown to some four hundred.

The final years of the Jesuit era in Arizona were marked by controversy. Spanish civil authorities, military and the padres clashed frequently over the welfare of the natives. Each blamed the other for transgressions, real or imagined. The native leaders, in turn, took advantage of this discord to further their political interests.

Ironically in 1767 when the ax fell on the Jesuits, it had little to do with affairs in the Pimeria Alta. With the stroke of a pen, King Carlos III expelled them from the Spanish realm. The Bourbon king wanted absolute rule, something adamantly opposed by the Society of Jesus. King Carlos had reason to fear the Jesuits were becoming too powerful, so he had them expunged. More than fifty Jesuit priests in the Pimeria Alta were secretly rounded up and deported to Spain. Some historians believe Spain removed the Jesuits from the Pimeria Alta because they feared the padres might provide strategic information about the area to their arch enemies: England and France.

The exodus of the black-robed Jesuits in 1767 was followed by the *entrada* of the brown-robed Franciscans a year later. Fray Francisco Tomas Garcés, a humble man, cut from the same cloth as the great Kino, was the man assigned to the Arizona missions. The intractable Apaches greeted the new padre on his arrival at San Xavier del Bac with a raid that destroyed part of the adobe church.

Despite the continuous raiding by Apache war parties, the tireless Garcés worked well among the natives. He sat cross-legged on the ground with them, ate their food and, although he was only thirty years old, earned the affectionate nickname "Old Man." Another priest described the humble friar aptly, saying, "God, in his infinite wisdom, must have created Garces for the place in which he served."

Like Kino, Garcés was the consummate missionary, always in search of souls to harvest. A year after his arrival, the gregarious friar spoke the Pima language fluently. In 1771, he headed west in search of a land route to Alta, California, which would link up with the missions recently established there by the legendary Junipero Serra. Using three Indian guides and a horse, he followed Kino's old trail, *Camino del Diablo,* to the Yuma villages on the Colorado. This expedition convinced Garces that a land route was possible. During the next five years he accompanied Captain Juan Bautista de Anza, commander at Tubac, on two major expeditions to California. On the second trip, in 1775-1776, 240 colonist-soldiers and their families were taken to the San Francisco bay where a new settlement was established. Most of the colonists were women and children. Only one of the thirty soldiers in the expedition was unmarried. Interestingly, most of the original settlers in the "City of the Bay" listed their birthplace as Tubac. Garcés didn't accompany de Anza to San Francisco. Instead he remained among the Yuma Indians at the historic river crossing establishing missions.

While de Anza was taking his colonists to Alta, California, Garcés set out on another of his epic journeys, this time up the Colorado River where he explored the westernmost reaches of the Grand Canyon. Heading east, he eventually reached the Hopi villages, becoming the first padre to visit in over seventy-five years. Time had not softened the Hopi stand on the white man's religion. The Hopi elders at Oraibi allowed the kindly priest to stay a couple of days before issuing a stern warning to get off the mesa. Garcés gave a short speech on peaceful co-existence and brotherhood before being forced to rapidly depart. Later he recorded the experiences in his journal and dates at the bottom, July 4, 1776.

That same year two other franciscans, Fathers Silvestre Escalante and Francisco Dominguez, were exploring a trade route from Santa Fe to California. The explorers trekked northeast across Four Corners into Utah around Provo before returning to New Mexico. On the way home they crossed the Colorado River near today's Page (the crossing of Vados de Los Padres is now buried beneath the water of Lake Powell) and then on to the Hopi villages before heading back to Santa Fe.

Garcés' journey into the wilderness lasted eleven months and covered some two thousand miles. During his absence, the presidio at Tubac had been moved farther north to Tucson.

During the de Anza expeditions to California, the natives living at the Yuma crossing were promised presents and missions in exchange for allegiance and cooperation. Their chief, Palma, was taken to Mexico City and given a hero's welcome before being baptised in the Cathedral of Mexico and given the name Salvador Carlos Antonio Palma. Chief Palma returned to his people with many promises but the Spanish failed to follow up. Following his great colonizing triumph, de Anza was named governor of new Mexico. Unfortunately for Spain, few commanders had de Anza's ability as statesman-soldier. Spanish travelers abused the natives at the Yuma Crossing. In August 1779 Garcés and another priest arrived at the Yuma villages without the lavish gifts promised. Chief Palma lost face and the natives grew more restive. When

Spaniards allowed their horses to graze on the natives' valuable source of food, the mesquite trees, Chief Palma decided it was time to rid his people of the unwanted interlopers.

The Yumas rose in rebellion against their Spanish oppressors in July 1781. One group vented their wrath on the padres at San Pedro y San Pablo Mission, killing father Juan Diaz and Matias Moreno. Moreno was beheaded with a crude ax. Most of the men were killed but the women and children were spared and later ransomed back to the Spanish. Father Garces was taken and for a time it looked like his life might be spared. In the end, the radical element held sway over the rest and the kind and daring priest was martyred. Afterward his body was buried and flowers were planted on his grave by the natives. Garces once observed, "We have failed. It is not because we haven't tried. It is because we have not understood." His words are timeless.

The Yuma Revolt of 1781 closed the land route to California for forty years. During this time, which was also the last days of the Spanish empire, settlement would be concentrated in the Santa Cruz Valley.

The Royal Regulations of 1772 called for a cordon of fifteen presidios from San Antonio, Texas, to Tubac. A red-headed Irishman in the Spanish army named Col. Hugo O'Conor was given the responsibility of selecting the sites. O'Conor chose Tucson over Tubac primarily because it was closer to Apacheria. Construction was begun in 1776 but proceeded slowly because most of the soldiers had gone to California with de Anza. The entire arsenal consisted of fifteen muskets and carbines, twenty-two sabers, ten six-ply leather vests, and six lances. The latter was considered the best weapon for Apache warfare. Discipline was lax at the new presidio until the arrival of Don Pedro Allande in 1777. Allande, a spit-and-polish officer destined to be one of Spain's greatest combat commanders, denounced the conditions at Tucson and took immediate measures to build a defensible fortress. He was a seasoned veteran of European wars and quickly adapted to the unorthodox manner in which the Apaches fought. His relentless campaigns into the heart of Apacheria eventually led to a peace that lasted forty years. Allande was also a fund-raiser for noble causes. In one of the more poetic ironies of Southwest American history the presidio commandant, in 1777, took up a collection among his humble settlers to raise money for the American colonists fighting for freedom far to the east. A total of 459 pesos was raised for the cause—a sizable amount when considering that four pesos would buy a cow and a good horse could be bought for seven pesos.

On May 1, 1782, a large war party of Apaches swooped down on Tucson. A desperate fight between the Spanish, their native allies, and the Apaches ensued. The Apaches' main thrust was at the front entrance and, fortunately, some of the soldiers were on the outside and caught the Apaches in a crossfire. Captain Allande and twenty soldiers made a gallant stand at the main gate. Although severely wounded, the captain refused aid and remained with his men. The discipline of Allande's men paid off and, in the face of superior firepower, the Apaches withdrew. An attack like the May Day battle was rare in the annals of Apache warfare. They usually preferred hit and run guerilla-style, raiding small settlements and running off with the livestock.

In 1784, a new Indian policy, the Galvez Plan, was formulated. Named for Viceroy Bernardo de Galvez, the plan combined aggressive military campaigns with bribery. The Apaches were encouraged to settle near trading posts where they would be rewarded with booze, food rations, and weapons (of an inferior quality). The plan worked wonderfully well and for the first time there was peace on the frontier.

The last thirty years of the Spanish empire (1790-1821) brought unprecedented prosperity to what would become Arizona. Gold and silver mines were opened, new settlers arrived, large herds of cattle were brought in to stock the ranges, and the beautiful missions of San Xavier del Bac and San Jose de Tumacacori were built, the former at the exorbitant cost of forty thousand pesos. The latter is today a national historic monument while the former is a "living" church to the Tohono O'Odham. The ornate structures, blending Moorish, Byzantine, and late Mexican architecture, are regarded as the most awe-inspiring in America. ♦

This painting by the late Theresa Potter depicts the expedition of Lt. Col. Juan Bautista de Anza crossing the Colorado River in 1775. The son of the Presidio Captain of Fronteras, Juan Bautista de Anza lived and served on the frontier for thirty-six years. Anza carried the dream of his father and uncle to conquer the desert. Commandant of the Presidio de Tubac, lieutenant colonel and governor, Anza became known as an explorer, colonizer, and statesman. Courtesy of the artist

The San Augustine Church, Tucson, was built of adobe in the early 1860s, but the church fell on hard times when its pastor, Father Donato, was killed by Apaches. In 1866 Father John Baptiste Salpointe arrived and, within two years, the church was completed. Hard times hit the church again in the 1930s when it became a garage and gas station. Saved again, today it graces the entrance to the Arizona Heritage Center in Tucson. Photo by Haynes, courtesy of the Arizona Historical Society/Tucson

The beautiful San Xavier del Bac, pictured here in 1890, replaced the first mission built in 1700 at the Papago village of Bac. Photo courtesy of the Arizona Historical Foundation

Artist Cal Peter's conception of the Royal Spanish Presidio of Tucson, circa 1795, looks southeast. Courtesy of the Arizona Historical Society/Tucson

This monument in honor of Francisco Garcés was dedicated in Yuma. Photo courtesy of the Arizona Historical Society/Tucson

1821·1854

Chapter 5

The Mexican Republic and Arizona

Mexico's struggle for independence from Spain began on September 16, 1810, when Father Miguel Hidalgo called upon the people to rally around the cause for freedom. Unfortunately, the upper crust of Mexican society failed to heed his call. Hidalgo was killed and his rebellion was short-lived. However, the seeds had been planted and by 1821 the new Mexican republic was born. During the next few years, one unstable government after another tried and failed. Many died by the gun in the turmoil. During one twenty-four hour period, three men held the office of president—one for only forty-five minutes. Finally, one man, Antonio Lopez de Santa Anna, proved strong enough to wrest control of the government, and he proved to be the biggest despot in Mexico's turbulent history. He was president-dictator eleven times and managed to lose or sell over half of Mexico to its neighbor, the "Colossus to the North."

During these unstable years, the payoffs to the Apaches ceased and, by the mid-1830s, war parties once again swooped down on Tubac and Tucson. Ranches and mines were abandoned. Church lands were secularized and sold at public auction. All priests were required to take a loyalty oath to Mexico or get out, and all foreign-born padres were deported. The once-beautiful missions were deserted and fell into disrepair.

The citizens in Tucson, the "post furthest out" knew little and cared less about the turmoil in Mexico City. In 1824, the state of Occidente was created. Sonora, Sinaloa, and the settled areas around Tucson and Tubac were included. A rift developed between Sonora and Sinaloa, and in 1831 the two split and southern Arizona became a part of Sonora.

The opening of a trade route between Santa Fe and St. Louis in the early 1820s played a significant role in the first American penetrations into Arizona. American traders, unwelcome during the Spanish colonial period, brought in much-sought-after merchandise from the United States to exchange for Mexican silver and fur. American fur trappers or mountain men moved their informal operations to Santa Fe and Taos. From these villages, trapping expeditions were launched into Arizona. Few records were kept since this was still Mexican territory and the authorities and the trappers played a running cat-and-mouse game.

Noteworthy among these fur trading entrepreneurs was Ewing Young. Young came down the Santa Fe trail with Bill Becknell in 1822, and soon was the central figure in the fur trade in the Southwest. He led one of the first American trapping expeditions into Arizona. A soft-spoken but determined frontiersman, Young feared neither man nor beast. He was the first American to trap along the Salt and Verde rivers and the first to explore the Gila to its mouth. Among his proteges was Kit Carson. No photographs or composite drawings of Young exist and he kept no journal, since Americans were usually not permitted to trap the area. While some gave up their citizenship and became Mexicans, Young, a staunch American, refused and took his chances with the authorities. The risks were great. Warrior tribes, the searing desert and grizzly bears took their toll. During the 1827-28 trapping season, somewhere near the junction of the Salt and Verde rivers, Apaches set an ambush, killing eighteen to twenty-four in Young's party. During one 1,000-mile expedition into Arizona, Young gathered in some $20,000 in beaver pelts, lost a third of his men in battle and, when he arrived at Santa Fe, Mexican authorities, claiming his license was void, confiscated all his furs. It seems a new law nullifying his license had been passed while Young was in Arizona. In order to avoid having their furs impounded, the Americans cached their pelts in the mountains near Taos then smuggled them over to Bent's Fort, a trading post on the north bank of the Arkansas River—in American territory.

The first written account of Arizona by an American was the journal of James Ohio Pattie. Pattie was only twenty years old when he arrived in Santa Fe with his father in 1824. Pattie's journal, written several years after his Arizona adventure, paints a rather vivid account of his trials and tribulations. It begins with our hero rescuing the beautiful young daughter of a

former New Mexico governor from rampaging Comanche raiders. In gratitude he was given a license to trap the Gila. Over the next few years he faced fearsome Apaches and Mojaves, hot, blazing deserts, cougars and grizzlies. Finally, James and his father, Sylvester, were jailed as trespassers in California where his father died. During a smallpox epidemic, James innoculated thousands and gained his freedom. He returned home to Ohio, a tired, beaten young man, lamenting, "The freshness, the visions, the hopes of my youthful days have all vanished and can never return."

Joe Walker, David Jackson, Jed Smith, Bill Williams, Pauline Weaver, Antoine Leroux, and a host of other explorers and mountain men passed through Arizona during these years, opening trails that others would one day follow. It is ironic that this reckless breed of men who went West in the first place to escape the restraints of the societies they despised, later opened the West for expansion and settlement of those beloved sanctuaries, ending a way of life that would never be seen again. ♦

From the journal of James O. Pattie comes this illustration of an Apache attack. The narrative was the first written material on Arizona by an American. Reproduction courtesy of Maricopa Community Colleges, Southwest Studies

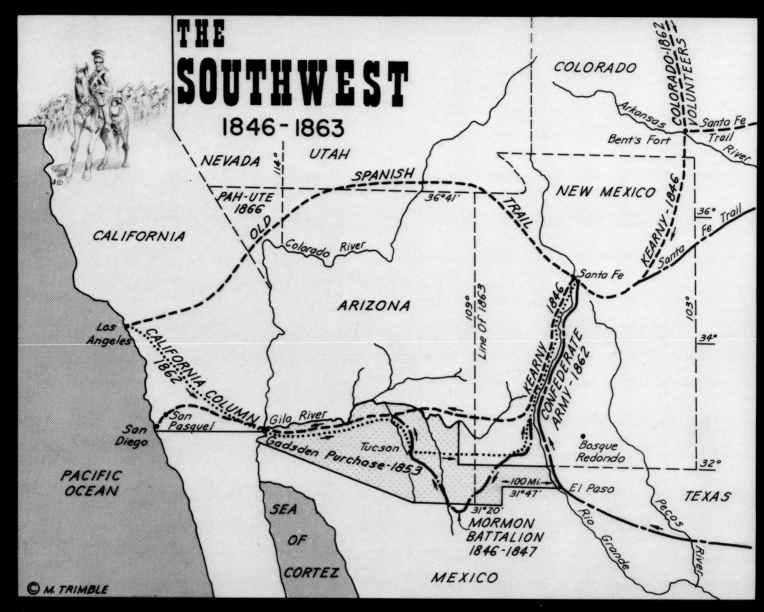

THE SOUTHWEST 1846-1863

NEVADA

UTAH

SPANISH

114°

36°41'

OLD

COLORADO River

CALIFORNIA

PAH-UTE 1866

TRAIL

COLORADO

Arkansas

Bent's Fort

COLORADO-1862 VOLUNTEERS

Santa Fe Trail

NEW MEXICO

36°

KEARNY-1846

Santa Fe Trail

103°

ARIZONA

Line of 1863

109°

Santa Fe

KEARNY 1846

Los Angeles

CALIFORNIA COLUMN 1862

34°

San Pasquel

Gila River

KEARNY 1846

CONFEDERATE ARMY-1862

San Diego

Gadsden Purchase-1853

Tucson

Bosque Redondo

32°

PACIFIC OCEAN

100 Mi.

El Paso

TEXAS

31°47'

Rio Grande

Pecos River

SEA

31°20'

OF

MORMON BATTALION 1846-1847

CORTEZ

MEXICO

© M. TRIMBLE

During the early 1840s the cry, "Manifest Destiny," rang far and wide. "It is our destiny," claimed American settlers, to reign from the Atlantic to the Pacific." But the Mexicans, equally adamant, boasted they'd plant the tricolors on the banks of the Potomac. The war began in some disputed land in Texas between the Nueces River and the Rio Grande. Map drawn by Dean Lyon, artwork by Jack Graham, courtesy of the author

Chapter 6

Manifest Destiny

During the early 1840s the cry, "Manifest Destiny," was ringing far and wide. "It is our destiny," advocates proclaimed, "to reign from the Atlantic to the Pacific." Some even went further, suggesting we take Canada and Mexico while we're at it. Texas won its independence from Mexico in 1836 and would join the Union nine years later. The same year Texas entered the union, President James K. Polk sent John Slidell to Mexico City with an offer to purchase California. The Mexicans, still smarting over the loss of Texas, refused to discuss the matter and made plans to go to war. Both young republics were spoiling for a fight. Mexicans boasted they'd plant the tri-colors on the banks of the Potomac and their American counterparts claimed they'd hang the Stars and Stripes above the Halls of Montezuma.

The war began in some disputed land in Texas between the Nueces River and the Rio Grande. Part of the American strategy was to send an army west, taking Santa Fe, then on to California. Colonel Stephen Watts Kearny was selected to head his so-called "Army of the West." Kearny was a veteran of many years of hard riding on the frontier and was known as the "Father of the U.S. Cavalry." His army consisted of three hundred regular cavalry, eight hundred boisterous, un-disciplined but rawhide-tough volunteers from Missouri and a sizable religious group whose job it was to build a road to California.

The Army of the West, numbering nearly seventeen hundred, followed the Santa Fe Trail to Bent's Fort on the Arkansas River, which bounded the Mexican border. There Kearny found some four hundred wagons loaded with millions of dollars worth of merchandise waiting to join him on the trek to Santa Fe. Since Santa Anna had closed the trade a few years

earlier, Kearny believed these merchants coveted their wares and would make the entrada of the American force easier. Kearny wisely sent one of his officers, Capt. Phillip St. George Cooke, and a well-known trader, Jim Magoffin, to hold secret talks with New Mexican governor Manuel Armijo. It is believed that Captain Cooke carried along a satchel full of hard cash as an added inducement. When the Army of the West entered Santa Fe on August 18, 1846, Governor Armijo and his force of dragoons had withdrawn to Chihuahua. Kearny's mission was achieved without firing a shot.

Meanwhile, in California, "Pathfinder" John C. Fremont and his ragtag band of mountain men successfully launched the "Bear Flag Revolt" and set up a provisional government. Kit Carson was given dispatches and ordered to ride cross-country to inform Washington.

Unaware of Fremont's Bear Flag takeover, Kearny took three hundred dragoons and set out from Santa Fe on his own con-quest of California. Near Soccoro, New Mexico, Kearny met Carson and learned that the war in California was over. It really wasn't. Carson couldn't have known that soon after he rode out, the *Californios* counter-attacked and regained control. Kearny, in a hurry to get to California, sent his wagons and two hundred of his dragoons back to Santa Fe, then ordered the famous scout to turn around and lead his small band west to California.

The Army of the West, now one hundred strong, had among its ranks two diarists, Dr. James Griffin and Capt. William Emory, and an artist, John Mix Stanley. These three men were awed by the flora and fauna encountered along the Gila River and spent many days taking copious notes. Stanley made the first detailed sketches in Arizona and Emory's scientific notes were later published worldwide. Militarily, the Army of the West impacted little on Arizona history. They stopped at the Pima villages and traded for pumpkins, melons, beans, and flour and seemed to have held the friendly natives in high regard.

Kearny's force saw no action until they reached the outskirts of San Diego and learned the hard way that the war hadn't ended.

The Army of the West lost a bloody battle to the Californio's at San Pascual on the outskirts of San Diego. A few weeks later, Kearny regrouped and joined forces with other Americans and marched to Los Angeles where, on January 13, 1847, General Andres Pico, head of the Californios, surrendered in the vicinity of today's Hollywood.

Following in the dust of Kearny's small army was the Mormon Battalion. Under the command of Capt. Phillip St. George Cooke, the Mormon volunteers were assigned the difficult task of building a road to California. Originally numbering some 500 men, 25 women and some children, Cooke started across Arizona with 340 men and five women; the remainder were too old, too young, or too sick for their assigned mission. Their road led farther south from Kearny's mule-back trail along the Gila. Guided by intrepid mountain men Pauline Weaver, Baptiste Charbonneau, and Antoine Leroux, the trail blazers skirted around the mountains, then turned north following the San Pedro Valley. The only action came near today's Tombstone, when they were attacked by a herd of wild bulls. Mules were gored, wagons rammed but none of the troops was injured seriously. The so-called "first battle of bull run" lasted about an hour; nothing more than a well-placed bullet to the heart would stop the hard-charging longhorns.

On December 17, 1846, the Mormon Battalion reached the dusty little adobe village of Tucson. The Mexican commandant at first refused to allow the Americanos to enter without a fight to the finish. However, when Cooke persisted, he took his small army of defenders and fled south a few miles to the Mission San Xavier. So, without firing a shot, the Stars and Stripes flew for the first time over an Arizona village.

The arrival of the Americanos caused the locals to charge "tourist prices" for their tortillas, grain, and other supplies. Not to be outdone, the Yanks paid in script redeemable only in the United States.

At the Gila River, Lt. George Stoneman decided to perform a naval experiment on that shallow stream. Lashing together some cottonwood logs, he set sail with about twenty-five hundred pounds of food and supplies. He hadn't traveled far when the craft sank. Stoneman went down with his ship, then walked ashore declaring the river unsuitable for navigation.

The Mormon Battalion reached California in January 1847, completing the longest infantry march in U.S. history. Shortly after the saints hacked and sawed their way across the wilderness of Arizona, James Marshall found gold at Sutter's Mill, altering the course of the westward movement from a slow, natural trickle into a stampede. During the next few years, thousands of emigrants would follow their path on what would be called the Gila Trail.

The passage of time does little to alter paths of least resistance from one place to another. Later, the Southern Pacific, U.S. Highway 80, then Interstate 10 and 8 would transport modern man along that same passageway. ◆

Jose' Romero, the "Mexican Juan Bautista de Anza," reopened the old overland trail to California in 1823. The road had been closed since the Yuma Massacre in 1781. The Yuma Indians were still unfriendly, so the explorers by-passed the historic Yuma Crossing. This diorama of the event is on display in the Arizona Historical Society Museum. Courtesy of the Arizona Historical Society/Tucson

Trappings of the mountain man. Photo courtesy of Gary M. Johnson

Pipe Springs National Monument. The Mormons established a fort and ranch here in the 1870s and the fort was called Winsor Castle for B. P. Winsor. The fort was built around the spring so the Indians couldn't poison it. Arizona's first telegraph office was located here in 1871 and the first telegrapher was Luella Stewart, grandmother of Stewart and Morris Udall. Photo courtesy of Maricopa Community Colleges, Southwest Studies

Early Mormon Missions on the

The first Mormon colonists from Utah arrived in Arizona in early 1854. The Navajos were on the warpath at the time and the saints were driven out a year later. Between 1858 and the early 1870s, Jacob Hamblin, the Mormon's greatest trailblazer, made several reconnaissance missions, locating river crossings, water holes and suitable trails. By this time the Navajos were at peace, thus making attempts at colonization safer. However, the greatest enemy facing the newcomers was the harsh, arid land and the fickle moods of the Little Colorado River.

Mormon settlements at Kanab (Utah), Pipe Springs, and Lee's Ferry were designated as bases from which to launch new colonies in Arizona. The primary mission of the church during these years was expansion. Under the dynamic leadership of Brigham Young, the Mormons were determined to establish a far-flung empire from their Utah base west to California and south to the Salt River Valley and eventually to Mexico.

A reconnaissance expedition was sent to the Little Colorado River Valley in 1873 to make a feasibility study for colonization. The scouts reported it unsuitable. A Norwegian missionary, Andrew Amundsen, pretty well summed up the bleak land. His spelling left a little to be desired but the meaning was clear: "From the first we struck the little Collorado...., it is the seam thing all the way, no plase fit for a human being to dwell upon." Amundsen concluded his report rather succinctly, calling it, "The moste desert lukking plase that I ever saw, Amen."

Despite this foreboding declaration, an expedition of some one hundred colonists left Utah in early 1873 headed for the Little Colorado determined to make a go of it.

They arrived on the Little Colorado in late May after a miserable, wind-blown journey down Moenkopi Wash. By this time the river was drying up. One journal entry referred to the Little Colorado, disparagingly, as "a loathsome little stream...as disgusting a stream as there is on the continent."

Jacob V. Hamblin, the "buckskin missionary," explored much of northern Arizona in the 1850s and 1860s. Hamblin spent much time among the Indians of the region, especially the Hopi. He worked with explorer John Wesley Powell and led Mormon settlers into Arizona in the 1870s. Photo courtesy of the Arizona Historical Society/Tucson

Iron-willed and purposeful as they were at the outset, the dispirited colonists soon packed their gear and returned to Utah. Undaunted, Brigham Young was determined to establish colonies in the valley of the Little Colorado River. Three years later he tried again, this time with success.

A major figure in the Mormon colonization along the Little Colorado River was a fiery red-headed frontiersman named Lot Smith. Smith is, perhaps, best remembered for his daring guerrila attacks on U.S. Army supply trains during the so-called Mormon War in 1857. In 1876, a mission was established at the ancient Hopi community at Moencopi and, over the next two years, Smith and other church leaders like William C. Allen, George Lake, and Jesse D. Ballinger led parties of colonists to the lower Little Colorado River Valley to the sites of today's Joseph City, Sunset Crossing (Winslow) and Holbrook. Town sites were marked, irrigation ditches were dug, dams erected, and crops were planted. The Mormons had, at last, taken permanent root in Arizona.

The four colonizing parties, each numbering about fifty, established camps and named them for their respective captains. Soon after the names were changed. Lake's Camp became Obed; Smith's Camp was changed to Sunset, for the river crossing nearby; Ballinger's Camp became Brigham City; and Allen's Camp, St. Joseph. (Since St. Joseph Missouri, was also on the Santa Fe line, in 1923, St. Joseph was changed to Joseph City).

As a precaution against Indian attacks, all four communities constructed forts of cottonwood logs and sandstone. These were self-containing units including communal mess halls and housing. The average size was about two hundred feet square with walls reaching a height of seven to nine feet. Elevated guardhouses stood at the corners. Each had shops, cellars, storehouses, and wells in case of prolonged siege.

Sunset and Brigham City were short-lived communities located on opposite sides of the Little Colorado near the site of present-day Winslow. In 1878, the two hardluck communities were ravaged by floods which destroyed the year's crops. Obed suffered the same fate. Within a year, malaria and flooding caused the colonists to pull up stakes. However, the sturdily built sandstone fort survived and was used as a stock corral by the Hashknife Outfit until it was torn down in 1895.

St. Joseph was the only one of the four commuties to survive. Despite numerous crop failures and dams destroyed by the rampaging Little Colorado, the gritty colonists won their battle against the elements. Today it holds the honor of being the oldest Mormon settlement in the Little Colorado River Valley. ♦

ittle Colorado River

Mormon Settler on the Colorado,
by Jack Graham

The Mormon Battalion faces the Gila River in December 1846. Mustered in at Council Bluffs, Iowa, in July 1846, the Mormons built a wagon road across Arizona. Much of today's Interstates 10 and 8 follow the old trail. During the California Gold Rush, thousands of emigrants made their way across Arizona following this route. Courtesy of Maricopa Community Colleges, Southwest Studies

Yuma's First Citizen

One of the most colorful ladies who ever rode the old West was Sarah Bowman of Yuma. She didn't fit the common frontier stereotype woman—calico dress, sunbonnet and a youngster hanging on each arm with another tugging at her skirt. In fact, there wasn't anything common about Sarah. They called her the "Great Western" after the biggest sailing ship of her day. Since she stood 6'2", that didn't seem to bother her; in fact she liked the comparison.

This red-haired lady with blue eyes was a Southwestern legend in her own time. She could literally sweep men right off their feet (and did on more than one occasion). Because of her bravery during the Mexican War at the battle of Fort Texas, the soldiers affectionately dubbed her the "American Maid of Orleans." The part about her being a "maid" was stretching things a bit but that happens a lot in Texas. Some folks might have questioned her morals—she had a long string of "husbands" during the war—but nobody ever questioned her bravery or generosity. During the seven-day bombardment of Fort Texas (later Fort Brown) by Mexican artillery, she dodged shells to serve hot coffee and soup to soldiers. Once she joined a battle charge declaring that if someone would loan her a pair of trousers she'd whip the whole Mexican army all by herself.

Sarah Bowman was born in Clay County, Missouri, in 1812 and seems to have led a rather uneventful life until the war with Mexico broke out in 1846. When her husband volunteered for service, she came along as a cook and laundress. He got sick and was put in a hospital, so Sarah left him behind and went on with the regiment to Fort Texas on the Rio Grande. During the siege she and nine other women, along with fifty men, were trying to hold against a superior Mexican force until the arrival of Gen. Zachary Taylor's army. Sarah was supposed to be sewing sandbags from soldiers tents but opted for more hazardous duty, defiantly dodging bullets to bring aid and comfort to the troops and earning their everlasting admiration. When Taylor's army advanced into Northern Mexico, she went along, setting up hostels along the way. For Sarah it was truly a labor of love. One "husband" died in the fighting around Monterey but the redoubtable "Great Western" continued to be the belle of Taylor's army.

During the two-day battle of Buena Vista, Sarah's commanding presence caught the attention of officers and men alike as, once again, she moved fearlessly around the battleground serving hot coffee to the weary soldiers.

When the war ended, Sarah loaded her wagons and decided to ride along with Major Lawrence Graham's dragoons to California. When told army regulations required that a woman couldn't travel with the troops unless she was married to one, she gave a snappy salute and announced with great alacrity, "All right, I'll marry the whole squadron." She climbed atop the hurricane deck of her Mexican donkey and rode down the line shouting, "Who wants a wife with $15,000 and the biggest legs in Mexico! Come my beauties, don't all speak at once—who is the lucky man?"

A fella named Davis took the challenge. "I have no objections to making you my wife," he said, "If there is a clergyman here to tie the knot." "Bring your blanket to my tent tonight," she laughed, "and I will learn you a knot that will satisfy you, I reckon!"

Sarah's "marriage" to Davis didn't last long. A short time later she cast her eyes on some mountain of a man her own size and fell madly in love—for a while. Actually, she switched husbands several times along the way.

Sarah got sidetracked in Franklin (El Paso), Texas, and spent the next few months running an eating establishment that offered the customers other amenities not usually found in restaurants. Later, on the way to California, Sarah stopped at Arizona City (Yuma) at the Colorado River crossing and decided to set up business in a "dirt-roofed adobe house." Author Raphael Pumpelly noted in 1861 that Sarah was the only resident in the eight-year-old town. He described her as "no longer young" and "was a character of a varied past. She had followed the war of 1848 with Mexico. her relations with the soldiers were of two kinds. One of these does not admit of analysis; the other was angelic, for she was adored by the soldiers for her bravery in the field and for her unceasing kindness in nursing the sick and wounded...."

Author-adventurer Capt. James Hobbs described her as "liked universally for her kind, motherly ways..." during the war.

Another observer, Jeff Ake, said she always packed two pistols, and "she shore could use 'em." He went on to say admiringly, "She was a hell of a good woman." According to Ake's father, Sarah was, "The greatest whore in the West." In the proper context, this appears to have been intended as a compliment.

Fort Yuma was evacuated briefly during the Confederate occupation, so when the soldiers prepared to march to San Diego, Sarah sent her "girls" home to Sonora and "followed the guidon" once more. She returned a few months later with the California Column. Time was catching up with the "Great Western." She died in Yuma on December 22, 1866. Years later, when the fort was abandoned, her remains and those of other soldiers who'd died at that post were taken and reburied at the Presidio in San Francisco.

Historians have used a lot of words, including generous, loyal, devoted and brave, to describe Sarah Bowman, the "Great Western." The community of Yuma, however, pays her the greatest compliment. Folks down there proudly call Sarah Bowman their "first citizen." (Originally published in the *Arizona Republic*)◆

Sarah Bowman Arrives in Yuma,
by Jack Graham

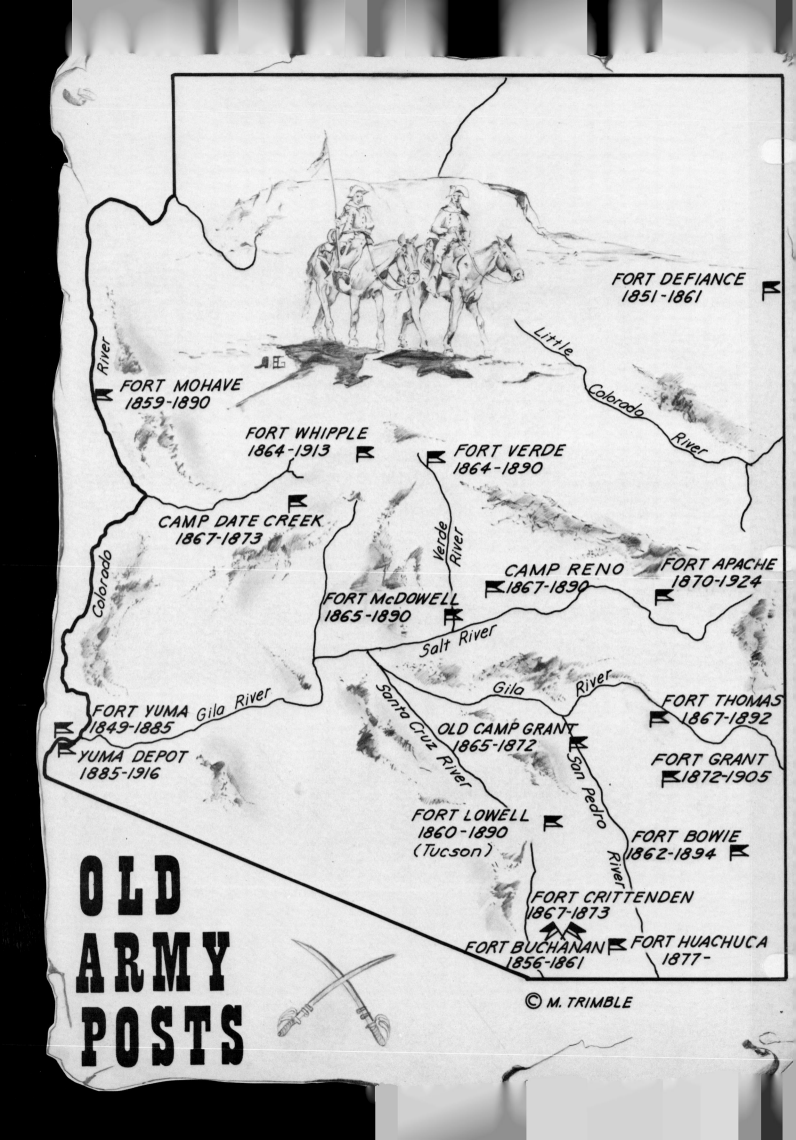

FORT DEFIANCE
1851-1861

FORT MOHAVE
1859-1890

Little Colorado River

FORT WHIPPLE
1864-1913

FORT VERDE
1864-1890

CAMP DATE CREEK
1867-1873

Verde River

Colorado

CAMP RENO
1867-1890

FORT APACHE
1870-1924

FORT McDOWELL
1865-1890

Salt River

Gila River

FORT YUMA
1849-1885

Gila River

Santa Cruz River

OLD CAMP GRANT
1865-1872

San Pedro River

FORT THOMAS
1867-1892

YUMA DEPOT
1885-1916

FORT GRANT
1872-1905

FORT LOWELL
1860-1890
(Tucson)

FORT BOWIE
1862-1894

FORT CRITTENDEN
1867-1873

OLD
ARMY
POSTS

FORT BUCHANAN
1856-1861

FORT HUACHUCA
1877-

© M. TRIMBLE

Chapter  7

Arizona in the 1850s

War with Mexico ended on February 2, 1848, when a treaty was signed at Guadalupe Hidalgo. Mexico agreed to give up its claims to Texas and ceded the lands including California, Utah, Colorado, Wyoming, New Mexico, and Arizona north of the Gila River.

The Mexican Republic received $15 million in recompense and the United States agreed to absorb more than $3 million in claims American citizens held against Mexico. Unfortunately, the new boundary was north of the Gila Trail, the only all-weather route to California. The problem was compounded by a boundary dispute in New Mexico. An inaccurate map used as the final authority placed El Paso about a hundred miles northeast of where it actually was. The American boundary commissioner, John Russell Bartlett, was completely outmaneuvered in establishing a suitable boundary by the clever Mexican engineer, Gen. Pedro Garcia Conde. Bartlett, a greenhorn political appointee with no knowledge of surveys, created such a controversy by his lack of interest and ineptitude, that he was eventually replaced by Maj. William Emory of the Army Corps of Topographical Engineers, a man of great ability.

The boundary controversy nearly boiled into open warfare between the United States and Mexico before President Franklin Pierce sent James Gadsden to Mexico with an offer to purchase more land. Gadsden arrived in Mexico City with five different offers. The largest, with a $50 million price tag, included a large chunk of northern Mexico that would have given Arizona a sizable seacost. However, it wasn't meant to be and the United States eventually paid $10 million for some 29,670 square miles and access to the Sea of Cortez. The important southern transcontinental railroad line along the Gila Trail was now possible.

Mexico might have sold more land had they not wanted to maintain the land bridge to Baja, California and a band of adventurers under William Walker hadn't made an ill-timed "invasion" of Mexico. That unfortunate incident raised the ire of Mexicans against selling any more than was necessary to build a railroad. The U.S. Congress was also divided on the issue. The Southerners wanted to acquire more land below the Mason-Dixon Line and Northerners were opposed. The final survey was completed by October 1855. On March 10, 1856, Capt. Hilarion Garcia lowered the Mexican flag at Tucson and moved his soldiers south. The following November, Maj. Enoch Steen and the First U.S. Dragoons arrived to take formal possession.

An old Arizona legend tells how the Arizonans missed out on having a seaport when engineers were surveying west of Nogales. It seems they were heading towards the Sea of Cortez when someone pointed out the nearest saloon was northwest at Yuma. The thirsty surveyors did a right oblique and marked a diagonal line towards the famous river crossing. Makes a good story but "it ain't true."

During the years preceding the Civil War, four military posts were established in Arizona. Fort Yuma, the first, was actually located on the California side of the Yuma crossing. Close on Fort Yuma's heels came the establishment of Forts Defiance, Buchanan, and Mojave. At the outbreak of the Civil War, all were abandoned and the civilian population, both Mexican and Anglo, were left to fend for themselves against hostile Apaches. Sonoran bandits and Anglo border ruffians. Map drawn by Dean Lyon; art by Jack Graham; courtesy of the author

John Russell Bartlett, 1805-1886, was U.S. boundary commisioner following the Treaty of Guadalupe Hidalgo in 1848. He badly bungled boundary operations and neglected his responsibilities but did manage to write an excellent narrative on the region. Photo courtesy of the Arizona Historical Society/Tucson

The Real Bill Williams

The picturesque town of Williams takes its name from Bill Williams Mountain which towers above and provides as beautiful a high country setting for a community as can be found in America. It's a fitting place-name for Ol' Bill Williams, the "greatest fur trapper of 'em all."

Ol' Bill was as colorful a man as any who ever forked a horse or mule and headed towards the setting sun. To those who knew the tireless old mountain man, he'd always seemed old—and eccentric. His drunken sprees around Taos set the standard others tried to match but never could. He rode alone into forbidding hostile Indian country.

Ol' Bill was a tall, skinny, redhead, with a high-pitched voice, his body battle-scarred and worn. He was known to run all day with six traps on his back and never break into a sweat. He had a peculiar way of walking, more closely resembling a stagger, and he never walked in a straight line. He fired his long-barreled "Kicking Betsy" with unerring accuracy in what was described as a "double wobble." On horseback he wore his stirrups so short his knees bobbed just beneath his chin. He leaned forward in the saddle, resembling a hunchback on horseback. All these eccentricities enhanced his reputation as the Old West's most unforgettable character. George Frederick Ruxton, an English adventurer who toured the West in the 1840s, wrote this colorful description of old Bill:

> Williams always rode ahead, his body bent over his saddlehorn, across which rested a long, heavy rifle, his keen gray eyes peering from under the slouched brim of a flexible felt-hat, black and shining with grease. His buckskin hunting shirt, bedaubed until it had the appearance of polished leather, hung in folds over his bony carcass; his nether extremities being clothed in pantaloons of the same material... The old coon's face was sharp and thin, a long nose and chin hob-nobbing each other; and his head was always bent forward giving him the appearance of being hump-backed. He appeared to look neither to the right nor left, but, in fact, his little twinkling eye was everywhere. He looked at no one he was addressing, always seeming to be thinking of something else than the subject of his discourse, speaking in a whining, thin, cracked voice... His character was well-known. Acquainted with every inch of the Far West, and with

Ol' Bill Williams, *by Jack Graham*

all the Indian tribes who inhabited it, he never failed to outwit his Red enemies, and generally made his appearance at the rendezvous, from his solitary expeditions, with galore of beaver when numerous bands of trappers dropped in on foot, having been despoiled of their packs and animals by the very Indians through the midst of whom old Williams had slipped.

They called him "Old Solitaire" for his lonesome ways (Bill wasn't that lonesome; he always seemed to have an Indian woman waiting somewhere). Fact is, he spoke several dialects and was more at home among the friendly tribes than he was with his own people. It was said he came west as a missionary to the Osage Indians but they converted him. He took an Osage wife and, after bearing two daughters, she died. So Bill headed for the mountains and became a trapper.

Bill had more lives than a cat, surviving one hair-raising adventure after another. His luck finally ran out after some thirty years in the wilds, when on March 14, 1849, a war party of Utes killed him and Dr. Ben Kern near the headwaters of the Rio Grande in southern Colorado.

Two years later, Richard Kern, a brother of Dr. Kern, was traveling with the Sitgreaves Expedition in northern Arizona. Kern took copious notes of everything he saw and heard on the journey. During the trip Kern and guide Antoine Leroux applied the name "Bill Williams" to the 9,200-foot range. Later the pair honored ol' Bill again by giving his name to the river that headwaters near Hackberry. Later it was changed to Big Sandy. Today, the stream becomes the Bill Williams River after it joins the Santa Maria River near Alamo Lake on its journey to the Colorado River.

Like the Indians, with whom they sometimes lived and sometimes fought, mountain men like ol'Bill were "nature's children." They loved the outdoors, hated fences and restrictions, respected grizzlies and rivers and rode anything that "wore hair."

Storing the knowledge of this vast *tierra incognita* in thier heads, they guided the storied Army Corps of Topographical Engineers on their historic surveys along the Thirty-second and Thirty-fifth Parallels during the 1850s. These trails or paths later became the trails that led emigrants to the promised land in what has been called the greatest mass migration of greenhorns since the children of Israel set out in search of Caanan. ◆

In 1850 Arizona became a part of the Territory of New Mexico. Since there weren't any non-Indian settlements north of the Gila, what was considered "Arizona" was, in reality, Doña Ana County, which extended across southern Arizona and New Mexico. The county seat was located at the small adobe village of Mesilla, along the Rio Grande. Feeling ignored by the government in Santa Fe, the citizens of Tucson began petitioning for separate status almost immediately after the Gadsden Treaty was ratified. In April 1860, an unofficial "Territory of Arizona" was created with the capital at Mesilla.

During the years preceding the Civil War, four military posts were established in Arizona. Fort Yuma, the first, was actually located on the California side of the Yuma Crossing. The hot desert was hell on humans and their livestock on their way to California. By the time they reached the crossing, most were in sad condition. To attend to these needs and keep an eye on the sometimes warlike Yuma Indians, a post was established on October 2, 1849 and called Camp Calhoun. A year and a half later it was renamed Camp Yuma. Getting supplies to the remote post was a major problem as they had to be hauled overland across the hazardous desert from San Diego. In 1852, the first steamboat loaded with supplies plowed its way up the muddy Colorado and the future of the fort was assured.

In 1851, Fort Defiance was built in the Four Corners country to keep an eye on the Navajos who, for generations, had raided the Hopis and the Spanish settlements along the Rio Grande. The isolated post was quickly dubbed "Hell's Gate" by the soldiers who were stationed there. The location of the fort was ill-planned. It was in a narrow canyon vulnerable to attack on three sides.

On April 30, 1860, a large war party made a bold attack on the fort. Stubborn resistance from the small force of defenders was all that prevented a massacre. Afterwards some fifteen hundred soldiers were assigned to the post to prevent a recurrence. The Civil War caused the post to be abandoned in 1861 and the Navajos resumed their raiding.

In 1856, Fort Buchanan was established to protect settlers and miners in the mountains south of Tucson. Three years later, Fort Mojave was built on the Colorado River as a shelter for emigrants following the old Beale Camel road across northern Arizona.

At the outbreak of the Civil War, all these posts were abandoned. Many of the officers and men who came from the South went home to fight for secession. Those loyal to the Union regrouped in California and New Mexico for the expected Confederate invasion. Naturally, the warrior tribes saw the retreat as a victory for their side and went on the warpath.

Most of this new land acquired from Mexico was *tierra incognita,* known only to a few mountain men. One of the first tasks for the U.S. government was to explore, map and survey routes for steamboats, wagons, and railroads. The responsibility for this giant undertaking was given to the Army Corps of Topographical Engineers, an elite, handpicked group of West Point graduates. Some of their names are stamped indelibly on the face of Arizona: Sitgreaves, Whipple, Ives, Beale, and Parke.

The first of these daring explorer-scientists was Capt. Lorenzo Sitgreaves. In 1851, he led an expedition of twenty men with an escort of soldiers and guided by the legendary scout Antoine Leroux along the Thirty-fifth Parallel. Their trek led some 650 miles across some of the West's most inhospitable land. During an attack by Yavapai warriors, Leroux was struck by three arrows. It was said the battle-toughened old scout was more chagrined at allowing himself to be shot than the physical pain inflicted by the wounds. The expedition's doctor, Sam Woodhouse, operated on Leroux with only one hand. Earlier

James Gadsden, U.S. Minister of Mexico, arranged the treaty in 1853-54 that bears his name, giving Arizona the land south of the Gila River to the present international boundary. Courtesy of the Western Archeological and Conservation Center, National Park Service

he'd been bitten on the other by a rattlesnake. The expedition suffered other hardships, including another savage attack by Yuma Indians, before reaching Fort Yuma bone weary and half starved.

The next group to run a survey along the Thirty-fifth Parallel (the future route of Interstate 40 and the Santa Fe Railroad) was led by Lt. Amiel W. Whipple in 1853. A few years earlier this young officer had won his spurs surveying the Arizona-Mexico boundary following the Treaty of Guadalupe Hidalgo. This time he was forging across northern Arizona. Again the expediton was guided by the redoubtable Antoine Leroux.

Whipple's small band spent a cold, wintery Christmas camped at the foot of the snow-covered San Francisco Peaks. Near the headwaters of the west fork of the Verde River, they turned south, then headed west to the Big Sandy River, thence to the Bill Williams Fork and on to the Colorado. His report proved that a railroad could indeed be built over the mountainous ranges of northern Arizona.

In 1858, Lt. Joseph C. Ives, former chief assistant to Whipple, was picked to chart the course of the unpredictable Colorado River. Steamboats had been plowing their way up the river as far as Yuma since 1852 when Capt. James Turnbull assembled a small, prefabricated sidewheeler called the *Uncle Sam.* The 120-mile trip from the mouth of the Colorado to Fort Yuma took two weeks. Progress was delayed by frequent stops for mesquite wood to fuel the twenty-horsepower, wood-burning engine. All hands had to go ashore and rustle up firewood. Later, local natives, after overcoming their initial fear of the smoke-belching creatures, sold firewood at "service stations" along the way. Incidentally, the swift current of the Colorado sped things

Major William Emory, soldier and scientist, led several boundary surveys in the 1850s. His writings did much to popularize Arizona for science. Photo courtesy of the Arizona Historical Foundation, Charles Trumbull Hayden University Library, Tempe

Gen. Sam Heintzelman was the most important figure responsible for the creation of the Arizona Territory in 1863. During the 1850s, he was post commander at Fort Yuma. During that time he also invested in Arizona mining ventures. Photo courtesy of the Arizona Historical Foundation, Sacks Collection

Amiel W. Whipple was a noted explorer and surveyor of the southwest during the 1850s. He rose to the rank of general and was killed at Chancellorsville in 1863. From the Photographic History of the Civil War, by F. T. Miller, courtesy of the Arizona Historical Society/Tucson

up a bit on the return journey. It took only fifteen hours.

The strategic Yuma Crossing at the confluence of the Gila and Colorado rivers provided a wonderful business opportunity for an entrepreneur named Dr. Able Lincoln. The lure of gold in California brought thousands of emigrants along the Gila Trail and they needed a way to cross the Colorado. Dr. Lincoln built a ferry and in 1850 made $60,000 in just three months. This lucrative business didn't go unnoticed by John Glanton and his band of scalp hunters. They horned in on the enterprise and soon incurred the wrath of the Yuma Indians, who commenced to massacre the whole bunch, including the unfortunate Dr. Lincoln.

Louis J. F. Jaeger reopened the ferry business a short time later and the establishment of Fort Yuma in 1852 served to protect the business from Indians and itinerant scalp hunters.

In 1853, Capt. George Johnson brought a sidewheeler dubbed the *General Jesup* to Fort Yuma. The fifty-horsepower paddlewheeler could haul fifty tons of freight. At $75 a ton, the *General Jesup* was soon grossing $20,000 a month and the steamboats on the Colorado became Arizona's main link with the outside world until the arrival of the railroad in the late 1870s.

Little was known about the navigability of the Colorado above Fort Yuma until 1858 when both George Johnson and Joseph Ives took their steam crafts up the river. The military steamer, piloted by Lieutenant Ives was an iron-hulled steamwheeler called the *Explorer*. It wasn't a graceful craft—one observer described it as a "water-borne wheelbarrow." Regardless, it did what it was supposed to do. In fact, both Johnson's civilian and Ive's military expeditions demonstrated the navigability of the silt-laden Colorado beyond today's Hoover Dam.

On the way back, Lieutenant Ives left his paddle wheeler and struck out east towards the Grand Canyon. With the help of some native guides, he snaked his way to the bottom, thus becoming the first white man to accomplish that feat. Ironically, his comments afterwards suggested that his was likely the last for a white man. "It can be approached," he wrote, "only from the south and after entering it there is nothing to do but leave. Ours has been the first and will doubtless be the last party of whites to visit this profitless locality." It's all in the eyes of the beholder.

A year previous to the Ives Expedition, Secretary of War Jefferson Davis selected a colorful adventurer named Edward (Ned) Fitzgerald Beale to build the first wagon road across northern Arizona. Beale, a former naval officer, was now a lieutenant in the Topographical Engineers. He was a hero of the battle of San Pascual in 1846 and had delivered the first dispatches of the California gold discovery to Washington three years later. Beale's expedition was unique in the annals of exploration in that camels were imported as beasts of burden. The camels' amazing ability to go great distances without

The Legend of Red Ghost

The great Camel Experiment in Arizona during the late 1850s produced a curious spinoff that has become one of Arizona's most enduring legends. Most folks know that just prior to the Civil War, camels were used as beasts of burden during the railroad surveys across the arid Southwest. They were ideally suited to the harsh desert environment and could outhaul and outdistance the best of pack mules. Their usefulness was championed by Lt. Edward F. Beale who wrote admiringly, "The harder the test they are put to, the more fully they seem to justify all that can be said of them. They pack water for others four days under a hot sun and never get a drop; they pack heavy burdens of corn and oats for months and never get a grain; and on the bitter greasewood and other worthless shrubs not only subsist but keep fat."

Unfortunately, the homely beasts, noted for their terrible halitosis and independence, never won general acceptance among Southwesterners. Although the camel surveys proved successful, the Civil War broke out and the critters were eventually sold at auction. A few got loose and ran wild and free in the desert regions where they became fair game for locals who used them for target practice. At least one fell victim to a more cruel and inhumane prank. Therein lies the basis for the Legend of Red Ghost.

Our story begins back in 1883 at a lonely ranch near Eagle Creek in southeast Arizona. The Apache wars were drawing to a close; however, a few renegade bands were on the prowl keeping isolated ranches in a constant state of siege. Early one morning two men rode out to check on the livestock, leaving their wives at the ranch with the children. About midmorning, one of the women went down to the spring to fetch a bucket of water, while the other remained in the house with the children. Suddenly one of the dogs began to bark ferociously. The woman inside the house heard a terrifying scream. Looking out the window she saw a huge, reddish-hued beast run by with a devilish looking creature on its back.

The frightened woman barricaded herself in the house and waited anxiously for the men to return. That night they found the body of the other woman, trampled to death. The next day tracks, cloven hoof prints much larger than those of a horse, were found along with strands of long, red hair.

A few days later a party of prospectors near Clifton was awakened by the sound of thundering hoofs and ear-piercing screams. Their tent collapsed and the men scratched and clawed their way out of the mess of rubble just in time to see a gigantic creature running off in the moonlight. The next day they too found huge cloven hoof prints and long reddish strands of hair clinging to the brush.

Naturally, these stories grew and were embellished by local raconteurs. One fellow claimed he saw it kill and eat a large grizzly bear. Another insisted he chased the Red Ghost only to have it disappear before his very own eyes.

A few months after the incident with the miners, a rancher on the Salt River, named Cyrus Hamblin, rode up on the animal while gathering cows. Hamblin recognized the beast as a camel with something tied to its back that resembled the skeleton of a man. Although Hamblin had a reputation as an honest man and not given to tall tales, many refused to believe his story. Several weeks later, over on the Verde River, the camel was seen again, this time by a group of prospectors. They, too, saw something attached to the animal's back and it wasn't just a hump. They grabbed their weapons and fired at the camel but missed. The animal broke and ran, causing a piece of the cryptic object to fall

to the ground. They discovered a sight that bristled the hair on their necks. On the ground before them was a human skull with some parts of flesh and hair still attached.

A few days later the Red Ghost struck again. This time the victims were teamsters camped beside a lonely road. They claimed to have been awakened in the middle of the night by a loud scream. According to the terrified drivers, a creature at least thirty feet tall knocked over two freight wagons and generally raised hell with the camp. The men ran for their lives and hid out in the brush. Upon returning the next day, they found cloven hoof prints and red strands of hair.

About a year later, a cowboy near Phoenix came upon the Red Ghost eating grass in a corral. Traditionally, cowboys have been unable to resist temptation to rope anything that wears hair, and this fella was no exception. He punched a hole in his rope and tossed a loop over the camel's head. Sudenly the angry beast turned and charged full bore. The horse tried to dodge the hard charging dromedary but to no avail. The horse and rider went down and, as the camel ran off in a cloud of dust, the astonished cowboy recognized the skeletal remains of a man tied to it's back.

During the next few years stories of the Red Ghost grew to legendary proportions, however, no more attacks were reported.

The Red Ghost appeared for the last time nine years later in eastern Arizona when a rancher awoke one morning and saw the critter casually grazing in his garden. He drew a careful bead with his trusty Winchester and dropped the animal with one shot. An examination of the corpse convinced all that this was indeed the fabled Red Ghost. The animal's back was heavily scarred from rawhide strips that had been used to tie on the body of a man. Some of the leather strands had cut into the camel's flesh.

How the human body came to be attached to the back of the camel remains a cruel mystery to this day. ◆

The Legend of Red Ghost, *by Jack Graham*

water, eating only the natural forage along the trail, offered a solution to the army's transportation problems in the arid southwest. Although Beale championed his illustrious camels, his hired hands scorned them. The muleskinners couldn't speak Arabic and the stubborn beasts wouldn't learn English. Furthermore, the animals' bad breath would peel the hide off a gila monster and they had a habit of spitting at anyone they didn't like. The problem was partially solved by importing North African camel drivers. Hadji Ali was the most famous. His name was quickly Americanized to Hi Jolly. Despite the foul-smelling camels, whose strange ways and appearances caused pack mules and wagon teams to panic, Beale successfully opened up his wagon road. But this romantic episode in Arizona history came to an end just prior to the Civil War. Hi Jolly remained in Arizona, got married and settled down. He is memorialized on a pyramid-shaped monument topped off with a lone camel at Quartzsite, Arizona.

While Sitgreaves, Whipple, Beale, and Ives were surveying routes across Northern Arizona, others were marking paths along the Gila Trail or, more scientifically, the Thirty-second Parallel. In 1854, Lt. John G. Parke of the Topographical Engineers was sent out to explore routes between El Paso, Texas, and the Pima villages near todays' Sacaton, Arizona. Parke was also a veteran of the Thirty-fifth Parallel country, having been with Sitgreaves in 1851. Since part of the trail blazed by the Mormon Battalion dipped into Sonora, Parke searched for shortcuts through the mountain passes inside the Gadsden Purchase. Assisted by Lt. George Stoneman, Parke mapped a route through Apache Pass, at the north end of the Chiricahua Mountains. This was the path followed a few years later by the famous Butterfield-Overland Mail. The pass had too steep a grade and too many arroyos for a railroad so Parke returned a year later and located a new route north of the Dos Cabezas Mountains. The Civil War delayed the building of a transcontinental railroad for many years, but when the Southern Pacific stretched its steel ribbons across Arizona in the 1880s, Parke's old survey was followed. Today, Interstate 10 passes along the same pathway.

Jesse Leach built the first wagon road across southern Arizona in 1858. Leach's road ran from El Paso to the San Pedro River, then turned north to the Gila River and followed that stream to Maricopa Wells, then on to Yuma. Although it was forty-seven miles shorter, Leach bypassed Tucson and doomed his road to failure.

In 1849, it took 166 days to travel coast to coast in a covered wagon. The same trip by stagecoach in the 1860s took sixty days. A decade later one could make the trip by rail in eleven days. By 1923, the time was shortened to twenty-six hours by airplane. A 747 could travel cross-country in five hours by 1975 and in 1980 the Space Shuttle made it in eight minutes.

Beginning in the late 1850s, in towns like Tucson, the sound of the bugle and the pounding of horses' hooves announced the arrival of the biweekly stagecoach. Small crowds gathered in the dusty streets to cheer the arrival of John Butterfield's Overland Stage. These leather-slung cradles on wheels were luxury liners compared to earlier times when men, women and children traveled afoot, on horseback or in some primitive wagon train. Newspapers as late as the 1870s still carried a long list of precautions for the prudent traveler. These included: If a team runs away, don't jump out—just sit tight and ride it out; don't discuss politics or religion with your fellow passengers; don't drink hard liquor in freezing weather; and don't grease your hair—too much dust.

In 1857, the first mail and passenger line across Arizona was chartered. It ran from San Antonio, Texas, to San Diego, California. The itinerary inspired one critic to mutter: "It ran from no place through nothing to nowhere." The line was

Taken captive by a band of nomadic warriors near Gila Bend in 1851, Olive Oatman endured six years of slavery until she was ransomed. During her captivity, Olive was tattooed on her chin, a custom among the people along the Colorado River where she was held. Olive later married lawyer John Fairchild, raised a family and died in 1903. She wore the tatoos as a badge of pride and testament to her survival. Photo courtesy of Maricopa Community Colleges, Southwest Studies

better known as the "Jackass Mail" because the coaches were pulled by mules and, west of Yuma, passengers were required to ride across the sand dunes on the hurricane deck of the long-eared critters. The stage rolled by day and stopped to camp each night; because of the weather, the routine was sometimes reversed. In one year of operation the Jackass Mail made only forty trips across Arizona before being replaced by the legendary Butterfield Overland Mail.

"Remember boys, nothing on God's earth can stop the U.S. Mail." So said John Butterfield—and hardly anything did. Butterfield had the first reliable stage line across Arizona. He had a government-subsidized operation that ran twenty-eight hundred miles from Tipton, Missouri, to San Francisco,

California. The line was quickly dubbed the Ox Bow because it swung south through Texas to Tucson, then Los Angeles and San Francisco. Butterfield was a logistical genius, building stations, hiring agents and teamsters, obtaining livestock and running his line with clock-like efficiency. The trip took about twenty-six days; the fare cost $200 plus meals, which usually consisted of coffee, beans, venison, mule meat, salt pork and heaps of mustard.

The twice-weekly stage ran twenty-four hours a day but the rough roads rendered a night's sleep impossible. To help pass the time, male passengers usually drank their way across Arizona, throwing their empties out alongside the trail. Modern pilots claim they can trace the old trail from the air because of all the glitter of broken glass.

The top line for the stagecoaches were the Concord coaches. They were sturdier and hand-crafted from the finest materials and assembled with more meticulous care than the most expensive of today's automobiles. All wood was first dried and sun-warped for three years so it wouldn't shrink in the hot, dry southwest. The Concord had no metal springs. Instead there were thick leather thoroughbraces supporting the body. These let it roll rather than bounce over the bumps. The Concords were used primarily in the eastern and western ends of the line. In Arizona, the lighter celerity wagon was used. It had wooden seats that folded into beds and canvas flaps that rolled down to keep the dust out. The wagon was pulled by mules and some were so wild they had to be blindfolded before they could be hitched.

Stations were located about twenty miles apart. In Arizona most of the stations were made of adobe and had protective walls in case of Apache attacks. And it could be dangerous work: 168 men died violently during those tumultuous years prior to the Civil War.

The Butterfield Overland Mail was stopped only once in its two-and-one-half year history. In 1861, Cochise and his Chiricahua Apaches went on the warpath around Apache Pass and did what nothing else on "God's earth" could: shut it down.

* * *

The winds of political change swept across Arizona in the mid-1850s. On the morning of March 10, 1856, Capt. Hilarion Garcia and his company of soldiers stood at attention while the tri-colors of the Mexican Republic were lowered for the last time over the tiny presidio at Tucson. It had been two years since the United States purchased the land from Mexico; however, Mexicans continued to man the small garrison. A small contingent of Americans living in the adobe commuity on the banks of the Santa Cruz River cheered heartily as the Stars and Stripes were raised. After the ceremonies Captain Garcia, along with his cavalry troops and their families in the wagons behind, rode south along the dusty road leading to Mexico.

Tucson, which had a population of some 1,000 during times of peace with the Apaches, had dwindled in recent years to about 350 residents due to the resumption of raiding and plundering. Early American explorers reported seeing decaying ruins of once-prosperous ranches and mines.

The wheels of bureaucracy turn slowly at times and, in spite of these Apache depredations, Tucson was without military protection from Captain Garcia's departure in March until Maj. Enoch Steen and his First U.S. Dragoons arrived eight months later.

During the time between the departure of Mexican soldiers from Tucson and the arrival of dragoons, a sizable party of American miners arrived under the leadership of an adventuresome young man named Charles Debrille Poston. They were headed for the mineral-rich Santa Rita and Cerro Colorado mountains, south of the old pueblo. During the next few years they would mine a king's ransom in silver.

Poston's company rested in Tucson for a couple of weeks. It was fiesta time, he wrote in his journal, and the men were allowed to "attend the fiesta, confess their sins, and get acquainted with the Mexican senoritas, who flocked there in great numbers from the adjoining state of Sonora." A few weeks later Poston established the company headquarters at the abandoned Spanish presidio at Tubac some forty-five miles south of Tucson.

The old fortress was still in pretty good shape. Most of the adobe buildings were still intact, but the doors and windows had been hauled away. Work crews were sent into the pine-studded Santa Rita Mountains to cut lumber; corrals were rebuilt and soon the historic old presidio was habitable once more. A short distance to the east flowed the cool waters of the Santa Cruz River, and nearby fields provided abundant grass. As soon as word reached Sonora, large numbers of Mexicans arrived seeking employment in the reopened mines. Next he purchased the twenty thousand-acre Arivaca ranch on the west side of the Cerro Colorado mountains. Old mines were reopened and soon Tubac was a bustling little community.

Tubac, with its low-lined adobe dwellings and dusty streets quickly took on the atmosphere of a pristine utopia. Far from cumbersome bureaucracy, cluttered cities and the influence of the Catholic church, Poston would later write, "we had no law but love and no occupation but labor. No government, no taxes, no public debt, no politics. It was a community in a perfect state of nature."

The young entrepreneur had a paternalistic fondness for the Mexicans, especially the women. "Sonora has always been famous for the beauty and gracefulness of its señoritas," he wrote admiringly. The gold rush had created a mass exodus of young men to California, leaving the ratio of women to men as high as twelve to one in some Sonora towns. Many of these unattached ladies headed north to the new American mining camp at Tubac, "when they could get transportation in wagons hauling provisions," he continued "they came in state." Others came on the hurricane deck of burros, and many came on foot. All were provided for.

"The Mexican señoritas really had a refining influence on the frontier population. Many of them had been educated at convents, and all of them were good Catholics."

Poston seems to have missed little in his observations. "They are exceedingly dainty in their underclothing, wear the finest linen when they can afford it, and spend half their lives over the washing machine."

The ladies of Sonora made a rich contribution to life in the community, not only providing companionship for the lonely miners, but assuming other responsibilities as well. "The Mexican women were not by any means useless appendages in camp." Poston noted. "They could keep house, cook some dainty dishes, wash clothes, sew, dance, and sing." They could give a good account of themselves in men's games also. ". . . they were expert at cards and divested many a miner of his week's wages over a game of Monte."

Poston was, in effect, the *alcalde,* or magistrate, of Tubac. Accordingly, under Mexican custom, he was in charge of all criminal and civil affairs of the community. "I was legally authorized to celebrate the rites of matrimony, baptize children, grant divorces, execute criminals, declare war, and perform all the functions of the ancient El Cadi. . . ."

Young couples who couldn't afford the twenty-five dollar marriage fee charged by the priests in Sonora came to Tubac where Poston not only married them for free but gave them jobs. In gratitude, many children were named Carlotta and Carlos in honor of the general *patrón.*

Life in Tubac went on its merry uncomplicated way until Archbishop Jean Baptiste Lamy of Santa Fe sent Father Joseph Machebeuf to check out the spiritual condition of Tubac. The

Fort Defiance was the first military post in Arizona. It was established as a base of operations for campaigns against the Navajo.

From an original sketch by Joseph Heger, 1860; courtesy of the Arizona Historical Society

priest was aghast upon learning the marriages hadn't been blessed by a priest. He quickly ruled all marriages null and void. "My young friend," the priest told Poston, "I appreciate all you have done for these people, but these marriages you have celebrated are not good in the eyes of God."

Poston defended his actions, claiming that he hadn't charged the couples any money and had even given them an official-looking marriage certificate. The couples were then given a ceremonious salute called "firing off the anvil" (a homemade tribute made by detonating a charge of blasting powder held in check by a huge anvil so as not to cause any damages). Father Machebeuf must have felt "bested" by the persuasive Poston for he agreed to do some horsetrading.

The marriages would be blessed on the condition that Poston would refrain from activity customarily performed by the church. A gala celebration was held; the couples were reunited in marriage. Guests included all the little Carlottas and Carloses. According to Poston, "it cost the company about $700 to rectify the matrimonial situation."

Poston enjoyed those halcyon days at Tubac. On Sunday mornings he relaxed in one of the natural pools of the Santa Cruz River, smoking good cigars and reading six-month-old newspapers.

Tubac had little government, few laws and no taxes. Employees were paid in company script called *boletas*. Since none of the Mexicans could read English, each *boleta* had a picture of a particular animal and each animal represented a specific amount. A calf represented twenty-five cents, a rooster was fifty cents and a horse was worth a dollar.

Food for the hungry miners was hauled in from Sonora.

Fresh fruit came from the orchards of the nearby mission at Tumacacori. Manufactured goods were hauled from St. Louis over the old Santa Fe Trail.

One of the freighters hauling trade goods in from Santa Fe was Charles Trumbull Hayden, father of the late senator Carl Hayden.

In 1857, the Heintzelman Mine in the Cerro Colorado Mountains hit a rich vein that yielded $7,000 to the ton. The ore was hauled by wagon to Guaymas, then by ship to San Francisco at a hefty 50 percent profit. In the fall of that year, Poston sent a wagon train loaded with rawhide bags full of ore, a ton to the wagon, over the Santa Fe Trail to Kansas City. The ore was widely distributed, giving the eastern United States its first look at the mineral potentials of Arizona.

But the good times couldn't last forever. A filibustering or looting expedition led by Henry Crabb attempted to take Sonora in 1857. The filibusterers were cornered at Caborca and killed, but the furor over the affair caused Mexico to place an embargo on commerce. For a while Americans crossing into Mexico did so at great risk. About the time tempers cooled, the Apaches heated up. Up to this time they had pretty much left the Americans alone, preferring to raid their traditional foes, the Mexicans. However, when a group of American newcomers who were not associated with Poston's mines joined a party of Mexicans and ambushed a band of Apaches, war was declared on all Americans in the area. In 1861 Cochise and his Chiricahua Apaches went on the warpath. Bands of marauding Apaches raided throughout the Santa Cruz Valley. That same year the Civil War broke out and the U.S. government focused its attention on more pressing matters.

This 1930 photo shows the ruins of walls of old Fort Crittenden built in 1856. It was built for troops who were to watch the Mexican border and assist in subduing hostile Apaches. Photo courtesy of the Arizona Historical Society

The Explorer, *shown here on the Colorado River in 1857, was the first U.S. military craft to sail the Colorado.* Sketch by Heinrich Baldwin Möllhausen, courtesy of Maricopa Community Colleges, Southwest Studies

Federal troops were removed from the area and Forts Buchanan and Breckinridge were abandoned. The civilian population, both Mexican and Anglo, were left to fend for themselves against hostile Apaches, Sonoran bandits, and Anglo border ruffians.

Poston later recalled how "the smoke of burning wheat fields could be seen up and down the Santa Cruz Valley, where the troops were in retreat destroying everything before and behind them. The Government of the United States abandoned the first settlers of Arizona to the merciless Apaches," he complained bitterly, adding that "armed Mexicans in considerable numbers crossed the boundary line, declaring that the American government was broken up and they had come to take their country back again.

"Even the Americans, the few Americans left in the country, were not at peace among themselves. The chances were if you met on the road it was to draw arms and declare whether you were for the North or the South.

"The Mexicans at the mines assassinated all the white men there when they were asleep, looted the place, and fled across the boundary line to Mexico."

The Apaches laid siege on Tubac and reduced it to rubble. There was nothing left for Poston to do but grab a few personal belongings and hightail it.

Poston left Arizona in 1861, barely escaping with his life. His personal loss was great. Earlier that year, a brother, John Lee Poston, had been murdered at the Cerro Colorado Mine.

The 1850s, born in hope and prosperity with the creation of the territory of New Mexico and enriched by the bold ventures of visionaries like Poston, died in those last dark days. Dreams of building a state in Apache land drifted hopelessly skyward, much like the billowing smoke that curled from the charred ruins of old Tubac. ◆

The Searchlight *is shown docked at Yuma in 1880-1916. The last survivor on the Rio Colorado, she made her last trip in 1916.* Photo courtesy of Maricopa Community Colleges, Southwest Studies

Louis J. F. Jaeger arrived at the Yuma crossing in 1850 to run the ferryboat operation. Later he was also a freighter. He became a millionaire in a very short time but lost much of his fortune in failed business ventures and river floods. He is shown here with Pasquale, a Quechan head-man or chief. Photo courtesy of the Arizona Historical Society/Tucson

Jaeger's Ferry at the Yuma Crossing. Photo courtesy of the Arizona Historical Society

THE LAST CAMP
OF
HI JOLLY
BORN SOMEWHERE IN SYRIA
ABOUT 1828
DIED AT QUARTZSITE
DECEMBER 16 1902
CAME TO THIS COUNTRY
FEBRUARY 10 1856
CAMELDRIVER — PACKER
SCOUT — OVER THIRTY
YEARS A FAITHFUL AID
TO THE U.S. GOVERNMENT
•
ARIZONA
HIGHWAY DEPARTMENT
1935

This tribute to "Hi Jolly," the legendary camel driver of the 1850s, stands in Quartzsite. His real name was Hadji Ali, but this was Americanized to "Hi Jolly" by locals. Since muleskinners and camels didn't see eye to eye, Arabs such as "Hi Jolly" were imported to do the job as part of the Army's famed "camel experiment" to use the critters as beasts of burden in the arid Southwest. The Middle Eastern drivers earned fifteen dollars a month. The experiment ended during the Civil War but "Hi Jolly" stayed, becoming a U.S. citizen in 1865. During the next twenty years he worked as a miner, married and finally settled in Quartzsite where he died in 1902. Photo by Jeff Kida

Camel Mail in Arizona *is a diorama in the Arizona Historical Society Museum. On July 18, 1859, on a prairie west of the San Francisco Peaks, camels arrived from California. In the recreation, Lt. Ned Beale and his beloved camels are surveying a route across mountainous northern Arizona.* Courtesy of the Arizona Historical Society/Tucson

This 1909 photo captures the fierce independence of William Hudson Kirkland, one of Arizona's most illustrious pioneers. His ranch at Canoa in 1857 was the first American ranching enterprise in Arizona. Of his many achievements, his proudest moment was the hoisting of the American flag over Tucson in 1856. Photo courtesy of Ben and Fern Allen

Williams, Arizona, is pictured here in 1893, long before it became famous as the "Gateway to the Grand Canyon." The town was named for the legendary free trapper and guide, Bill Williams. Old Bill rode through here many times and, when Army surveyors were mapping the region, trail guide Antoine Leroux, a friend of Bill's, mentioned that the old trapper had camped at the site. Thus, Bill Williams Mountain got its name and the town that grew up here in the 1880s followed suit. Photo by C. R. Allen, courtesy of the Arizona Historical Society/Tucson

Charles D. Poston, promoter, entrepreneur, and leader in the fight for territorial status is known today as the "father of Arizona." Photo courtesy of the Sharlot Hall Museum

WILLIAMS ARIZONA 1893

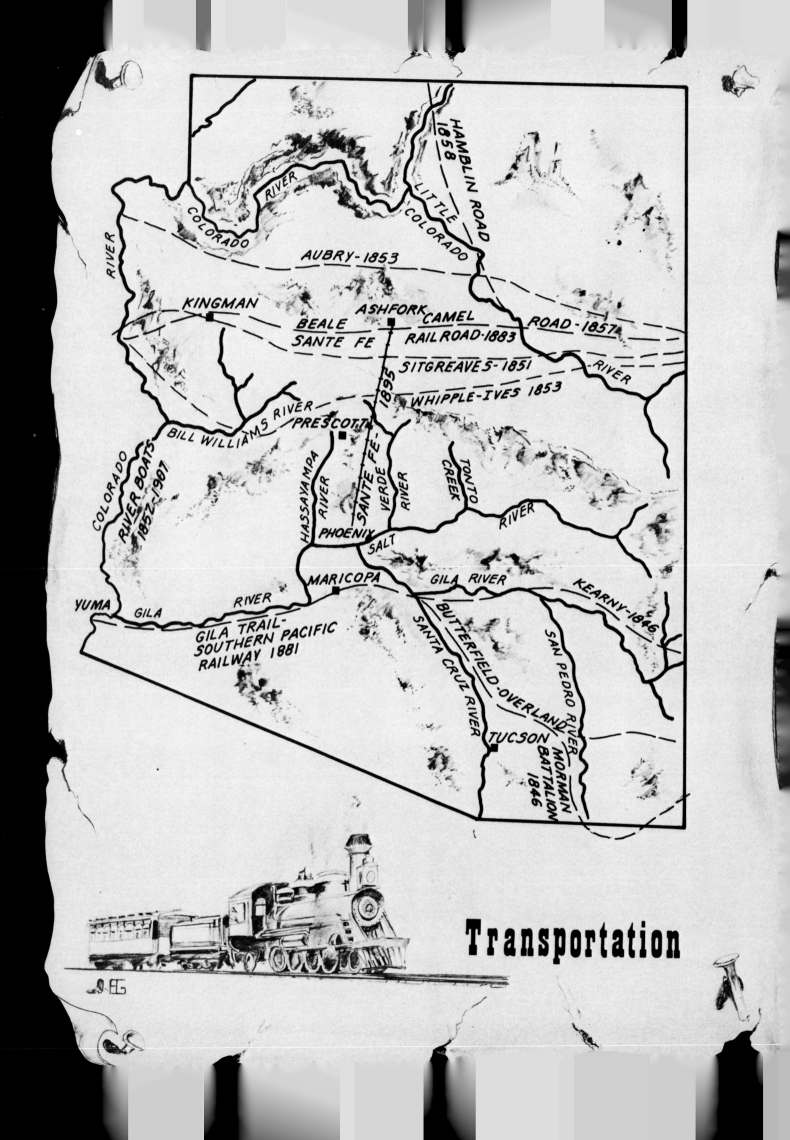

Transportation

Chapter  8

Steel Ribbons

Since the first prospector's pick struck paydirt along the Gila River in 1858, roadways following paths of least resistance were essential to get supplies in and ore out of the rugged mountains of Arizona. In 1852, steamboats began churning their way up the muddy Colorado River. These paddle wheelers hauled freight, passengers and soldiers to ports like Yuma, Ehrenberg, and Hardyville. From there, roads that weren't much more than cattle trails headed into central Arizona. These steamboats were the main supply link with the outside world until the arrival of the railroads in the late 1870s. From that time on, the days of the paddle wheeler were numbered. Historically, America's western roads ran east and west, and there wasn't much demand for riverboats that ran north and south far from the population centers.

Naturally, there was always much cause for celebration with the arrival of a new railroad. Anyone who had crossed the desert afoot, on horseback or mule, rocked and rolled on the leather-slung thoroughbraces of a stagecoach, or in a wagon

without shock absorbers, was bound to appreciate the wonders of riding in a steam car.

In the spring of 1877, Arizona's citizens at Yuma were anxiously awaiting the arrival of the first railroad. Construction was delayed when the Southern Pacific, building eastbound from California, reached the Colorado River and ran into some Washington-style bureaucratic politicking. Earlier, permission had been granted from Gen. Irwin McDowell to build the bridge. However, the secretary of war overruled the department commander and refused to allow the railroad to cross a federal stream until some red tape was untangled. Permission was granted to build the bridge—they just couldn't stretch any steel rails across it.

Chinese workmen spent the hot summer months laying a grade while pile drivers were busily constructing a 667-foot bridge across the Colorado. On September 29, 1877, the bridge was complete except for the rails.

The new line ran close to the old military post at Fort Yuma,

Camels, stagecoaches, ox-drawn wagons and paddle wheelers, all had a hand in linking the Arizona Territory with the outside world. But none was met with such celebration, or controversy, as was the iron horse. Map drawn by Dean Lyon; art by Jack Graham; courtesy of the author

In 1877, Southern Pacific crews complete the rail bridge across the Colorado to reach Yuma. Photo courtesy of the Arizona Historical Society

Bungled Burglaries

Nefarious ne'er-do-wells bent on leading a life of crime in the Arizona territory knew their stock in trade had a few risks. It was hard to look innocent and inconspicuous while driving a herd of stolen horses or cattle. The incumbered perpetrators were also quite vulnerable to being pursued by an angry rancher and his hired hands. Whiskey running and small-time holdups brought little return for the risk involved. Banks had lots of money but they were located in towns where people didn't take kindly to having their savings robbed and posses could be formed quickly. That left stagecoaches and trains as likely victims. Both were especially vulnerable when pulling long grades or stopping at some remote station.

The arrival of the railroads in the 1880s opened up new career opportunities for these ubiquitous desperados. Towns were few and far between, the Mexican border was close, the rough country provided a sanctuary, and local peace officers didn't have the resources for lengthy manhunts.

One of Arizona's earliest train robberies occurred on the evening of August 10, 1887, at Pantano, a few miles east of Tucson. The gang leader was a tough, cocky outlaw recently exiled from New Mexico named Larry Sheehan. Sheehan and his gang were captured at Stein's Pass, along the New Mexico border, by Sheriff John Slaughter's posse. However, before they could be tried and given room and board at the Yuma Territorial prison, a lenient Tucson judge released the gang on bail. Unreformed, they wasted no time in returning to a life of crime, robbing the Southern Pacific at Stein's Pass, then hightailing it to Mexico. This time they were pursued by U.S. marshal W. K. Meade. Marshal Meade unwisely led his posse across the Mexican border in hot pursuit and found themselves pursued and captured by the *rurales* or state police and locked up in a Mexican jail. For two weeks, U.S. and Mexican authorities exchanged diplomatic acupuncture before the embarrassed and ruffled marshal and his men were released at the border sans guns and horses. Incidentally, the Sheehan bunch was hunted down and executed by the *rurales* shortly afterward.

One of Arizona's zaniest robberies took place five miles west of Willcox on January 30, 1895, when two cowboys named Grant Wheeler and Joe George decided to raise their station in life by robbing the Southern Pacific.

Since neither had ever heisted a railroad before, there was going to be a degree of on-the-job training. The novice train robbers purchased a box of dynamite in Willcox under the pretense of going prospecting. They cached their blasting powder and hobbled their horses some seven miles west of town, then walked back a couple of miles to meet the train. West of Willcox was a long grade that slowed the train enough that the two itinerant cowpunchers jumped aboard with ease. It didn't take much persuasion to entice the engineer to stop the train, especially when he was looking into the muzzle of a .45 revolver. One of the desperados jumped down and uncoupled the passenger cars and signaled the obliging engineer to pull forward with the mail and baggage cars to where the dynamite was waiting.

They broke into the express car and found the messenger had slipped out the door on the opposite side and skedaddled back to the passenger cars. Undaunted, Wheeler and George placed sticks of dynamite around the two safes, lit the fuses and ducked out the door. The first blast destroyed the door on the smaller safe but the prize, a large Wells Fargo safe, remained intact. They tried again, this time adding a couple of extra sticks for good measure, and got the same results. The big safe reappeared, unblemished in a haze of smoke and splinters. Finally, the frustrated would-be desperados piled the rest of their blasting sticks around the safe and packed eight large sacks, each containing one thousand Mexican silver pesos, on top to act as ballast. They struck a match to the fuse and lit out running for the nearest cover. The resounding blast shook the ground from the Dragoons to Dos Cabezas. The entire express car was blown to splinters. Pieces of lumber mixed with thousands of "dobe dollars" (short for adobe) were flung far and wide.

It was something of a miracle that Wheeler and George survived the blast of silver coins that spewed from the exploding car, impregnating everything they hit, including the telegraph poles alongside the track. When the smoke cleared the two amateurs entered the car and found the durable safe door blown off but only a few dollars tucked inside. The real booty was the Mexican silver used as ballast and it was scattered off all over the countryside. They stuffed a few coins in their pockets and rode off into the night, no doubt, to re-evaluate their *modus operandi.* When word of the dobe

dollar fiasco reached town, most of the population of Willcox took their rakes and hurried out to the scene of the crime. Old timers said people were still raking the ground and uncovering silver coins thirty years after the robbery.

The Wheeler-George venture had gotten off to a shaky start but the two erstwhile cowboys decided to persist in their new career. On the evening of February 26, they stopped another Southern Pacific train, this time at Stein's Pass, a popular place for train robbers. To their surprise, the fireman and engineer were the same crew from the previous robbery. "Well, here we are again," Wheeler grinned.

Since the only part of the game plan that failed previously was the extravagant application of blasting powder, Wheeler and George decided to use the same set up as before: uncouple the passenger cars and move the express and mail cars down the track a couple of miles to where the dynamite was waiting. While George kept the crew covered, Wheeler went back to uncouple the cars. That done, he climbed back on the engine and ordered the engineer to pull ahead (by now, it's likely the four were on a first name basis).

When they reached the dynamite, the engine was halted and the two headed for the express car and discovered—horrors!—in his haste Wheeler had uncoupled the wrong car. The express car, the one with the *dinero,* was still hitched to the passenger cars, two miles down the track.

Wheeler and George looked at each other with resigned frustration, shrugged and sheepishly ordered the engineer to go rejoin his train.

After the train left, the much-chagrined badmen lit the fuse on the unused dynamite and rode off in disgust.

This story should have a happy ending, but it doesn't. Wheeler and George should have gone back east and formed a vaudeville team or something more suitable to their natural talents. Wells Fargo and the Southern Pacific failed to see the humor in these frivolous escapades, nor did they take kindly to having their property tampered with in such an irreverent manner. Both Wheeler and George were eventually tracked down and died with their boots on. ◆

on the California side of the river. The entire garrison at the time consisted of a Maj. Tom Dunn, a sergeant, a private, and a prisoner.

Major Dunn's orders were not to allow any track laying on the bridge, and the major was determined to see that the railroad remained on the California side, even if it meant putting his entire command on military alert. He surveyed the construction crew. All hands appeared to be complying with the secretary's orders.

In fact, things appeared too quiet for the suspicious officer. That evening he decided to post a sentry at the entrance to the bridge. At 11:00 p.m. the guard went off duty and, within an hour, dark, shadowy figures seemingly appeared out of nowhere. With a flamboyant display of the stealth and cunning of an Apache war party, the gandy dancers began laying track across the bridge. All went well until about 2:00 a.m. when some careless pick and shovel men accidentally dropped a rail. The resounding clatter woke up the sleeping soldiers and the four-troop garrison of Fort Yuma sprang into action. With bayonets fixed, Major Dunn and his men (minus the prisoner;

presumably he remained in his cell) grimly stood their ground, the major bravely stationing himself on the tracks. Suddenly, a rumbling sound came out of the darkness and the major found himself staring into the headlights of an iron-bellied locomotive. Quickly determining that discretion was the better part of valor, the major and his men made a hasty retreat to the confines of the fort.

Along about sunrise the next morning, old Engine No. 31 came rolling into Yuma with her whistle screaming. The whole town turned out to witness the historic occasion. The locomotive crept slowly along, blowing off steam while the gandy dancers strung track ahead of her along Madison Avenue.

The Southern Pacific and the federal government each accused the other of being highhanded in the matter. General McDowell was much-chagrined and quickly reinforced Fort Yuma with a dozen more soldiers to thwart any further usurping of his military authority. Most folks around Yuma found the incident humorous and were glad that the railroad had, at last, arrived.

The Arizona Lumber Company, co-owned by Mike and Tim Riordan, was the first major manufacturing industry in Arizona. The company supplied railroad ties, telephone poles, and lumber for the towns that sprang up in Northern Arizona with the arrival of the Santa Fe Railroad. Photo courtesy of Northern Arizona University, Blanche Riordan Chambers Collection

The brothers built a log mansion for their families on the outskirts of Flagstaff. The families lived in separate residences at each end of the mansion with a common social gathering place in the center. The home is a state park today. Photo courtesy of Maricopa Community Colleges, Southwest Studies

Horses pull a load of logs, circa 1890s. Photo courtesy of the Reynolds Collection, Arizona Historical Society/Tucson

Holbrook was a major freighting center in northern Arizona after the arrival of the Santa Fe Railroad in 1881. The rail yard bustles with activity in this 1902 photo. Goods were hauled south to the Mormon colonies and Fort Apache and to the Navajo and Hopi people in the north. Photo courtesy of the Arizona Historical Foundation

In this 1882 photo of Flagstaff, Santa Fe Avenue, fronting along the railroad tracks, is in the foreground. Then as now, the city sits gloriously beneath the spectacular San Francisco Peaks. Photo courtesy of Maricopa Community Colleges, Southwest Studies

Three Finger Jack Fingers the Alvord Gang

Burt Alvord was a stockily built, swarthy-looking character with a bald pate and and I.Q. that was considerably less than his age, which was about thirty. Alvord did have a few positive attributes. He was usually cheerful, had a sense of humor and was a mighty popular fellow in Cochise County during the 1890s. He'd been a deputy for County Sheriff John Slaughter. Slaughter pronounced him fearless.

Burt was as good a brawler as they come. The citizens of Pearce hired him as constable and in no time he'd pacified the two-fisted miners. When things got out of hand at the rollicking cow town of Willcox, Burt was called in to tame it. Again he was up to the task.

I reckon things were getting too easy for the good-natured constable and he felt a need to broaden his dimensions. That's when he decided to go into the lucrative business of robbing trains. He could use his job as a peace officer to screen these nefarious activities and no one would suspect. Besides, he was too well liked by the local citizenry. Also, it might be added, no one figured him to be smart enough to pull off a crime and get away with it.

Alvord rounded up a few cronies to assist in these endeavors. He'd plan the crimes and establish alibis while they'd execute them. The gang included a pugnacious kid named Billy Stiles; Bill Downing, a surly ne'er-do-well; Matt Burts, a not-too-bright cowboy; and Bravo Juan Yoas and Three-finger Jack Dunlap, a pair of saddlebums who'd do anything for money except work.

The first robbery took place at Cochise Station on the evening of September 11, 1899. The take has been estimated as high as $30,000 in gold.

Alvord's alibi was cleverly planned. He, Matt Burts, Stiles, and Downing were playing poker in the back room of Schwertner's saloon when the robbery occurred. Every few minutes a porter would carry a round of drinks into the room and then emerge with a tray of empty glasses and announce to the local imbibers that Burt and the boys were having a serious game of poker behind those closed doors.

Meanwhile, Alvord and his pals had exited a side window, slipped into the darkness and headed towards Cochise Station.

When word of the robbery reached Willcox, someone suggested they notify Constable Burt Alvord who was involved in a poker game at Schwertner's saloon. Burt was noticeably shocked upon learning that the Southern Pacific had been held up. He immediately deputized his poker partners and off they rode. naturally, the trail was lost on the outskirts of Willcox.

Just to make sure the boys didn't start squandering their new wealth around town and arouse suspicion, Burt took the gold to a secret hiding place and buried it. He was feeling pretty good about his perfectly executed train robbery and the alibi he'd established. It sure looked like good ol' Burt had planned and executed the perfect crime.

However, Alvord didn't count on the persistence of Wells Fargo detectives and a suspicious lawman named Bert Grover. Grover suspected the constable of Willcox early on. Perhaps he acted a little too innocent. Grover cajoled the porter at the saloon into confessing to his role in establishing Burt's alibi, but before he could bring charges, his star witness got cold feet and left the territory. Having no other witnesses, investigators could only hope for a break in the case.

Meanwhile, Burt was feeling so confident about his debut as a mastermind of crime that he decided to plan another. This time he let Bravo Juan, Three-Finger Jack, Bob Brown, and the Owens brothers do the dirty work.

The daring robbery took place at the train station at Fairbank on the evening of February 15, 1900. This time something went awry. The outlaws didn't figure on the legendary former Texas Ranger Jeff Milton being in the express car.

Posing as drunken cowboys, the five bandits opened fire on Milton who was standing in the open door of the car as it pulled into the station. Seriously wounded, Milton fell back inside. The experienced old gunfighter had the natural instinct to grab his trusty Wells Fargo shotgun as he dropped. The five desperados charged through the door just as Milton rose and cut loose with his ten-gauge. Bravo Juan saw it coming and turned his backside just in time. he caught a load of double-ought shot in the seat of the pants. He lit out on the run and didn't stop until he hit the Mexican border. Three-Finger Jack wasn't as lucky. He was hit full force.

The outlaws went away empty-handed; that is, if you don't count the Wells Fargo lead two of 'em were carrying.

Three-Finger Jack was mortally wounded and, a few miles from Fairbank, his compadres left him beside the trail to die. Back at Fairbank a posse was organized. Trackers easily picked up the bloody trail leading to where Dunlap lay. The dying outlaw was much-chagrined at being left behind by his cronies and only too willing to give testimony, not only for the details surrounding the Fairbank robbery, but the one at Cochise Station as well.

As a result of Three-Finger Jack's confession, Wells Fargo got the break they needed to crack the case, and the citizens of Willcox had to find a new constable. Burt Alvord eventually did his time at the Yuma Territorial Prison. Incidentally, the recovery of the loot remains a mystery. Old timers around Willcox said that after Burt was released he came back to town to say "howdy" to his old friends, then left for Central America where he bought a large cattle ranch. Who grubstaked him? *Quien sabe,* (who knows) although one can't help but wonder if he might have stamped a "WF" brand on the hides of those critters in honor of his unwilling benefactors. After all, Burt did have a grand sense of humor.◆

Three Times en Yer Out

On the evening of April 27, 1887, southern Arizona's only passenger train, the Sunset Express, was making its run towards Tucson. The train was a few minutes behind schedule, so the engineer gave her a little more steam to make up time. About twenty miles east of Tucson, the yellow streak from the headlight picked up a figure standing on the track waving a red lantern. About that same time the big drive wheels ran over a torpedo. The bomb-like blast served as a warning of trouble on the line. The engineer slammed on the brakes and stopped just before crashing into some upraised railroad ties jammed between the tracks.

Out of the darkness rifle shots cracked and several holes suddenly appeared in the engine's boiler. Two masked men appeared beside the locomotive and ordered the engineer, Bill Harper, to step down off the train. They took him back to the express car and told him to have the Wells Fargo express messenger open the safe, then unlock the door and get out.

"Or what?" the stubborn engineer asked.

"Or we blow it up," one of the bandits replied, holding up a stick of dynamite.

Inside the express car, Messenger J. E. Smith heard the conversation and unlocked the safe. Then he removed $5,000, took it over to the cold, potbellied stove, lifted the lid and stuffed it in. The money safely hidden, the resourceful messenger unlocked the door and jumped out.

The robbers, members of the Doc Smart gang, found only a few scattered bills in the safe. Disappointed, they took their meager haul and, after a few hurried instructions on how to run a locomotive from Engineer Harper, climbed aboard and headed for Tucson.

Later that night, when the Sunset Express failed to show, a relief train was sent out from Tucson. About fifteen miles east of Tucson, they discovered the abandoned steam engine and its ransacked express and mail cars. A few miles farther down the track, they found the anxious crew waiting by the passenger cars.

The next day a posse, led by Papago Indian trackers, went to where the engine was found to pick up the trail of Doc Smart and his desperados. They searched in vain but found no tracks. It was as if the gang had vanished into thin air.

It wasn't until several months and several robberies later, after Doc Smart and his gang were captured at El Paso, that investigators learned what happened. It was really quite simple. The outlaws merely rode the locomotive into the outskirts of Tucson, then put ol' iron-belly into reverse and sent it eastbound. The perforated boiler ran out of steam about ten miles down the track, and that's where it was found—with no tell-tale tracks to follow.

Clever fellows, those outlaws, except they didn't get much loot since J. E. Smith had so cleverly hidden the money in the stove. The newspapers made a big deal out of it and Smith was quite a local celebrity for a spell.

On August 10, the Doc Smart gang struck again. Same train, same location, same *modus operandi,* but a different crew except for Messenger J. E. Smith.

This time the train didn't stop in time and the engine jumped the tracks and flipped over on its side on the edge of a steep embankment. Out of the darkness, the outlaws opened fire. One bullet passed under the nose of Fireman R. T. Bradford, burning off part of his mustache. Engineer Jim Guthrie hopped out of the prostrate locomotive and fell down the bluff. Fortunately, he landed in the top of a mesquite tree.

Doc and the boys weren't taking any chances this time. A stick of dynamite blew open the door of the express car. Inside was their old adversary, J. E. Smith. One of the robbers pointed the business end of his .45 at the messenger and hissed, "Smitty, that stove racket don't go this time."

The gang got away with $3,000 that time and, while lawmen scoured the Arizona country, Doc Smart and the boys were livin' it up in Texas.

Things went so well the last time, two of the outlaws decided to rob the Southern Pacific outside El Paso a couple of months later. Ironically, J. E. Smith was in the express car again. By now the feisty messenger was getting tired of getting held up. This time he greeted the train robbers with his guns blazing. In a few brief moments, outlaws Kid Smith (no relation) and Dick Meyers were laid out stone cold on the ground.

Lawmen in El Paso located the boarding house where the two outlaws were staying and were able to round up the rest of the gang, including the notorious Doc Smart.

Doc Smart was given a life sentence for his part in the three train robberies. Somehow he got his hands on a six-shooter and tried to commit suicide. Doc fired three slugs into his head but the soft lead collided with his hard head and couldn't penetrate. Doc Smart got nothing for his efforts except a severe headache. ◆

Three Times 'en Yer Out, *by Jack Graham*

By March of 1880, the Southern Pacific and its indefatigable Chinese laborers had stretched its ribbons of steel eastward to Tucson. A gala celebration was held as Tucsonians turned out to witness the event. The citizens of Tombstone presented a silver spike to ceremoniously nail down the last steel rail. There was a great deal of speechmaking, socializing and imbibing spiritous beverages. Self-congratulatory telegrams were being wired to distant American cities. Some wag conceived a brilliant notion that the pope should be notified of the historic occasion. The others agreed, and Mayor Bob Leatherwood quickly penned the following:

To His Holiness, the Pope of Rome, Italy:

The mayor of Tucson begs the honor of reminding Your Holiness that this ancient and honorable pueblo was founded by the Spaniards under the sanction of the Church more than three centuries ago, and to inform Your Holiness that a railroad from San Francisco, California now connects us with the entire Christian World.

R. N. Leatherwood, Mayor

A few minutes later Mayor Leatherwood was interrupted by a young telegrapher who handed him a telegram and quickly departed.

The mayor didn't take time to read the message but called the informal gathering to order. Then he read the "Pope's Reply":

His Holiness the Pope acknowledges with appreciation receipt of your telegram informing him that the ancient city of Tucson at last has been connected by rail with the outside world and sends his benediction, but for his own satisfaction would ask, where the hell is Tucson?

"Antonelli"

It's highly probable the "Pope's Reply" was conjured up by more discreet and sober celebrants but it added considerably to the festivities. It is a matter of historical record that on March 20, 1955, the seventy-fifth anniversary of the railroad's arrival, the pope did send a congratulatory message to all the folks in Tucson.

Phoenix had a big turnout in 1887 when the first steam engine from the Maricopa, Phoenix and Salt River Railroad arrived. At the time, the future capital only rated a branch line from the Southern Pacific station at Maricopa. Phoenix wasn't quite ready for the big time. A turntable hadn't been built yet, so after the ceremonies, the train had to make the thirty-five mile trip back to Maricopa in reverse.

One of the most exciting finishes to the building of a railroad line occurred at Prescott in 1886. Tom Bullock, a former bartender on Whiskey Row, proposed a line to link Prescott with the Santa Fe mainline at Seligman.

Prescottonians raised $300,000 for constructing the seventy-five miles of track. Bullock had to reach Prescott no later than midnight, December 31, or face a stiff $1,000-a-mile penalty. No sooner had construction begun when railcars loaded with beer were being shipped in to mobile tent saloons set up along the way. Cattlemen, angry over the railroad right of way across their grazing lands, had their cowboys stampede cattle through the construction sites.

Meanwhile, in Prescott the betting was heavy as to whether Bullock would meet his deadline. Some folks tried to hedge their bets by vandalizing the line. Someone tried to blow up a caboose. Another group of reprobates set fire to a trestle but, thanks to some divine intervention, a rainstorm doused the flames.

Other vandals tried to derail the work train by removing a section of track. The plot was foiled when the engine ran aground before reaching the damaged area.

Working feverishly against the clock, the track layers reached Granite Dells with one day to go. By the evening of the final day they were only two miles from Prescott. Odds against the Bullock line reaching Prescott on time had gone as high as twenty-to-one and those who had taken the bet shouted encouragement from the sidelines. Others couldn't restrain themselves and joined the work crews.

The Bullock line reached Prescott with five minutes to spare. Throngs of locals cheered as the territorial governor, Conrad Zulick, drove a gilded spike into a rail tie painted red, white, and blue.

Prescott, at last, was linked by rail to the outside world. ♦

The Atcheson and Topeka (later Santa Fe) crosses Canyon Diablo in the 1880s. Photo courtesy of Maricopa Community Colleges, Southwest Studies

Willcox was the freighting center for southeast Arizona after the arrival of the Southern Pacific Railroad in 1880. In this 1894 photo of Main Street in Willcox, Harry Park's family store can be seen behind the windmill. Photo courtesy of the Arizona Historical Society/ Tucson

The Gila Valley Globe and Northern Railway reaches Globe for the first time. The town was "rescued from obscurity and decay" on Saturday, December 6, 1898, when the first train on the new Gila Valley Globe and Northern Railway line reached town. During those days, a railroad represented the difference between continued prosperity and economic ruin to communities in remote regions. Photo courtesy of the Arizona Historical Society/ Tucson, Woody Collection

The Yuma Territorial Prison opened in 1876. Although the prison was no worse and better than most prisons of its time, the hot, dry climate in southwestern Arizona gave it a reputation as a "hell hole," as these prisoners (pictured below) lined up in the uncovered, dusty, barren courtyard could testify. It was said that one prisoner died and went to hell but came back and requested blankets because, after living in Yuma, hell was too cold for him. This 1890 photo shows the south side of the prison area, with guard tower, ventilators, and the women's yard at night. The door to the library can be seen to the left of the pole. Both photos courtesy of the Arizona Historical Society/Tucson

The riverboat Aztec *heads upriver along the east bank of the Colorado River, passing through the open span of the Southern Pacific Railroad bridge circa 1892. Yuma Territorial Prison is perched on the hill in the distance. Beyond the hill, the Gila River flows into the Colorado River.* Photo courtesy of the Reynolds Collection, Arizona Historical Society/Tucson

President William McKinley visits Congress, Arizona, May 7, 1901. Photo courtesy of the Reynolds Collection, Arizona Historical Society/Tucson

S.P. DEPOT
PATAGONIA ARIZ.

A.T.& S.F. DEPOT
ESCALANTE HOTEL
ASHFORK ARIZ.

The Southern Pacific Depot in Patagonia, Arizona, circa 1905-6. The old line ran from Benson, on the Southern Pacific mainline, through Patagonia to Nogales. Photo courtesy of the Arizona Historical Society/Tucson

This grand old building, the Escalante, built by Fred Harvey in Ashfork, was one of several constructed along the Santa Fe mainline around the turn of the century. The author shined shoes here duirng the late 1940s. Photo courtesy of Maricopa Community Colleges, Southwest Studies

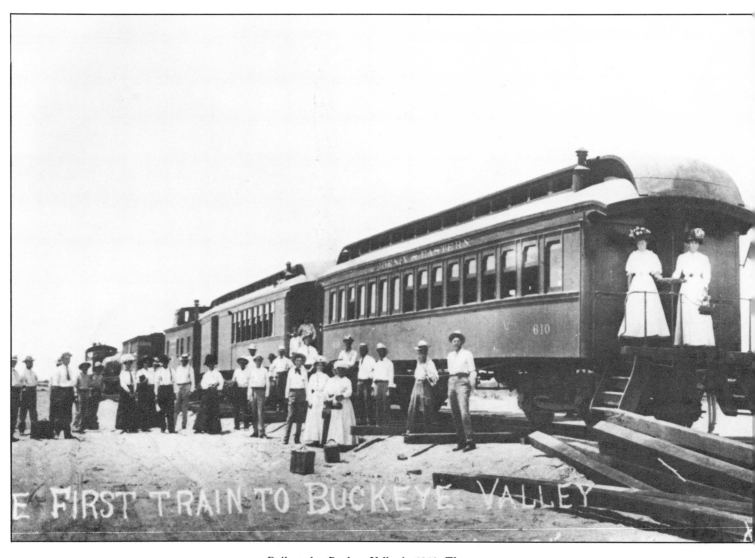

E FIRST TRAIN TO BUCKEYE VALLEY

Rail reaches Buckeye Valley in 1910. The cars still bear the name of Phoenix and Eastern, a line acquired by Southern Pacific more than three years earlier. The town got its name in 1898 when M. Jackson of Sydney, Ohio, built a canal in the western part of the Salt River Valley and named it for the nickname of his native state. Photo courtesy of the Arizona Historical Society/Tucson

This photo of Burt Alvord (standing) with Billie Hildreth was taken while Alvord was a cowboy on the Mexican Border. Photo courtesy of the Arizona Historical Society/Tucson

October 1926 marked the completion of a Phoenix leg of Southern Pacific's second mainline across Arizona. It touched off this celebration at the Union Station in Phoenix. No longer was it necessary to travel south to Maricopa to board the mainline. Photo courtesy of the Arizona Historical Society/Tucson

Chasi-ta, son of Bonito, was a well-known chief of the Warm Springs Apaches. Photo by Ben Wittick, courtesy of the Arizona Historical Society/Tucson

Chapter  9

Turbulent Times: The Inevitable Clash of Cultures

The 1860s began three decades of turbulence in Arizona. The discovery of gold and silver brought a rush of prospectors and settlers into what had been previously all Indian lands, evoking an inevitable clash of cultures. Army troops from Fort Buchanan led by Lt. George Bascom rode into Cochise's stronghold at Apache Pass and accused the Chiricahua chief of kidnapping a youngster from a ranch near Sonoita Creek. Cochise denied the charge (it turned out he was telling the truth) and, when the soldiers tried to take him hostage, he escaped and took some hostages of his own. The eyeball-to-eyeball confrontation ended when Cochise executed his prisoners. When the mutilated bodies were found, the soldiers retaliated by hanging an equal number of Apache prisoners, including some of Cochise's relatives. The angry bands under the great Apache chieftain Mangas Coloradas, Cochise, and several others, combined to form a formidable force the terrorized southern Arizona for the next decade.

Yavapai and Tonto Apaches living in the central mountain range saw their traditional grounds invaded by prospectors and settlers after the discovery of gold in the Bradshaw Mountains in 1863. Vigilantes from Prescott, Wickenburg and other settlements embarked on relentless campaigns. Unlike the regular army, they took no prisoners and sought vengeance: an eye for

an eye. The barbarism of some shocked others. A ruffian known as Sugarfoot Jack was reported to have picked up a baby during a raid and tossed it into a burning wickiup. Later, he found another toddler crying in the aftermath of battle. He picked up the child and placed it tenderly on his knee and began rocking. When the baby began to smile he drew his revolver and fired point-blank into the tot's face. The sight of such cruelty shocked the battle-toughened veterans of Indian fighting. Had he not run off, Sugarfoot Jack might have been lynched by his own men.

The Navajos also resumed their raiding during the Civil War, choosing to ignore treaties previously signed. Since they regarded a treaty as binding only by the party signing it, most weren't worth the paper they were written on. Also, the army made a practice of handing out gifts at these signings, something the Navajos regarded as a sign of weakness. In 1863, Col. Kit Carson called upon the Navajos to surrender and move to a new reservation at Bosque Redondo, New Mexico. A large number retreated into their historic sanctuaries in Canyons de Chelly and del Muerto. The canyons were thought to be impregnable but, in January 1864, Carson wisely sent troops in from both ends and destroyed the Navajos' horses and crops, breaking the spirit of the warriors. More than eight thousand

White Mountain Apache Indian women.
Photo by Ben Wittick, courtesy of the Arizona
Historical Society/Tucson

The party, which included ninety-four Papagos, forty-eight Mexicans and six Anglos, nearly wiped out the band in a few furious moments. Most of the Apache men were away at the time so women, children, and elderly took the brunt of the attack. When the smoke had cleared, about a hundred were dead. All but eight were women and children. Those taken alive were given to the Papagos as slaves.

The Tucsonians took great satisfaction in the success of the raid since for years they'd been at the mercy of the fierce Apaches. Nearly every citizen had experienced the loss of a friend or family member. Juan and Jesus Maria Elias, two of the leaders, had been driven out of Tubac and three members of their families had been murdered by Apaches.

While the Tucsonians were celebrating, Washington politicians and Indian proponents were outraged. President Grant called the Camp Grant incident "murder" and ordered a trial. The trial was held in Tucson and, not surprisingly, the verdict was not guilty. No jury in the Arizona Territory would find anyone guilty of killing an Apache.

In the aftermath of the Camp Grant Massacre, President Grant ordered a two-pronged program to end the Apache wars. With one hand he extended the olive branch in the person of Gen. Oliver Howard, a one-armed Civil War officer with a reputation for honesty and integrity. Howard would negotiate treaties with the tribes. In case Howard failed, the president carried in his other hand the sabre as personified by the greatest Indian fighting officer in the army, George Crook.

General Howard was able to link up with a lanky redhead named Tom Jeffords, superintendent of a mail line and a man who'd become friendly with old Cochise. A few years earlier, Jeffords had boldly ridden into Cochise's stronghold and negotiated a treaty with the chief to protect his mail riders. Cochise respected Jefford's bravery and honesty. Their friendship lasted despite the continued animosity between their respective races. Jeffords led the general into Cochise's camp where a treaty was negotiated ending the ten-year war. Next, Howard approached the Yavapai and Tonto Apaches in the central mountains. They defiantly rejected the peace proposals and president Grant had no choice but to order Crook into battle.

Crook's famous winter campaign of 1872-73 was one of the most successful in military history. He sent his troops into the field, guided by Apache scouts during the time of year when most of the bands preferred to hole up in the steep, twisting canyons around the Tonto Basin.

Military columns swept through the central mountains, keeping the bands on the move. Led by the scouts, they ventured into places where no white man dared tread. The following spring, most of the bands agreed to move onto reservations.

Following his great success, Crook was promoted to general and transferred out of Arizona. For a time it seemed the Apache wars were over. Unfortunately, reservation life didn't appeal to all Apaches. Following the death of Cochise, the Chiricahuas were moved from their traditional lands to the San Carlos reservation to live. Also, the Yavapais, who weren't Apaches, were taken on their own long walk from fort Verde to San Carlos or "Hell's Forty Acres," as it became known.

Before he left in 1875, Crook protested these moves but to no avail. This consolidtion was supposed to make administration more efficient. Instead, the bands fought like cats and dogs. This led to the emergence of troublemakers like Geronimo. During the next few years the wily renegade and his followers bolted the reservation several times and headed for their former haunts in Mexico.

In September 1882, General Crook was recalled to Arizona to bring in Geronimo. Once again Crook gathered his trusty

were taken on the "Long Walk" of some four hundred miles to Bosque Redondo.

Life was tough for the Navajos there. Hundreds died of smallpox. Cutworms and poor irrigation caused massive crop failures and, for reasons only a Washington bureaucrat could explain, they were placed among the Mescalero Apaches. The two groups got along like cowboys and sheepherders. Finally, in 1868, the government realized the Bosque Redondo Reservation project was a failure and the Navajos took another long walk, this time a happier trek, back to their beloved Four Corners country where a new reservation was established.

Indian raiding and depredations were so bad around Prescott that on January 22, 1870, the *Prescott Miner* published a list giving dates and locations of three hundred whites killed in the area. The massacre of Aravaipa Apaches at Camp Grant in 1871, focused national attention on the Indian problem in Arizona.

On April 30, 1871, a group of vigilantes from the Tucson area attacked a band of Aravaipa Apaches living near Camp Grant.

scouts, equipped his pack trains and headed out on the campaign trail. Crook's relentless tactics were successful once again and by January 1884 the Apaches agreed to return to San Carlos.

When Geronimo's plunder was taken and returned to its owners, he grew bitter and began looking for a reason to gather a few braves and escape again. Following a drinking bout in May 1885, Geronimo and a small band headed south, leaving in their wake death and destruction. Crook took up the chase, sending his hardriding cavalry and Apache scouts in pursuit.

In March 1886, at Cañon de los Embudos, Geronimo agreed to surrender. That evening a whiskey peddler sold the band a barrel of mescal. A drunken Geronimo, convinced Crook meant to kill him, gathered a few braves and bolted once more.

The latest broken agreement by Geronimo was an embarrassment for Crook. When General of the Army Phil Sheridan questioned his placing too much trust in Apaches, including the loyal scouts, Crook resigned.

Crook's replacement for the final stages of the Geronimo Campaign was another soldier of proven ability, Gen. Nelson Miles. In other aspects, the two were quite different. While Crook was an outdoorsman with little interest in pomp and ceremony, Miles was egotistical and politically ambitious. Miles continued Crook's tactics in the field while loading up the peaceful Chiricahua's at San Carlos and Fort Apache and shipped them by rail to Florida.

In early September, Lt. Charles Gatewood and two Apache scouts, along with interpreter Tom Horn, rode into Geronimo's lair in Mexico's Sierra Madre and arranged a final surrender. In the aftermath, General Miles took most of the credit for Geronimo's capture and used it to advance his career. Eventually he became army chief of staff. Unfortunately, the real heroes, Gatewood and his two Apache scouts, fared much worse. Gatewood was transferred to an obscure army post out of reach of the press. He died many years later, forgotten and unrecognized. The two scouts, Martine and Kayitah, were imprisoned along with the renegade Chiricahua and sent to prison in Florida. Tom Horn, a frontier legend, left the army and became a lawman, range detective and regulator, eventually moving to Wyoming where he became involved in a range feud and was accused of murdering a thirteen-year-old boy. Horn was hanged in 1903. His guilt or innocence is still debated by historians.

Although General Miles had promised the Chiricahua a two-year term in Florida and then freedom to return to Arizona, they were held in Florida and Alabama for nearly a decade before being moved to Fort Sill, Oklahoma. Eventually, around 1915 a few were allowed to return to southern New Mexico. Unwelcomed by Arizonans both Indian and white, the door to their eventual return to this land had been closed permanently. ◆

Pima elder statesman holds his calendar stick, a recording of historical events in tribal life. Photo courtesy Maricopa Community Colleges, Southwest Studies

Despite the harsh Arizona life, this wizened old Apache woman had reached age 106 when this photo was taken. Courtesy of Maricopa Community Colleges, Southwest Studies

Old Nana, noted Apache leader during Indian Wars. Photo courtesy of Maricopa Community Colleges, Southwest Studies

Nahlekadeya, wife of Cochise. Photo by Ben Wittick, courtesy of the Arizona Historical Society/Tucson

Mangas inherited the role of chief of the Mimbres Apaches in 1863 when his father, Mangas Coloradas, died. Photo by Ben Wittick, courtesy of the Arizona Historical Society

Na-buash-i-ta was an Apache medicine man. Photo by Ben Wittick, courtesy of the Arizona Historical Society/Tucson

Not even a formal photograph interrupts "chow time" for this Apache infant. Photo by Ben Whittick, courtesy of the Arizona Historical Society/Tucson

This photo of Tom Jeffords was taken at his ranch late in life. As a mail superintendent between Lordsburg, New Mexico, and Tucson, he negotiated a treaty with Cochise to allow his mail riders safe passage. The two became friends. Their story was dramatized in the movie Broken Arrow *starring Jimmy Stewart as Jeffords and Jeff Chandler as Cochise.* Courtesy of the Arizona Historical Society/ Tucson

Mickey Free, aka. Felex Telles, as a youth was kidnapped from a ranch in Sonoita Creek. Cochise was accused of the crime, touching off the Bascom Affair at Apache Pass in 1861. His alleged kidnapping by Cochise set off a long and bitter war in southeast Arizona. He later became a scout for the Army during the Geronimo Campaign. Photo courtesy of Maricopa Community Colleges, Southwest Studies

This Apache camp proudly displays its white captive, Jimmy McKinn. Note the negro captive on the far left. Children were raised to endure the hardships of Apache life. Some remained with the tribes after the close of the Apache Wars. Others like McKinn, returned to life in the "white man's world." McKinn died in Phoenix in the 1950s. Courtesy of Maricopa Community Colleges, Southwest Studies

William Neal, better known as "Curly Bill," rode with Bill Cody during the Indian Wars on the Great Plains. Born in Oklahoma Territory, his mother was Cherokee and his father black. His Indian name was "Bear Sitting Down." He spent little time living up to that name as he ran a prosperous operation that included a freight business, resort, stageline and cattle ranch. Photo courtesy of the Arizona Historical Society/Tucson

Navajo men pose for a photographer. Each seems to reflect a different opinion of having his picture taken. Courtesy of the Northern Arizona University Library, Northern Arizona Pioneers' Historical Society Collection

Papago wood carier. Photo courtesy of Maricopa Community Colleges, Southwest Studies

Although the cradleboards look binding and uncomfortable, infants like this Navajo Indian baby found them a source of warm security. Photo by Mishler and Walker, courtesy of the Arizona Historical Society/Tucson

Pima girl. Photo courtesy of Maricopa Community Colleges, Southwest Studies

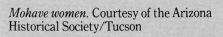

Fort Apache, 1870s. Courtesy of Maricopa
Community Colleges, Southwest Studies

Apache scouts. Photo courtesy of the Arizona
Historical Society/Tucson

Camp Grant was the site of the infamous massacre in 1871 when more than one hundred Apaches were killed. The photo at bottom was taken during the trial of several Tucson citizens for their part in the Camp Grant Massacre. Pictured is the first Pima County Courthouse, 1871, at the corner of Church and Ott streets.

Photo courtesy of the Arizona State Library

Photo courtesy of the Arizona Historical Society/Tucson

John Clum arrived in Arizona in 1874 as Apache agent at San Carlos. He preached self-government for the Apaches and organized a native police force. Once he and his police made a daring capture of Geronimo and Victorio. In 1877 Clum resigned because of military interference with his agency. He went to the new boom town of Tombstone and declared, "every Tombstone needs an epitaph." As editor of the Tombstone Epitaph *and mayor, he was a prominent figure and staunch supporter of Wyatt Earp in the famous feud.* Photo courtesy of Maricopa Community Colleges, Southwest Studies

Chow time in the old Army was an informal affair. This photo aptly fits the old adage that the cavalry traveled "forty miles a day on beans and hay." Photo from the Owen Wister collection, courtesy of the Arizona Historical Society/Tucson

Martha Summerhayes arrived in Arizona by steamboat in August 1874. As a young army bride she lived on several remote military posts. Later she wrote about her life on the frontier in her book. Vanished Arizona, Recollections of my Army Life, *in which this photo originally appeared.* Courtesy of the Arizona Historical Society/Tucson

Yours Sincerely
Martha Summerhayes

The guns were never far away in this military-style family outing in the 1870s. Courtesy of Maricopa Community Colleges, Southwest Studies

Soldier and his Indian wife. Courtesy of the Arizona Historical Society/Tucson

Fort Huachuca was established at the foot of the picturesque Huachuca Mountains in 1877 to thwart attempts by renegade Apache bands to slip into Mexico. It is the only Arizona frontier military post that is still active. This muster of Company C, First Infantry at left of line, Troops I, H, and L, Sixth U.S. Cavalry at right, occurred in November/December 1883. Courtesy of the Arizona Historical Society/ Tucson

Fort Thomas in the 1880s. Courtesy of Maricopa Community Colleges, Southwest Studies

This rare photo shows Gen. George Crook, the "greatest Indian-fighting general" in the army. He was also one of the few to win the trust and respect of the Indian. Photo courtesy of the National Archives

Military pack trains were essential to the success of the campaigns against the Apaches. Techniques developed in Arizona during the 1880s were still in use during World War II. Photo from the Owen Wister Collection, courtesy of the Arizona Historical Society/ Tucson

Peaches, Crook's guide. Photo by Ben Wittick, courtesy of the Arizona Historical Society/ Tucson

The historic parley between General Crook and Geronimo took place in 1886. Photo by C. S. Fly; courtesy of the Arizona Historical Society/Tucson

The grateful citizens of Tucson presented Gen. Nelson Miles a silver sword as the "man who captured Geronimo." Actually there was so little enthusiasm from contributors for the vainglorious Miles that he had to make a sizable contribution to his own trophy. Pictured is Miles responding to the speech of Judge W. H. Barnes who presented the sword to him at a ceremony Nov. 8, 1887, at 3 p.m. at Levin's Park, Tucson. Courtesy of the Arizona Historical Society/Tucson

A soldier was naked without his weapon.

Army life on Arizona's remote military posts could be tedious, especially after the Apache wars ended. Long hours were spent drilling and preparing for inspections. Card games such as this one at Fort Grant in 1890 were a popular form of recreation, especially around payday. Courtesy of Maricopa Community Colleges, Southwest Studies

Top to bottom:
Colt Third Model Dragoon .44 Caliber. This model was made after 1849 and was called the Dragoon Colt because it was issued mainly to this branch of service. U.S. Dragoons were the forerunners of the U.S. Cavalry.
Colt 1860 Army with cuts for shoulder stock. The army model was the largest of the new series of revolvers released around 1860. This was a .44 caliber six-shooter.
Remington 1858 .44 Caliber. Second only to

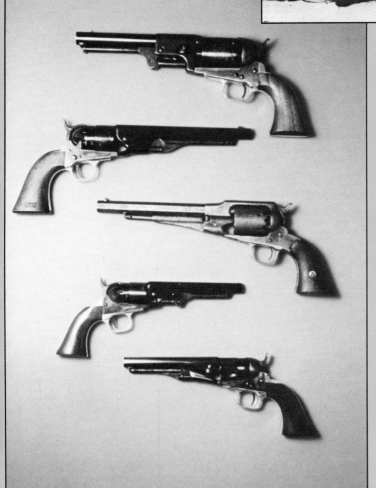

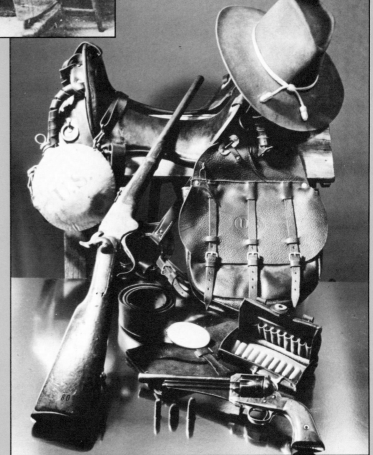

Colt in popularity, the Remington saw wide use in the Civil War and on the frontier during the Indian Wars.
Colt 1862 Pocket Navy .36 Caliber. Called "pocket pistols" because of the shorter barrels, a few were issued to unmounted officers during the Civil War.
Colt 1862 Pocket Police .36 Caliber. This model was similar to the above and came out the same time as the pocket navy. It was more handy than the regular navy version and saw wider use. This series was the last of the Colt's percussion-cap arms to be sold.

101

Thomas V. Keams established a trading post in a canyon a few miles east of the Hopi mesas in 1872. Keams, an Englishman, rode with Col. Kit Carson during the Navajo Campaign in 1864. A Hopi agency was located at the trading post, pictured at bottom in 1889 and today Keams Canyon is the site of the Hopi tribal headquarters. Photo courtesy of the Arizona Historical Society/Tucson

"Don" Juan Lorenzo Hubbell, shown here in this circa 1885-1888 photo, reflected the best in the frontier Indian trader. He dealt with open honesty and fairness. The natives relied on him as a trusted go-between in dealings with the federal bureaucracy. When disputes arose between clans, they came to him for settlement and his decisions were usually accepted as fair and final. Courtesy of the Arizona Historical Society/Tucson

Apache Indians wait to be fed at San Carlos, Arizona, 1894. Photo from the Owen Wister Collection, courtesy of the Arizona Historical Society/Tucson

Hopi Indian girls grinding corn in a home scene at Shonghopavi, Arizona, circa 1903. Courtesy of the Arizona Historical Society/Tucson

Drying corn hangs on the walls of this Hopi village home. Photo courtesy of the Arizona Historical Foundation

Walpi Village, circa 1920. Hopi Indians live atop three mesas jutting out on the southside of Black Mesa. They are called First Mesa, Second Mesa, and Third Mesa. Several villages are located on all three. Walpi was first settled in the 1600s. A few families still reside in the picturesque village today. Walpi is also well known, as is the rest of the First Mesa villages, for its beautiful pottery. Photo courtesy of the Arizona Historical Foundation

This photo, of a Navajo Indian camp with an Apache basket in the foreground, was taken in the Grand Canyon, 1932. Photo courtesy of the Arizona Historical Society/Tucson

These reconstructions of desert brush and earthen dwellings are part of an exhibit at the Gila River Cultural Center near Sacaton on the Pima Indian reservation. Photos by the author

Jack Swilling, right, erstwhile Indian fighter, Confederate officer, prospector, and entrepreneur, organized an irrigation and canal building company in the 1860s in the Salt River Valley. Swilling mixed drugs and alcohol as a painkiller for an old wound and was prone pneumonia serving time for a crime he probably didn't commit. He is shown here with his sidekick Tonto. (It's not known whether or not Jack wore a mask and rode a horse named Silver.) Photo courtesy of Maricopa Community Colleges, Southwest Studies

Chapter 10

The Civil War in Arizona

Arizona was a far cry from glorious-sounding names like Shiloh, Missionary Ridge, Gettysburg, and Chancellorsville, yet it too played a small part in the war between the Blue and Gray. Confederate President Jefferson Davis was well aware of the mineral-laden mountains in the western part of the new Mexico territory which included Arizona. The land was also a link between Texas and what he hoped to become the Confederate state of California.

In July 1861, three hundred Texans led by Colonel John Baylor rode hellbent-for-leather into New Mexico, taking the sleepy town of Mesilla by storm. On August 1, he declared himself governor of the "Confederate Territory of Arizona" and, since he couldn't find any Yankees to fight, opened a war of extermination on the Indians. Baylor's extermination orders got him relieved of command by Confederate leaders who considered him something of an embarrassment.

On Febraury 14, 1862, fifty years before statehood, Arizona was officially declared a Confederate Territory. That same month, Gen. Henry Sibley led his Texas army into New Mexico. Sibley sent Capt. Sherod Hunter, a resourceful young officer, west with a company of cavalry to occupy Tucson, then turned the rest of his boisterous army north towards Santa Fe. He won a hard-fought victory at Valverde, then marched through Albuquerque and took possession of Santa Fe.

Sibley had served as a U.S. officer in New Mexico before the war and knew that vast amounts of critical military supplies were stored at Fort Union, a hundred miles up the Santa Fe Trail. He was determined to get his hands on them. Also, he knew that once he took Fort Union, there was nothing to keep him from marching north to Denver, then on to the Oregon Trail, effectively cutting off the entire West from the Union.

Sibley's best laid plans got waylaid by a bunch of rough-hewn miners known as the Colorado Volunteers. They marched out of Denver under the dynamic leadership of a Bible-thumping ex-Methodist preacher named John Chivington. The Coloradans, known as "Pike's Peakers" engaged the Texans at Glorieta Pass, a few miles outside Santa Fe, in late march. For three days the two armies locked horns like a pair of old Texas steers.

Finally, a young officer named Manuel Chavez, who had been raised in the area, led Chivington and his men along a ridge that led behind the Texas lines. The Pike's Peakers blew up the supply wagons and killed hundreds of horses and mules. With victory within their grasp, the Texans were forced to withdraw and were soon in a full-scale, every-man-for-himself retreat down the Rio Grande. The so-called "Gettysburg of the West" ended forever hopes of a Confederate empire in the West.

While General Sibley was making dubious history in northern New Mexico, Capt. Sherod Hunter was enjoying success in Arizona. He was welcomed joyfully by the grateful citizens of Tucson when he rode into town on February 28, 1862. Most were happy to see soldiers, no matter what color the uniform. The next few weeks were spent campaigning against Apaches and expelling from the old Pueblo those who refused to swear allegiance to the Confederacy. It wasn't long before he learned that the Confederates had failed to gain control of California and a two thousand-man volunteer force led by a flinty-eyed professional soldier named Jim Carleton was heading towards Arizona. Already, advance elements were storing supplies along the Gila River.

By a series of brilliant maneuvers, Hunter created an illusion of having a much larger force than his small company of

Texans. He sent small, mobile patrols out to destroy the Union supply stores. At the Pima villages near Sacaton, he arrested a miller named Ammi White who'd been processing grain and gathering supplies for the Californians. Hunter gathered fifteen hundred sacks of wheat and presented it to the Pima Indians. A few days later Capt. William McCleave and his nine-man force unwittingly rode into White's mill. The man they believed to be Ammi White was Capt. Sherod Hunter dressed in civilian clothes. After the Union soldiers relaxed their guard and informed "Mr. White" there were no other Union troops near, Hunter drew his revolver and took them prisoner. McCleave was so chagrined at his blunder he challenged Hunter to a fist fight—winner go free. Hunter, no doubt, admired the young man's spunk but politely refused the offer. Instead, he ordered Lt. Jack Swilling to escort the prisoners to Texas.

A rescue party sent out to secure McCleave got there too late but did manage to encounter some Confederates at Stanwix Station on the Gila River (near today's Sentinel) about eighty miles east of Yuma. Several shots were exchanged and a Union soldier was wounded before the two patrols broke off the battle. Some historians call this the westernmost battle of the Civil War. Others say a gunfight near the Goldwater store in La Paz on the east bank of the Colorado River holds that honor.

Neither of these can be considered much of a "battle." A better case can be made for the fight that took place at Picacho a few days later. Two Union patrols were sent south from the Pima villages in hopes of capturing the Confederates camped there. On April 15, young Lt. Jim Barrett surprised three Confederates and took them prisoner, then carelessly allowed his own force to be ambushed. A furious ninety-minute firefight took place in the thick chaparral and when the smoke had cleared Barrett and two enlisted men were dead and three were wounded. Two Confederates who were also wounded would die from their injuries. The Union force retreated back to the Pima Villages and the Confederate pickets carried the news to Captain Hunter at Tucson that the California army was approaching. Hunter gathered his troops, lowered the colors, mounted up and rode east.

On May 20, 1862, the California Column entered Tucson. Colonel Carleton, still smarting over the exasperating young Texas captain, and needing an ego booster, delayed his entrance until June 7 so the artillery units could get set up and give him a fitting and proper salute.

Colonel Carleton's orders were to proceed on to New Mexico. Several weeks before he moved his forces east from Tucson, Apache scouts were sent out from the lair of Cochise and Mangas Coloradas in Apache Pass to keep an eye on the bluecoats. When an advance force of 126 California volunteers under Capt. Tom Roberts approached the watering hole in the pass, they were ambushed. The Apaches held the high ground but Roberts' thirsty men fought desperately to reach the spring. The soldiers opened fire with howitzers, scattering schrapnel on the warriors along the edge of the canyon rim. After several rounds of devastating fire, the Apaches picked up their dead and wounded and withdrew. Roberts' men, having gone some seventeen hours without water, drank eagerly from the spring.

The next day, July 16, the Apaches regained the high ground and resumed their attack on the soldiers. Meanwhile, a supply train under Capt. John Cremony, had joined the beleaguered troops who were holed up in the old Butterfield Stage Station. Once again Roberts opened up with his howitzers, scattering twelve-pound spherical shot among the Apaches. When the battle ended, the Californians had regained the spring. Roberts lost only two men in the battle and claimed to have killed more than sixty Apaches. Historians have revised the Apache losses to about ten.

Carleton arrived at the pass a few days later and realized its strategic importance. On July 28, 1862, Fort Bowie (named after Col. George Washington Bowie) was formally established on a site overlooking Apache Spring. It was later moved to its present site a half-mile farther east. Two decades later, during the Geronimo Campaign, Fort Bowie was one of the most important posts in the Southwest. It was abandoned in 1894 and lay in crumbled ruins. The old fort became a National Historic Site in 1964. ◆

Picacho was the site for this recent re-enactment of the Civil War battle of 1862 that is regarded as the westernmost battle of that war. Memorial units of Union and Confederate soldiers dramatize the clash of April 15, 1862, at Picacho Pass. Union troops under Lt. James Barrett surprised a small party of Texans and were then in turn ambushed by a larger Confederate force. The battle lasted about an hour and a half. Lieutenant Barrett and two Union soldiers were killed. The Confederate losses were two wounded. Both died later on the trail. Although the Texans won the battle, a large Union force advancing from California forced them to withdraw from Arizona. Photos by the author

The Reverend Charles Logan York came to
Arizona in 1913 as minister of the Chandler
Mission. Settling in Tempe, he traveled far and
wide in the remote parts of Arizona. He always
carried a camera along and had a photogra-
pher's sense of the historical value of his work.
A few of his photos are presented in this section.
Photos courtesy of Trudy Murphy

113

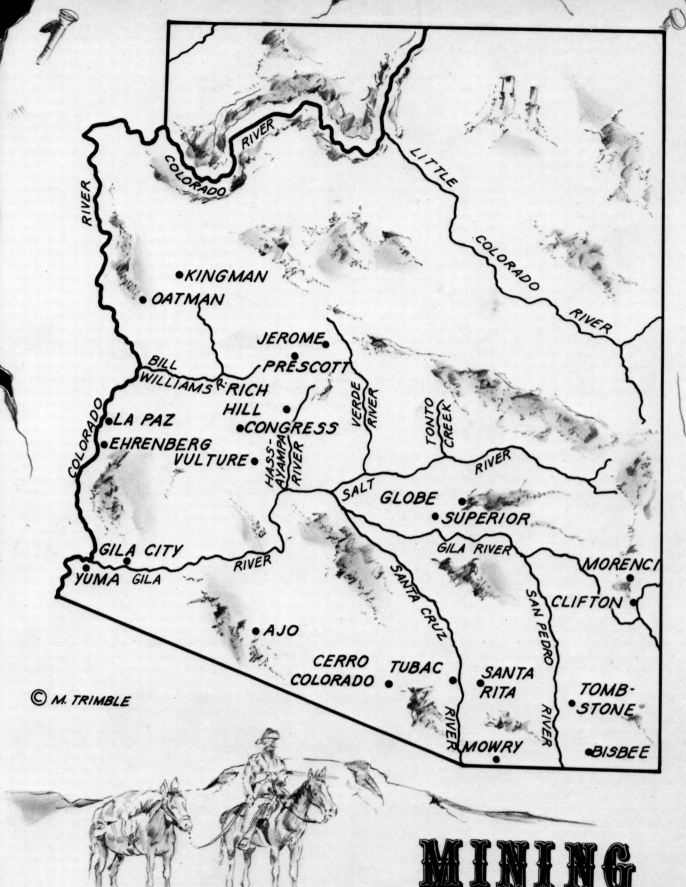

KINGMAN
OATMAN

JEROME
PRESCOTT
BILL
WILLIAMS RIVER
RICH
HILL
LA PAZ
CONGRESS
EHRENBERG
VULTURE
VERDE RIVER
TONTO CREEK
COLORADO RIVER
HASS-AYAMPA RIVER
SALT RIVER
GLOBE
SUPERIOR
LITTLE COLORADO RIVER
RIVER
COLORADO

GILA CITY
YUMA GILA RIVER
GILA RIVER
MORENCI
CLIFTON

AJO

CERRO COLORADO
TUBAC
SANTA CRUZ RIVER
SANTA RITA
SAN PEDRO RIVER
TOMB-STONE

© M. TRIMBLE

MOWRY
BISBEE

MINING

Chapter 11

"If ya stumble on a rock, don't cuss it—cash it!"

The gold and silver rushes, more than anything else, created the dramatic changes that affected nineteenth-century Arizona.

With a single lucky break a man or woman could make more money in an instant than they could lend or spend in a lifetime. So it was off to "Arizoney with my washpan on my knee." "Lynx Creek or Bust, Rich Hill or Bust, Tombstone or Bust," cried the jackass prospectors. "If ya stumble on a rock, don't cuss it, cash it," and "If ya wash yer face in the Hassayampa River, you can pan four ounces of gold dust from yer whiskers," claimed the burro men with some credibility. Wherever there was a "rumor and a hole in the ground," as Mark Twain said, "someone built a town around it." And each one claimed it was built right smack on top of the mother lode. The rusted ruins and weathered headframes are still out there—epitaphs marking the high water mark of someone's aspiration.

They gave the towns picturesque, whimsical names like Oro Belle, Placerita, and Total Wreck. Born in boom, most faded back into the adobe dust whence they came, a metropolis that didn't "metrop." Others like Prescott possessed staying power and grew into thriving cities. Tombstone, "the town too tough to die," almost did. With a grand display of remarkable grit, the community hangs on. The earliest residents of these boom towns were aptly described as "unmarried, unchurched and unwashed." The streets were ankle-deep in dust in dry weather and a quagmire when wet. They weren't passable; in fact, most

of the time they weren't even "jackassable." Many towns were perched on mountain slopes. "It was about as close to heaven as any of 'em got," said one. "It was no place for a Presbyterian," Mark Twain wrote wryly, "so, therefore, I did not remain one for long."

After the surface mineral played out, a new breed of men arrived: hard rock miners. Rawhide-tough, they hammered, chiseled, and dug into the innermost reaches of the mountains, revealing riches beyond the most optimistic dreams of the *conquistadores*. Boom camps like Bisbee, Tombstone, and Jerome bcame household words in board rooms in New York, London, and San Francisco. This new breed of miners brought their families into the boisterous, devil-may-care camps and soon the cry was heard, "We need schools, churches, law and order." And so they did. The bawdy towns began to take on respectability—oh they still knew how to let their hair down once in a while, but like the rest of raucous Arizona, they were starting to grow up.

The earliest mining ventures in Arizona, excepting explorations by Coronado, Onate, and Espejo, came during the mid-1700s. The famous Planchas de Plata discovery in 1736 led to other discoveries in the mountains straddling the Santa Cruz River. These were abandoned a century later when the Apaches went on the warpath and drove the Mexicans out. Charles Poston, Pete Brady, Sylvester Mowry, and a few others reopened those old mines in the mid-1850s but they too were

The first important gold discovery came on the Gila River about twenty miles east of Yuma in 1858. The town of Gila City materialized overnight. What followed afterwards was a string of gold and silver rushes which, more than anything else, created the dramatic changes that affected nineteenth-century Arizona. Born in boom, most of the towns, like Oro Belle, Placerita, and Total Wreck, faded back into the adobe dust whence they came. Others, like Prescott and Tombstone, possessed staying power and grew into thriving cities. Map drawn by Dean Lyon; art by Jack Graham; courtesy of the author

driven out by Apaches when the American troops were withdrawn at the outbreak of the Civil War.

The first important gold discovery came on the Gila River about twenty miles east of Yuma in 1858, when a colorful Texan named Jake Snively swished the water in his pan and saw gold nuggets glittering in the sun. A town materialized overnight and was soon peopled with would-be millionaires who ran the wide gamut of frontier society. Gila City had everything, one wrote, except "a church and a jail." Placer miners, using everything from skillets to wash pans, were panning out $20 to $125 a day in gold dust. In 1862, about the same time the gold played out, the Gila River went on a rampage and wiped out the town. Two years later, all that was left, according to one writer, was "three chimneys and a coyote."

The second major gold strike was made on the Colorado River at La Paz in 1862. Redoubtable mountain man, Indian scout and guide, Pauline Weaver, found gold in *Arroyo de la Tenaja* on January 12, at *El Dia de la Fiesta de Nuestra Señora de la Paz* (The Day of the Feast of Our Lady of Peace). By the time the La Paz strike played out, miners using pans, rockers and sluices had taken out $8 million in gold. In 1864 the town just missed by a few votes becoming the territorial capital of Arizona.

The legendary Goldwater family's mercantile enterprise got its start in that same year when Mike Goldwater hauled some much-needed goods across the desert from California and opened a store at La Paz. Later, he and his brother Joe freighted goods over the dangerous wagon road to Prescott.

The fabled Bradshaw Mountains would provide the source of the greatest gold and silver discoveries during the next few years.

In 1863, noted mountain man Joe Walker led a party of some thirty prospectors up near the headwaters of the Hassayampa River. The miners' picks and shovels turned over rich deposits of gold along Granite, Lynx, Big Bug, Turkey and a host of other creeks in the area. Gen. Jim Carleton dispatched a company of soldiers to protect the miners and, at the same time, convinced the gubernatorial party of the brand new territory of Arizona to locate the capital in the wilderness instead of Tucson. Thus, Prescott, as it came to be called, became the only wilderness capital in U.S. history.

Following on the bootheels of the Walker party was the ubiquitous Pauline Weaver. Weaver was guiding a party of prospectors up the Hassayampa when gold was discovered atop a lofty knoll a few miles north of the soon-to-be-established Wickenburg. Needing nothing more than jackknives to pry the nuggets loose, the prospectors gathered gold valued at more than $100,000 in just a few weeks. The richest single placer discovery in Arizona history became known, for good reason, as Rich Hill.

Henry Wickenburg wasn't far behind Weaver and Walker in the quest for gold along the Hassayampa. Wickenburg's gold turned out to be a fabulous ore discovery rather than placer. Placer gold could be mined with the toe of your boot or a jackknife but ore or lode gold was still attached to the rock and had to be pulverized and separated. Wickenburg's Vulture Mine was located about eleven miles from the Hassayampa and the ore had to be hauled overland to the river where *arrastras* or mule-powered ore crushers had been built. He sold the ore for fifteen dollars a ton to others who hauled it over to the river. Soon a town was established and named in old Henry's honor. Unfortunately, things didn't pan out for Henry Wickenburg. He sold out to some eastern financiers who promised him a peice of the action, then swindled him out of his profits. In 1905, broke and downtrodden, Henry Wickenburg took his own life.

This photo of Bisbee miner George Warren was used on the design of the Arizona state seal. According to local legend, George once wagered a drunken bet that he could outrun a horse. He bet his share of what became the legendary Copper Queen Mine. Naturally, he lost the race up Brewery Gulch and the mine later produced millions. George died broke but all was not lost as the town of Warren, Arizona, was named for him. Photo courtesy of Maricopa Community Colleges, Southwest Studies

A prospector's dream! Photo courtesy of Maricopa Community Colleges, Southwest Studies

An Arizona prospector pauses for posterity, but not necessarily for prosperity, before striking out in search of the mother lode. Photo courtesy of Maricopa Community Colleges, Southwest Studies

A miner's Saturday night usually began with a bath to scrape off some of the week's dust. Photo courtesy of the Arizona Historical Society/Tucson

Prescott's First Citizen

When old Joe Walker, a big, strapping, ex-mountain man, and his party of prospectors arrived at Granite Creek in the spring of 1863, another old mountain man, Pauline Weaver, was already camped there. The area where the future territorial capital city of Prescott would be founded was the stomping grounds of the Yavapai and Tonto Apaches. Both groups had a reputation as formidable foes of the whites who asked no quarter and gave none. Surprisingly, the earliest days of Prescott's history were relatively free of bloodshed and the credit goes to Pauline Weaver.

Weaver was one of those ubiquitous characters who best fits the description of one who never had time to write or narrate early Arizona history. He was too busy making it. Born in Tennessee around 1800, he was the son of a white father and Cherokee mother. For a time he worked for the Hudson Bay Fur Company but preferred warmer climates, so he headed for the Southwest. He first arrived in Arizona in the late 1820s and over the next few years established a reputation as a first-rate mountain man, coming to know Arizona's mountains, deserts and rivers like the back of his hand. Somebody scratched his name on the Casa Grande ruins in 1832. Since Weaver made his mark with an *X* until his dying day, the signature is but one more mystery at that site.

During the Mexican War, Gen. Stephen Watts Kearny, commander of the Army of the West, hired Weaver as a guide for the Mormon Battalion on their historic road building trek along the Gila Trail. Weaver spent the 1850s trapping for beaver along the river streams in Arizona where he got on friendly terms with most of the tribes. In 1862, some natives along the Colorado River in western Arizona showed him some rich gold placers at La Paz not far from today's Ehrenberg. Before the gold played out, some eight million dollars worth of the yellow metal had been panned out. The boom town of La Paz that sprang up nearby, almost became the capital city of the Arizona territory. Sometime later, the capricious Colorado changed its muddy course, bypassing La Paz and leaving a couple of steamboats sitting high and dry in the desert. The town picked up and moved over to the river and renamed itself Ehrenberg.

The same year Weaver discovered gold at La Paz he hired out as a scout for the California Volunteers. A small force of Confederates from Texas had occupied Tucson and were probing their way along

Pauline Weaver, mountain man, scout, and gold prospector, was one of Arizona's most prominent trailblazers and was named Pres- *cott's "first citizen."* Photo courtesy of Maricopa Community Colleges, Southwest Studies

the Gila towards the strategic river crossing at Yuma. A few weeks later they retreated back to the Old Pueblo in the face of the two thousand-man California Column that was planning to reoccupy Arizona. The hard-riding mountain men led Capt. William Calloway and 272 men up the Gila to the Pima Villages at today's Sacaton-Bapchule (Interstate 10 at the Gila).

Two detachments from Calloway's Cavalry headed to Picacho where they fought a battle with the Confederate's rear guard in what is called the "Westernmost Battle of the Civil War."

Not long after the Walker Party found gold in the Bradshaw Mountains, Weaver guided the Abraham H. Peeples Party up the Hassayampa River in search of another *madre del oro*. A few miles north of Wickenburg they stumbled upon a treasure trove of gold nuggets lying atop a rocky knoll that was rightfully named Rich Hill. It was the richest single placer strike in Arizona history and how it got deposited up there is still an enigma, but gold, as they say, is where you find it.

During those first months, Weaver worked tirelessly to negotiate a treaty between the native tribes and newcomers and succeeded for a spell. The Indians used the password *Paulino-Tobacco,* which was to indicate to the whites they were friendly. *Tobacco* was a word nearly every Indian knew and understood and it was always given by whites during a parley as a token of friendship. As more whites poured in who weren't aware, or didn't care about the arrangement, the treaty became meaningless. Too many cultural differences and mutual mistrust caused the inevitable outbreak of hostilities. In the mid-1860s Weaver himself was jumped by a war party outside Prescott and seriously wounded. The old scout thought he was a goner and went into his "death song," a custom he'd

adopted from the Plains Indians. The suspicious warriors, not familiar with the ritual, believed he'd gone crazy and left him alone. When Weaver saw he wasn't going to die, he got up and casually walked home. The wound did, however, continue to trouble him for the remainder of his days.

It is said the natives were remorseful about shooting Weaver and during friendly parleys always asked how "Powlino" was getting along.

When the first settlers moved into the Verde Valley, the army was called in to provide protection from a growing number of attacks. The officers wisely brought Weaver in to bring about a peace

treaty. His service, according to military records, was invaluable but ol' Dad Time was catching up. His health deteriorated and, on June 21, 1867, Pauline Weaver died. He was buried at Fort Verde (Lincoln) with full military honors. Later, when the post was abandoned, his remains were taken to California. In 1929, poet-historian Sharlot Hall organized a campaign to have Weaver's remains returned to Prescott. Thanks to the Boy Scouts and Prescott school children, funds were raised and Weaver was re-buried on the grounds of the old territorial capital. Ms. Hall declared him "Prescott's First Citizen," a title he richly deserved.

La Paz was the site of a rich gold strike in the 1860s near the Colorado River. Pauline Weaver discovered gold near here in 1862. The town boomed for a time and nearly became the territorial capital. In 1863, the Colorado River changed its course and this river port literally *dried up. A new community was established at the river and named Ehrenberg for the noted Arizona adventurer and mining engineer, Herman Ehrenberg.* Courtesy of the Arizona Historical Foundation

The granddaddy of all silver strikes came in 1877 when a persistent sourdough named Ed Schieffelin struck it rich on a limestone mesa east of the San Pedro River. For years Schieffelin had endured the rigors and disappointments that come with the quest for the illusive *madre del oro*. He had nothing to show for his efforts and had become something of a joke around Tucson when he decided to try his luck over in the San Pedro Valley. Apache chieftain Victorio and his warriors were on a rampage at the time and one soldier warned, "all you'll find out there will be your tombstone." Ed went anyway and eventually convinced his brother Al and a reknowned assayer named Richard Gird to join him. Dodging Apaches while he scoured the rocky crags, Ed searched and found nothing of value. His conservative sibling protested the fruitless search, preferring to give up the quest and take a two-dollar-a-day job in the mines. Then one day Ed brought in some new specimens. "You're a lucky cuss," Gird smiled as he handed Ed the results of his assay. And that's how the fabulous Lucky Cuss mine got its name. A town grew up nearby and the folks didn't have any trouble picking a name. Ed Schieffelin had, indeed, found his Tombstone.

By the time Tombstone's heyday had drawn to a close, copper was becoming an important natural resource. America was entering the age of electricity and buried beneath the gold and silver deposits lay a king's ransom in copper just waiting to be dug. The colorful jackass prospector had become a vanishing breed. His place was taken by the hardrock miner, and a new era was aborning. By the early 1900s Arizona had become the copper king of America. During World War I the industry would reach its zenith. Towns like Jerome, Bisbee, Clifton, Morenci, and Ajo boomed, and the likes of them would never be seen again. Copper towns, like their gold and silver predecessors, had a life span. Some of those early-day camps lasted only a few weeks before they played out and became ghost towns. The life span of the copper towns was much greater—about a century. But it was only a matter of time till the inevitable demise came.

Still, they left behind a rich, colorful history and a powerful legacy. Mining was the foundation on which twenty-first-century Arizona would be built. As one old third-generation miner said, "Well, it's all over, ain't it. But it was sure one hell of a time and we won't ever see anything like it again."♦

It was a solitary life for this unidentified miner (possibly near Clifton). Photo courtesy of the Arizona Historical Society/Tucson

This is Glory Hole, also called Copper Queen Cut, where the first ore was taken from the Copper Queen claims near Bisbee. Photo courtesy of the Arizona Historical Society/Tucson

This early 1900 photo shows Bisbee looking east. That cone-shaped mountain in the center is today replaced by a huge open pit mine. Photo courtesy of the Arizona Historical Foundation

Crazy Horse Lil

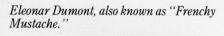

Eleonar Dumont, also known as "Frenchy Mustache."

Big Minnie

Boom Town Belles: *The "soiled doves" of the boomtowns used different tools to strike it rich.*

Photos courtesy of Maricopa Community Colleges, Southwest Studies

Snake Hips Lulu

D. May Davenport of May's Place, Cananea, Sonora, Mexico

Blonde Marie

This saloon was typical of those in the late 1800s. Photo courtesy of the Arizona Historical Society/Tucson

The Silver King Mine, the richest silver vein in Arizona history, was a "lost mine" that was found again. When the original discoverer, a man named Sullivan, returned many years later and told his tale of finding, then losing the location, sympathetic owners gave him a life-time pension and a job. Photo by E. A. Bonnie, courtesy of the Arizona Historical Society/Tucson

Shady Deals

Today's disreputable land promoters selling lakeshore lots on the edges of mirages are mere amateurs when compared to some of the wheeler-dealers of yesteryear. The lawless Arizona territory attracted a wide gamut of frontier con men ranging from tin horn gamblers to stock swindlers.

Most Arizona history buffs are familiar with the notorious James Addison Reavis, the self-styled "Baron of Arizona," who tried to steal some twelve million acres of prime Arizona territory by forging some old Spanish land grants. For a time he was successful and amassed quite a fortune, all of which was quickly squandered on an opulent lifestyle and, later, on attorney's fees.

Another was Doctor Richard Flower. "Doc" Flower wasn't really a doctor. He earned his living for a time selling cure-all bottled medicine. Although Doc Flower claimed his recipe could cure everything from baldness to toothaches, it really had no redeeming medicinal value. It did contain enough alcohol to mellow its imbibers enough that nobody felt ripped-off. Anyhow, that's how he came to be called "Doctor" Flower.

Doc Flower eventually grew weary of small time scheming and decided to play for higher stakes. Fortunes were being made in the Arizona mines and, since Doc Flower didn't have a bona fide mine of his own, he decided to create one. He'd never been to Arizona and wouldn't have known a nugget from rolled oats but that didn't stop him. He erected a phony, movie set-looking mine, complete with headframe, east of Globe, bought a few samples of ore from a producing mine and headed back east to promote his strike.

He called the company the Spendazuma, something that indicates old Doc Flower did at least have a wry sense of humor. *Mazuma* was a slang term for money, so in effect he was promoting the "spend yer money" mine—and noboby caught on. Would-be millionaires were waiting in line to buy stock in Doc's mine.

The balloon burst when a reporter from the *Arizona Republican* (today's *Republic*) named George Smalley, rode out to have a look at this mine that was creating such a stir back east. The property was being guarded by one of Doc's hirelings, a hard-bitten character named Alkali Tom. Tom tried his best to keep the snoopy reporter from getting too close to Doc's imaginary gold mine, but Smalley was not to be denied. Workers were about as scarce as horseflies in December, and Smalley became suspicious. A closer examination revealed the

whole setup was a phony.

When Smalley's expose made the papers, Doc's lawyer indignantly threatened to sue for a hundred thousand dollars and demanded a retraction. Smalley could hardly keep from laughing, so they offered him five thousand to rewrite the story and admit he made a mistake. When the spunky reporter assumed a pugilist's pose, the lawyer retreated and Doc Flower's blossoming Spendazuma scheme withered away.

Bret Harte spent enough time around mining camps to become an authority on the art of selling worthless claims to unsuspecting tenderfeet. He wrote rather poetically on the subject:

> The ways of a man with a maid be
> strange, yet simple and tame
> To the ways of a man with a mine
> when buying or selling the same.

One overzealous promoter distributed brochures back east extolling the mineral riches in the Bradshaw Mountains. On the cover was a picture of an oceangoing, ore-laden vessel steaming down the normally dry Hassayampa River.

Unscrupulous prospectors upgraded their dubious mining properties in a manner contrary to nature by a process known as salting. Since gold was malleable, it could be loaded in a shotgun shell and impregnated into the rocky walls of a worthless tunnel, creating a glittering Golconda.

One careless victim bought a silver mine laden with chunks of blackened native silver from an honest-looking dealer. A closer examination of one of the nuggets revealed the partially melted words "United States of America."

Sometimes the property owner became the victim in cases of salting. One of the most unusual happened to a man named Julian, who owned a rather large operation.

When a rich body of ore was found in one of the tunnels, the price of the stock rose dramatically on the local exhcange. Three employees offered to sell their inflated stock back to the boss. That alone should have made Julian wary but he eagerly purchased the stock. A few days later the "vein" played out and the stock went back down. Julian lost a tidy sum on the stock drop and became suspicious. When the three miners were asked if they had salted the mine, each innocently denied guilt.

"Would you swear to that on the Holy Bible?" Julian asked. The miners shrugged their shoulders and agreed, whereupon Julian produced an ornate Bible and had each man declare himself innocent. "I believe those men," Julian declared. "No good Irish-Catholic would dare place his hand upon the Holy Bible and deliberately lie."

Julian might have gone right on believing their innocence had he not dropped the Bible while returning it to the bookshelf. The book jacket flopped open to the title page. Julian looked once, blinked, then looked again. Instead of "Holy Bible" it said "Webster's Dictionary." Those Irish miners had anticipated what Julian would do and had "salted" his Holy Bible.

Julian didn't fire them. He had too much admiration for their resourcefulness. He did, however, demote the trio to menial tasks to discourage any future tampering with the stock market.

Up in old Yavapai County, they tell of an incurable sourdough who worked tediously to salt a worthless claim he wanted to unload. Quite literally, the prospector left no stone unturned. His foolproof work carefully completed, he urged a prospective buyer to bring in his own assayer to run tests. The prospector had done his work well, for the rsults of the assay showed the claim to be a rich one—so rich, in fact, that the old prospector changed his mind and refused to sell. ♦

Sylvester Mowry was a flamboyant ex-Army officer, mining entrepreneur and promoter of territorial status for Arizona. Photo courtesy of Maricopa Community Colleges, Southwest Studies

Nellie Cashman, prospector and restauranteur was known affectionately throughout the west as the "Miner's Angel." Although a pretty woman, she never married. Nellie preferred the free life of a prospector and adventurer. Her travels took her from Mexico to the Arctic Circle. Photo courtesy of the Arizona Historical Society/Tucson

This was the site of Sylvester Mowry's famous lead and silver mine during the 1860s. Union Army Col. James Carleton accused Mowry of *siding with the Confederates. Mowry was arrested and sent to Yuma and lost his mine.* Photo courtesy of the Arizona State Library

The Good Ol' Days in Jerome

Jerome, perched precariously on the slopes of Cleopatra Hill, is a popular tourist attraction today. It's also a quiet community most of the time, and that's a far cry from those halcyon days around the turn of the century when there was, roughly, one saloon for every one hundred residents.

The town took on quite a personality during those years. Payday came once a month and the mines closed for a couple of days to let the rough and tumble miners have time to spend their hard-earned wages. Things got pretty western for a few days and the old jail, which looked more like a concrete bunker, was usually overflowing. Legend has it the jail had spikes on the floor to keep the occupants from getting a good night's sleep.

The plucky miners never let incarceration keep them from having a good time. Once, when the jail was already filled, the town constable chained twelve unruly drunks to a huge mill wheel. Undaunted, the brawny, bibulous reprobates picked up the wheel in unison and hauled it to the nearest saloon where they demanded an ax to widen the door so they could get in.

Lewis St. James was the local magistrate. He was totally deaf and couldn't hear the testimony, but he seemed to know most of the defendants personally and ruled accordingly. Like most judges, he had an uncanny ability to know just how much money they were carrying and set the fine thusly.

The town dentist was Dr. Lee Hawkins. He'd never been to medical school, but folks liked him and, since his remedies were harmless, they let him practice (literally). Eventually, Doc Hawkins became a pretty good dentist. When he wasn't pullin' teeth, Hawkins was an inventor of gadgets that usually didn't work.

Jennie Banters was the town's most prominent and prosperous madam. It was said she was the wealthiest businesswoman in Arizona around the turn of the century. She was also the most resourceful. Once when the town was having one of its periodic holocausts, she went to the volunteer hose company and offered them lifetime free passes to her establishment if they'd put the fire out at her place. It was said the red-blooded volunteers rose to superhuman efforts as they charged up the hill and extinguished the flames.

Jerome's citizens never missed a chance to celebrate some festive occasion, and the Fourth of July was always the favorite. Everybody turned out to watch the volunteer hose companies run races. A great deal of pride was at stake, since fire in the hillside town built of wood-framed structures was a constant threat and the hose company judged fastest was held in the highest esteem among town folks, not to mention braggin' rights until the next contest.

Drilling contests were the most popular. Hard rock miners competed for some two hundred dollars in prize money, no small amount since a miner only earned about three dollars a day. Each contestant or team had fifteen minutes to drill a hole in a block of Gunnison granite. Naturally there was a lot of betting on the outcome.

Baseball, the great American pastime, always generated a lot of excitement. Fierce rivalries were established between towns like Prescott and Clarkdale. The company bankrolled the local team and imported some of the best players money could buy. Hal Chase, banned from major league baseball for accepting a bribe, was brought to Jerome but didn't last long. One story has it he was bought off by gamblers in Clarkdale, a far cry from the World Series but no less scandalous to the rabid fans at Jerome.

Jerome never recovered from the stock

Jerome was a billion dollar copper town perched on the side of Cleopatra Hill. By 1923 the town was on the decline in more ways than one. Blasting beneath the town caused the buildings to slide downward. That, along with hard times, led to a new town motto: "Jerome is a city on the move." It was, but unfortunately all downhill. The city peaked during World War I, declined during the Great Depression, rose again during World War II, then closed its mines in 1953. It almost became a ghost town. Photo (A) courtesy of the Arizona Historical Foundation; Photo (B) courtesy of Maricopa Community Colleges, Southwest Studies

market crash in 1929. A few years earlier, the United Verde Extension had discovered a rich body of ore directly below the town. Hundreds of thousands of tons of earth-shaking dynamite were used to wrest the ore from the mountain's clutches. Above the ground, years of choking smelter smoke had destroyed the flora on the mountain. With nothing to hold the soil, Jerome began to slide.

Despite hard times and the new catastrophe, Jerome's hardy citizens never lost their sense of humor. Mayor Harry Mader coined a new phrase when he proclaimed "Jerome is a city on the move." It was, but unfortunately all downhill. ◆

The pride of each mining community was its firefighters. The combination of coal oil lamps and wooden structures burned most towns to the ground at least once. Jerome burned three times in three years. Once during a fire the town's most prosperous madam, Jennie Ban- *ters, told the firemen she'd give lifetime free passes if they'd put out the fire at her house first. Legend has it they charged up the hill with superhuman effort to save Jennie's place.* Photo taken 1906, courtesy of the Arizona Historical Society/Tucson

Henry Wickenburg discovered Vulture Mine near the town that bears his name. Swindled out of his rightful fortune, Wickenburg later committed suicide. Photo courtesy of Maricopa Community Colleges, Southwest Studies

The tall building with the flag is Schieffelin Hall, the tallest adobe structure in Arizona. The photographer shot this 1882 view at the site of the gunfight at the O. K. Corral which occurred a year earlier. Photo courtesy of the Arizona Historical Society/Tucson

Ed Schieffelin located rich silver lodes at Tombstone. Shown here in a studio photo, Schieffelin represented the highest ideals in a prospector. After many years of luck he struck it rich in the mountains of southwest Arizona, but continued to search for more rich mines, preferring the lonely life of a prospector. His last request was to be buried at the site of his fabulous find in Tombstone. Photo courtesy of Maricopa Community Colleges, Southwest Studies

The Congress Mine opened in 1883 and soon about four hundred miners filled the town. The mine was so rich, the Santa Fe Railroad located its line from Prescott to Phoenix nearby. President William McKinley visited the town in 1900. Photo courtesy of the Arizona Historical Foundation

Hardrock miners work the five-foot vein of argentiferous galena at the five hundred-foot level of the Tombstone Consolidated Mines. Photo by Hadsell, courtesy of the Arizona Historical Society/Tucson

Morenci, shown here between 1905 and 1913, was called "Joy's Camp" in 1871. It was later changed to honor Bill Joy's hometown in Michigan. About 1871 William "Slim" Joy staked claims in this area. A decade later he offered them as collateral in seeking a $50,000 loan from the Phelps Dodge Mining Company. The company bought him out in 1887. Phelps Dodge became the major copper producer in Arizona with operations in such other rich mining districts as Bisbee and Jerome. An open pit mine eventually swallowed up old Morenci and a new town had to be built nearby. Photo courtesy of the Arizona Historical Society/Tucson

Black Jack Newman wasn't black and his name wasn't Newman. His skin was dark and his Polish name too difficult to pronounce. He was the newest arrival in the area so they called him "New Man" or "Newman." He wanted to name the community Mima after his fiancé, Mima Tune. Another group from Miami, Ohio, opted for their hometown. A compromise was reached and the town was spelled Miami *and pronounced "Mima." This photo of the town shows Sullivan Street.* Photo courtesy of the Arizona Historical Society/Tucson

Tombstone Lawyers

Soon after a prospector's pick struck paydirt in some remote, rocky crag, a town was sure to spring up nearby. A host of new arrivals would be on hand to help separate some poor sucker from his poke sack. They called it "mining the miners" and the whole wide gamut of frontier society was well-represented. Among the first to arrive were the whiskey peddlers. All one needed for furnishings were two empty barrels and a couple of boards. Next came the gamblers, soiled doves, and land speculators, with all their virtues and vices. If the boisterous boom camp had any staying power—that is, if the ore deposit was sufficiently large enough to last a few years—merchants, hard-rock pick and shovel men and their families, preachers, and teachers arrived to make up the next wave of new residents.

Quite naturally it was only a matter of time before disputes over boundaries of mining claims and real estate properties required the presence of the much-maligned frontier lawyer. Litigation became the single most lucrative, money-making scheme in this frontier society dedicated to the principles of getting rich without working.

Lawyers weren't always welcomed in these raw boom camps. Locals figured they'd managed reasonably well before their arrival. "We didn't need laws," one observer said, "until the lawyers got here."

Still, someone had to settle these complex disputes over claims and someone had to represent the poor, defenseless tinhorn gamblers, con men, cow thieves, stage robbers, and murderers. And someone had to represent the decent people, too. Like any other profession, the lawyers who came to territorial Arizona represented the best and worst when it came to ethics and morals.

Many were well-educated scions from established eastern families who had become a source of embarrassment and were exiled to practice in the raw, western towns, while others came in search of adventure. Some of the most eminent legal minds in the territory were also some of the most colorful characters to ever make the Arizona scene.

Since Tombstone was the granddaddy of all silver strikes in the early 1880s it became a favorite gathering place for lawyers hoping to cash in on the wealth and perhaps launch a political career. The lawyers' offices occupied a row of low-slung adobe buildings along Fourth Street between Tough Nut (named after the hard diggin' required for mining) and

Proprietors discovered that some of the richest deposits could be found "mining the miners." Photo courtesy of Maricopa Community Colleges, Southwest Studies

Allen streets, bounded on the north side by Allen Street, Tombstone's notorious bibulous Babylon. The county courthouse was a block west on Tough Nut, so they were conveniently situated midway between. Residents dubbed the area inhabited by the lawyers "Rotten Row." Local punsters noted that very few of Tombstone's astute attorneys could pass the "bar" and resist the temptation to "belly up."

Back in 1942 this writer's favorite writer, Dr. C. L. Sonnichsen, penned an Arizona classic called *Billy King's Tombstone: The Private Life of an Arizona Boom Town*. The book is a rich treasure-trove of stories about some of Tombstone's characters who didn't receive the notoriety of Wyatt Earp, Johnny Ringo, Curley Bill, and friends. Among these were lawyers such as Mark Smith, Ben Goodrich, William C. Staehle, and Allen English.

Foremost among the attorneys who hung their shingles out on Rotten Row in the 1880s was the distinguished Marcus Aurelius Smith. He was tall, handsome and colorful, a consummate politician, imbiber, gambler, and "good ol' boy." Mark, as he was known to his many friends and constituents, fit in quite well with Tombstone's society. His imposing,

gregarious figure was a permanent fixture in the bars and casinos on Allen Street. He made friends easily and was a formidable attorney for the defense. His greatest flaw was an addiction to the game of chance. Mark loved to gamble and he didn't seem to mind the odds. One time some of his friends tried to drag him away from a rigged game at the Pony Saloon. "You haven't got a chance to win," they warned. "What of it," he replied with grim determination, "it's the only game in town, ain't it?"

When Smith left Tombstone for bigger political stakes, he penned his own appropriate epitaph. "Here lies a good man—a lover of fast horses, pretty women, and good whiskey." One can see why his departure saddened Tombstone's sporting crowd. He was the territory's perennial delegate to Washington for sixteen years and then served an additional eight years as U.S. Senator when Arizona became a state in 1912.

If Mark Smith epitomized the hard drinkers and high rollers of his profession, his counterpart was his own partner, Ben Goodrich. Goodrich was regarded as a bit eccentric. He didn't drink, smoke, hang out in the red-light district, or play games of chance. Stranger yet, with all those peculiarities one would suspect Ben would have had some virtuous propensity such as going to church, but he didn't do that either. Tombstonians were a pretty tolerant bunch in those days though, and they accepted Goodrich despite his "vices."

Perhaps the strangest member of the society on Rotten Row was William C. Staehle. Staehle was a cultured connoiseur of classical music, an accomplished violinist who proudly boasted his Germanic heritage, referring to himself as the "German Warrior." He was strongly addicted to the liquid refreshment dispensed on Allen Street, so much so that locals insisted his middle initial stood for corkscrew. For a time he was married to a fickle lady named Gussie, but she ran off with somebody else, leaving Corkscrew Staehle to seek solace in redeye and violin music.

Staehle's jingoistic Teutonic pride increased with each downing of a shot glass. He boasted of Germany's superiority in everything from culture and music to military might. Occasionally he went too far and felt compelled to prove his own pugilistic abilities against some of the barflies on Allen Street. One night he tried to pick a fight but couldn't find any takers. Finally he was escorted to the door by the saloonkeeper and given a gentle kick in the seat of the pants. The German Warrior resented this affront to his dignity, complaining to anyone who'd listen that he didn't mind being kicked in the seat of the pants, "but the dirty son-of-a-gun kicked me with a pair of dollar-and-a-half shoes."

Another time he invited himself to a brawl between some soldiers from Fort Hauchuca in an alley behind the Crystal Palace. "Count me in," the German Warrior said, raising his forefinger in the air. Before he could assume a pugilistic pose, a fist caught him beside the head and sent him sprawling. Just before the lights went out, he gamely pointed his forefinger skyward again and mumbled, "Count me out."

Of all the attorneys to hang their shingles on the adobe walls of Rotten Row, none was more capable or better liked than Allen R. English. His contemporaries described him as standing well over six feet, with a sweeping mustache, a neatly-trimmed Vandyke beard, and a magnificently-adorned head of thick hair. Providence had endowed him with handsome features and a deep, resonant voice. He was fond of dressing in a cutaway coat and striped trousers. His stately appearance was comple-

mented by a formidable wit and an intellectual mind. He had a great sense of humor, made friends easily, and was one of the most popular personalities in Cochise County.

Allen R. English was one of Arizona's great oratorical lawyers. And he was colorful. When a Tombstone judge fined him twenty-five dollars for contempt of court because he appeared in court intoxicated, English roared indignantly, "Your Honor, twenty-five dollars wouldn't pay for half the contempt I have for this court." A stranger in town remarked to a weary prosecutor, "Mr. English is certainly an outspoken man." "Mr. English," the prosecutor replied, "may be out-thought, out-maneuvered, out-smarted, but believe me, he is never out-spoken." Photo courtesy of the Arizona Historical Society/Tucson

English was born into an affluent eastern family. He displayed signs of brilliance early on, receiving a law degree while still in his teens. He arrived in Tombstone in 1880 at the age of twenty. Surprisingly, he didn't go into the practice of law but took a day job as a hardrock miner. He made the nightly rounds of the honky-tonks where he met Mark Smith. Smith took a liking to the young man and talked him into quitting the mines and coming in as a law partner. Smith groomed his young protege well, both in the practice of law and the night life on Allen Street. In time, English's reputation both as a drinker and lawyer was well known throughout the territory.

Once the Santa Fe railroad offered him $25,000 as a retainer on one condition: that he refrain from drinking.

"What," he bellowed indignantly. "Give up my inalienable rights to a bloodless corruption. Hell no!"

Despite those remarks, English represented many large corporations and accumulated a small fortune for his efforts. Unfortunately his free-spending habits kept him broke most of the time.

My great uncle, Frank Gilpin, was a peace officer in Bisbee during English's heyday. Among the many Allen English anecdotes he passed on to me was this: Phelps Dodge kept English on a retainer and, every time a case was pending, they'd lock him up in the Copper Queen Hotel and post a guard outside the door in an effort to keep him sober for the trial. Without fail, some cronie would figure out a way to smuggle a bottle up to his room and English would appear before his honor "under the influence."

Once he appeared for a case so plastered the judge fined him twenty-five dollars for contempt of court. English, with a great display of his inimitable, rapier wit, replied. "Your Honor, twenty-five dollars wouldn't pay for half the contempt I have for this court."

Although Allen English was a popular man among juries and courtroom spectators, his clever courtroom antics and florid use of the English language made him the nemesis for judge and prosecutor alike.

Some courtroom novice once remarked, "My, that Mr. English is certainly an outspoken man." A somewhat jaded prosecutor heard the remark and corrected. "Mr. English may be out-thought, out-maneuvered, out-smarted, but believe me, he is never out-spoken."

English was in his greatest glory when performing in front of the jury box. This courtroom colossus moved with the grace of a cat, his rich, sonorous voice indignant one moment, pleading the next. He directed juries like a conductor leads a symphony. He could laugh, cry, and make a sentimental appeal to motherhood and the American Flag all in the same paragraph. English punctuated his remarks wth lofty quotes ranging from Greek and Latin poetry to Shakespeare, all for the benefit of a jury held spellbound by his ornate oratory. And he knew how to be homespun. "Got a chew, Jim?" he'd say, leaning on the rail grinning at an acquaintance on the jury.

Somewhere along the way, English had developed a talent for spitting tobacco juice with all the expertise of a mule skinner. They said he could stand blindfolded and unload a brown stream, hitting a spittoon ten feet away with unerring accuracy. His favorite target was the judge's own private cuspidor next to the bench. During heated debates his aim sometimes became capricious and spattered the bench. These exhibitions came to be called "English's Great Expectorations" (with all respect to Dickens, of course).

At times strong liquor seemed to improve his ability to try a case. One time he was defending a gunslinger named Wiley Morgan on a murder charge and at the same time nursing a painful hangover. The court recessed for lunch just before the closing arguments, so Mr. English went to his favorite watering hole for more of the "hair of the dog that bit him."

By the time court was ready to convene, he was passed out on the barroom floor. Somebody brought a wagon to the front door and English was stretched out in back and hauled to the courthouse, then carried up the back stairs, arriving just in time for the closing arguments. English opened his eyes, then slowly stood up, focused on the jury and went into the most masterful piece of oratory folks in those parts had ever heard. When it was over, the jury found his client innocent of all charges. Afterwards, friends and admirers who gathered around to offer congratulations found English still totally inebriated. ♦

A Memorial Day parade meanders along notorious Allen Street in Tombstone during the 1880s. The O. K. Corral stands near the half-mast flag in the top center. Less than a block down the street is Hatch's Saloon where Morgan Earp was murdered. Photo by C. S. Fly, courtesy of the Arizona Historical Society/Tucson

The old Clifton Jail cells were carved out of solid rock. When the San Francisco River flooded, prisoners had to be evacuated quickly. Local legend has it that the miner who carved the new jail took his money and went to a local bar to celebrate. He proposed a toast to himself as "the world's greatest jail builder." Patrons weren't impressed and refused to toast. He raised a ruckus, shot up the place and became the first resident in his own jail. Photo courtesy of the Arizona Historical Foundation

A court scene in Tombstone, Arizona Territory, circa 1883. Photo courtesy of the Arizona Historical Society/Tucson

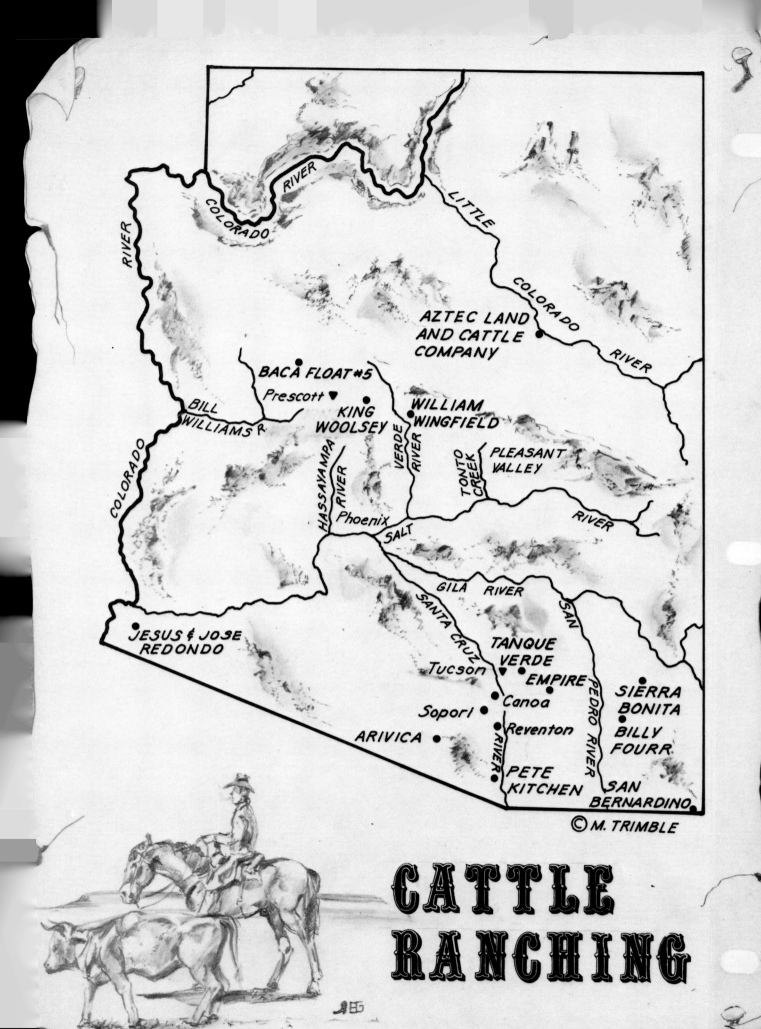

COLORADO RIVER

RIVER

LITTLE

COLORADO

RIVER

AZTEC LAND
AND CATTLE
COMPANY

BACA FLOAT #5

Prescott ▼

BILL
WILLIAMS R.

KING
WOOLSEY

WILLIAM
WINGFIELD

COLORADO

HASSAYAMPA RIVER

VERDE RIVER

TONTO CREEK

PLEASANT
VALLEY

Phoenix

SALT

RIVER

GILA RIVER

SAN

JESUS & JOSE
REDONDO

SANTA CRUZ

TANQUE
VERDE

PEDRO RIVER

Tucson ▼

EMPIRE

SIERRA
BONITA

Sopori

Canoa

BILLY
FOURR

ARIVICA

Reventon

RIVER

PETE
KITCHEN

SAN
BERNARDINO

© M. TRIMBLE

CATTLE
RANCHING

Chapter  12

The Cowboys

The men and women of the Old West are among the most cherished figures in Americana—the rugged symbols of the making of a country, hard-working, self-reliant, with honest determination and independence. In short, all those virtues that people like to see in themselves, not just in this country, but throughout the world. Among these figures, the most beloved and enduring are the cowboys, America's legends in Levis. Their brash, rebellious years were short; only a couple of decades made them immortal. Yet they cut a deep trail in the illustrious history of the West. "He made tracks in history," wrote cowboy artist Charley Russell, "that the farmer can't plow under."

The cowboy seems so indigenous to our culture that, had he never existed, we would have invented him. "To become a cowboy," someone wrote, "all you needed was guts and a horse. And if you had guts, you could steal a horse." They came from varied backgrounds. Kids ran away from home and walked down to the cattle country in south Texas to fulfill that dream of being a cowboy. Blacks, escaping slavery and prejudice, found what really counted on the open range was not the color of one's skin, but his ability to handle a lariat and work with horses and cattle.

Some modern-day critics have criticized the romantic image of the cowboy, claiming he was little more than an illiterate laborer on horseback differing little from factory hands in Eastern cities. The subject has been cussed and discussed among iconoclastic scholars at university seminars. However, in reality the cowboy had much greater responsibility than his fellow laboring class. A small handful were oftentimes charged with driving up the trail to market a large herd that represented the life savings of a group of ranchers. They might be called upon to defend the herd with their lives from predatory outlaws or Indians. And they might have to risk their necks turning the herd in a stampede, or swim dangerous swollen rivers. Many lost their lives in lonely places trying to protect their employer's investment. With the exception of the fabled mountain man, the cowboys shared freedoms enjoyed by few others in the laboring class. Granted, they worked for bosses who might be autocratic but, away from the ranch headquarters, they were pretty much their own boss and they had the wide-open spaces to ride and planty of clean air to breathe. It's doubtful if any of them would have traded places with a laborer in some stagnant, throat-choking factory town.

Their days might be spent under a blazing desert sun or in a

A few punchers from the Diamond A outfit in Cochise County ham it up for the cameraman. They bear little resemblance to the Hollywood version of cowboys. Photo courtesy of Maricopa Community Colleges, Southwest Studies

Huge land grants during the golden years of the Spanish empire created ranches so large, "you had to grease the wagon twice to get from the front porch to the front gate." Northern Arizona's most spectacular enterprise was established in 1884, however, when Edward Kinsley formed the Aztec Land and Cattle Company, better known as the "Hashknife," on a million acres of land. Map drawn by Dean Lyon; art by Jack Graham; courtesy of the author

bone-chilling blue Montana norther, and their nights were spent in exhausted slumber. The body took a merciless beating from the pounding of a bronc. Skin weathered prematurely from exposure to the elements. It was a tough life and it bred an indomitable character that is deeply ingrained in our culture. Hollywood transformed the real working cowpuncher into a tight-lipped, tight-trousered puppet who was quick-on-the-draw, straight-shooting and always on the side of right. Often viewed in an overly romantic light, the cowboy has been lionized, analyzed, and psychoanalyzed. We've had the lonesome cowboy, hero cowboy, anti-hero cowboy, tragic cowboy, singing cowboy, drugstore cowboy, electric cowboy, Coca-Cola cowboy, midnight cowboy, urban cowboy, rhinestone cowboy, and a host of others.

Few realize that a cowboy gave this country its first job description. The hours spent in the great out-of-doors gave them plenty of time to reflect on the work and if anyone should ask just what the job required, a cowpuncher had this stock reply:

> Cowboys is noisy fellers with bow-legs and brass stomachs that works from the hurricane deck of a u-necked cowpony and hates any kind of work that can't be done atop one.
>
> They rides like Comanches, ropes like Mexicans and shoots like Arizona Rangers.
>
> They kin spit ten feet into a stiff wind, whup their weight in wildcats, fight grizzlies bareknuckled, bites on the tail of live cougars, takes on the whole Apache nation armed with one sixshooter and kin ride anything that wears hair.
>
> They lives in and loves the outdoors, hates fences and respects rivers.
>
> And they's independent too. You jest throw one of 'em into a river and he'll naturally float upstream.
>
> The only way to tame one of 'em is to cut off his head and bury it someplace where he can't find it.

Cowboys were also well known for thier extreme self-confidence. One time an unemployed puncher stopped off at a lumber camp in northern Arizona and inquired about a job. The strawboss, a big strapping hunk of a man, looked down at the wiry, 140-pound waddie and said, "Why you looks like a piece of second growth timber to me. You ever done any lumberjackin' before?"

The cowboy looked nonplussed and replied, "Have you ever heard of the Sonoran Forest?"

The strawboss raised a hand and said, "Now wait a minute, don't you mean the Sonoran Desert?"

The cowboy nodded confidently and replied, "Yup, it is now."

Cowboys liked horses, dogs, and children and were well known for their generosity. They also had a reputation for being kind-hearted to the downtrodden.

One time over in Cochise County, a fellow was on trial for first-degree murder and he knew his goose was cooked—that is until he learned there was a cowboy on the jury. During a recess he asked the cowboy to hold out for manslaughter. "Please hold out for manslaughter," he pleaded, "and I'll walk the straight and narrow. I'll never go wrong again." Well, the cowboy said he'd do the best he could. When the verdict came in, sure enough, it was manslaughter. The defendant could not believe his good fortune. He ran up to the cowboy and pumped his arm like an old well handle. "I can't thank you enough," he exclaimed, "but you must have had a hell of a time."

"I sure did," the cowboy replied, "the rest of 'em wanted to acquit you."

Rustling cattle was a serious offense in old Arizona, especially if the culprit was a stranger or a nester. However, big

outfits took a more philosophical view. Two old ranchers had been neighbors for thirty years and hadn't socialized much, so one day one decided it was time to invite the other to dinner. He planned to throw the biggest barbeque southern Arizona had ever seen as a tribute to his old neighbor. Folks from three counties showed up to partake of the free beef and booze. Along about sundown the guest was feeling pretty mellow as he cut into another slice of beefsteak. "Ya know ol' pard," he said, "we've been neighbors for thirty years and I've got a confession to make. In all this time I've never eaten one of my own cows."

The host was unflapped by the revelation. He looked out at all the tables heaped with beefsteak, smiled and replied "eat hearty 'cause ya are now."

Throughout all the myth-making and hype, the real working cowpuncher endures, the only one of this nation's folk heroes who can legitimately make that claim. Although they are few in number, cowboys still work cattle on the ranges in Arizona much the same as their ancestors a century ago.

Arizona's first cowboy was the famed Jesuit padre, Eusebio Kino. He drove the first herds of cattle into the Santa Cruz valley from Sonora in the late 1600s. Spanish rancheros hadn't settled in this area yet and Kino's herds were distributed among the Pima and Tohono O'Odham (Papago) peoples.

During the "golden years" of the Spanish empire, 1790-1821, rancheros stocked the ranges with large herds of cattle. Huge land grants with romantic sounding names like Boquillas, San Rafael, Sonoita, Babocomari, Canoa, and Buena Vista, occupied the best grazing lands in southern Arizona. The outfits were so large that, as the old saying goes, "you had to grease the wagon twice to get from the front porch to the front gate."

The peace treaty with the Apaches broke down in the 1830s and by 1840 all of these beautiful ranches lay in ruins.

Ranching resumed in the 1850s after the American occupation. Mexican rancheros like, Bernabé Robles, Pedro and Yjinio Aquirre, Juan Elias, Manuel Amado, and Sabino and Teofilo Otero started big outfits and resumed ranching in southern Arizona. They were joined by Americans Bill Kirkland, Pete Kitchen, and Bill Oury. These bold men held stubbornly to the land despite frequent raids by roving bands of Apaches.

During the early days of the California gold rush, herds were gathered in Texas and driven along the Gila Trail to the mining camps. In 1849, a three dollar steer in Texas sold for five hundred dollars a head in California. A cattleman could lose most of his herd to raiders or the blistering desert and still turn a huge profit. Many cattle strayed from the herds during the drive and lost themselves among the tules along the Gila River where they became wild as deer. Years later, after the Apaches, Yavapais, and Mojaves were located on reservations, cowpunchers rode into the brush and gathered these wild cattle. They provided the seed crop for many a rancher who had the temerity to go after them.

The Apache Wars caused a number of military posts to be established in the Arizona territory. By 1886, one-fifth of the entire U.S. Army was in Arizona trying to bring in wily old Geronimo and his band.

The military posts, Indian reservations and blossoming mining towns like Tombstone created a huge market for beef. By the mid-1870s, most of the tribes were on reservations, and ranchers were able to graze their cattle in southern Arizona without much fear of large scale losses from raiding war parties. However, as large herds were driven into the pristine ranges from Texas another kind of raider made his appearance: the cattle rustler. The proximity to the Mexican border and the rough, uncurried land provided an excellent refuge for large gangs of rustlers well into the twentieth century. At one point the president of the United States threatened to declare martial aw on the whole territory if the rustler element wasn't retrained by local authorities.

The gangs were so well organized that cattle were stolen in southern Arizona and driven to the Tonto, Bloody, or Horsehief Basin where their brands were altered. Then they were driven as far north as Utah, Colorado or northern New Mexico where they were sold. Then, as if not to show favoritism, the rustlers stole horses up north and sold them down south.

The building of the Atlantic and Pacific Railroad (Santa Fe) across northern Arizona in the early 1880s inspired the first large ranching enterprises to locate there. In 1881, John Young, a son of the Mormon leader, began the Mormon Cattle Company. The headquarters were located at the foot of the spectacular San Francisco Peaks. A year later, he teamed with some eastern investors to form the Arizona Cattle Company or the A1 brand as it was better known. Iron-bellied locomotives hauled thousands of cattle to market and by 1883 the price of beef was fifty dollars a head, up fifteen dollars from just two years earlier.

Northern Arizona's most spectacular enterprise was established in 1884 when Edward Kinsley, one of the owners of the railroad, made a trip west to inspect the new line. He noted the grass-carpeted ranges between the junction of the Rio Puerco and Little Colorado rivers and Flagstaff and declared he could raise enough cattle out there to feed a nation.

Back in New York he joined with others to form the Aztec Land and Cattle Company. The company purchased a million acres from the railroad for fifty cents an acre, bought a herd in Texas and shipped it by rail to Horsehead Crossing, which was now being called Holbrook. Eventually, the ranch which, because of its brand, was called the Hashknife, ran sixty thousand head on the ranges.

In 1886, five young brothers from Cincinnati, Ohio, named Babbitt invested their life savings in a small cow ranch east of the new town of Flagstaff. They branded a CO Bar, for their home town, on the hides of some twelve hundred cows.

Within a few years the enterprising young men diversified their cattle operation into other businesses, including mercantile stores, trading posts, a bank, an opera house, and even a mortuary. By the end of World War I, Babbitt Brothers was one of the most prominent corporations in the entire West. It was said the Babbitts "fed and clothed and equipped and transported and entertained and buried Arizonans for four generations, and they did it more efficiently and more profitably than anyone else."

The hellbent-for-leather, freewheeling days of the open range came to an end in the 1880s. A series of long droughts coupled with overstocking the ranges spelled disaster for cattlemen. By the turn of the century, erosion and vegetation destruction had destroyed what had been rich valleys where once grass grew "stirrup high." Cattle died by the thousands and many ranchers had to sell out. The ones who survived had to sell steers cheap to cut their losses and reduce the size of their herds. Ranges were fenced, watering holes were dug, windmills were erected, and cattlemen became more selective in their breeding.

Weather, especially prolonged drought, was the nemesis of Arizona cattlemen. "It always rains after a dry spell," one waxed dryly. Arizona's capricious weather had a way of scattering its rainfall. It seemed to always rain on the other fellow's range while your own baked in the relentless sun. Some resorted to a higher being to bring moisture to the dry ranges. Back in the 1880s, during a particularly long period without rain, Daniel Houston Ming was asked to deliver the opening prayer at a cattlemen's convention.

"Oh Lord," he began matter-of-factly, "I'm about to round you up for a good plain talk. Now Lord, I ain't like these fellows who come bothering you every day. This is the first time I ever tackled you for anything and if you will only grant this, I promise I'll never bother you again. We want rain, good Lord, and we want it bad, and we ask you to send us some. But if you can't or don't want to send us any, for Christ's sake don't make it rain up around Hooker's or Leitch's ranges, but treat us all alike. Amen." ◆

Rob Roy McGregor, left, and John Wisener while away the hours on the Jim Hancock, Wood Canyon Ranch, in the Chiricahua Mountains twelve miles southwest of Fort Bowie. Photo courtesy of the Arizona Historical Society/Tucson

Jim Roberts Last Gunfight

The legend of the Old West was fading by the mid-1920s. Most of the bona fide gunfighters were gone and Hollywood took up the chore of telling us how it really was. Tom Mix was earning over $17,000 a week performing superhuman feats from atop his famous horse, Tony, and the public loved it. Nobody seemed to care much for the way it really was out in lotus land, so Americans were fed a heavy dose of tight-trousered, fast-drawing, hard-riding heroes.

As late as 1928, though, a few of the real straight-shooting lawmen of old still walked the beat in Arizona. One of them was Jim Roberts. "Uncle Jim," as folks called him was almost seventy and walked with a stoop. The older folks around Clarkdale remembered him as the deputy sheriff in the rough and tumble town of Jerome nearly forty years earlier. Singlehandedly he'd tamed the town, taking on all troublemakers with fearless abandon.

One night three men holed up on the outskirts of town after killing another in a card game. They sent a defiant message to Roberts and his young deputy to "come and take 'em."

"You take the one in the middle and I'll get the other two," Roberts said quietly as the two moved towards the desperadoes. Suddenly the young assistant's hands began to tremble. Roberts looked at him and said in a kind but firm tone," Get out of the way, sonny, and I'll take 'em all." Moments later all three killers were down.

Before his long and illustrious career as a lawman, Jim Roberts had been deeply involved in the notorious Graham-Tewksbury feud at Pleasant Valley. Thirty men died over several years as a result of this bitter battle, better known as the Pleasant Valley War. Roberts rode with the Tewksburys and all agreed he was the most dangerous man with a gun in either faction.

But that was a long time ago and now the legendary gunfighter of the Old West was a kindly, stooped old gentleman known around Clarkdale affectionately as "Uncle Jim."

Youngsters had heard all the stories of this old man, but in their eyes he didn't seem to fit the image of a Tom Mix, or even a Buck Jones or Hoot Gibson. Why, Uncle Jim didn't even carry his nickel-plated revolver in a fast-draw holster; he packed it in his hip pocket. When they asked him to tell stories about the Pleasant Valley War or his famous shootouts

Even without his nickel-plated revolver and fast-draw holster, "Uncle Jim" Roberts seems ready to out-draw the photographer in this 1929 photo. As a young man, Roberts was known as "the best gunfighter in the Pleasant Valley War." In 1928, at the age of seventy, Roberts proved he was still a gunfighter without peer as he singlehandedly stopped a pair of notorious outlaws. Photo courtesy of Ben and Fern Allen

as a lawman, he'd just smile and change the subject. Another thing that bothered the kids was that Uncle Jim didn't dress like a cowboy. One day, after much prodding he agreed to draw his famous revolver.

Those used to seeing Tom Mix fast draw and fire forty rounds from his six shooter without reloading were disappointed when the old man reached into his hip pocket and, with slow deliberation, drew the six shooter. Gripping it with two hands, he carefully aimed at an imaginary target.

Well, needless to say, there were more than a few youthful doubters in the gathering. "Maybe," they thought, "those stories about Uncle Jim were nothing but tall tales." To some it was kind of like waking up on Christmas Eve and catching Santa Claus kissing your mother next to the Christmas tree.

All those doubts about Uncle Jim were laid to rest one day in 1928 when two Oklahoma bank robbers held up the Bank of Arizona (First Interstate Bank) in downtown Clarkdale. The two walked out the door with $40,000 in payroll for the mines, the largest heist in Arizona history at the time. Old Jim Roberts was making his rounds just as the two robbers jumped in their getaway car and started to speed away. One turned and fired a shot at the old man. With that same slow deliberation, Roberts reached into his hip pocket, drew his nickel-plated revolver and, with a firm-two handed grip, took a bead on the driver.

The pistol bucked in his hand as a bullet struck the driver in the head. The car went out of control, jumped the curb and landed against an electric pole. The other outlaw climbed out of the wreck, stunned. He took one look at the old man with the two-handed pistol grip and meekly surrendered.

There wasn't any doubt among the youngsters of Clarkdale after that. It wasn't the clothes that made the man. As far as they were concerned, Jim Roberts could outshoot, outthink, and outfight Tom Mix or any of those other Hollywood shooting stars any day of the week.

On January 8, 1934, Jim Roberts died of a heart attack while making his rounds in Clarkdale. It was fitting somehow that one of the Old West's greatest lawmen, and the last gunfighter in the Pleasant Valley War, should die with his boots on. But wait a minute. One other thing needs mentioning: Uncle Jim didn't wear boots. ♦

Pecos Edwards and John Young shoe Old Hoggie at the Blue River Horse Camp on the Apache Reservation around 1911. The boys were employed by the famous CCC, Chiricahua Cattle Company. Photo courtesy of the Arizona Historical Society/Tucson

Dad Hardiman and uncle Hal Young oversee the CCC horse herd at Apache reservation, circa 1911. Photo courtesy of the Arizona Historical Society/Tucson

Will C. Barnes, circa 1885, was a cowboy, soldier and author-authority on Arizona place names. Photo courtesy of Maricopa Community Colleges, Southwest Studies

Cattle hands from the CO Bar (CO) Ranch near Flagstaff gather 'round the chuck wagon in 1909. The brand stood for Cincinnati, Ohio, hometown of the Babbitt brothers, owners. By World War I the ranch was one of the largest in the Southwest. Photo by Earle R. Forrest Collection, courtesy of the Museum of Northern Arizona

Earle R. Forrest worked as a cowboy for the CO Bar Ranch. He carried a camera on horseback and recorded a rich part of northern Arizona's cattle history. Later he authored an important book on the Pleasant Valley War. Photo by Earle R. Forrest, courtesy of the Museum of Northern Arizona

These industrious young men from Cincinnati, Ohio, created a family dynasty in Northern Arizona the likes of which will never be seen again. The five Babbitt brothers, pictured here in 1908, are (from left) George, Charles J. ("C.J."), Edward, William, and David. Former Governor Bruce Babbitt is the grandson of "C.J." Photo courtesy of Maricopa Community Colleges, Southwest Studies

Even a cowgirl needed her trusty steed. Photo courtesy of Maricopa Community Colleges, Southwest Studies

This young Arizona cowgirl's name seems lost in history. She's known now only as the "Sunbeam Girl." Photo courtesy of the Arizona Historical Society/Tucson

Cowboys with young calf "stretched out, tailed down" and branded. Photo courtesy of Maricopa Community Colleges, Southwest Studies

George Ruffner, longtime sheriff of Yavapai County, was the first Arizonan admitted into the National Cowboy Hall of Fame at Oklahoma City. Photo courtesy of Maricopa Community Colleges, Southwest Studies

Felix Ruelas won a horse race near Patagonia around 1880 on this stalwart steed. Photo from the Buehman Collection, Arizona Historical Society/Tucson

Commodore Perry Owens was sheriff of Apache County during the Pleasant Valley War. In 1887, Owens had a celebrated shootout with members of the Blevins family in Holbrook. In just a few brief but furious moments, the sheriff shot and killed three men and seriously wounded another. Photo courtesy of Maricopa Community Colleges, Southwest Studies

Cowboys and their "hayburners"—horses— kept farmers busy gathering hay in northern Arizona. Photo courtesy of the Arizona Historical Society/Tucson

William J. Flake at age ninety-three. Even then he was still able to fork a horse. Flake provided one-half of the town name of Snowflake. Erastus Snow, a Mormon apostle, provided inspiration while Flake provided the land where the town was founded. Courtesy of the Arizona State Library

Grace Sparks (1893-1963) was the straw boss of the Prescott Frontier Days Rodeo for many years. She was known throughout the West as "the gal who bosses two hundred bronco busters." During her life, Grace was active in a multitude of community services in Yavapai County. Photo courtesy of the Arizona Hall of Fame

147

Arizona's first territorial officers were sworn in in 1863. They are, standing: H.N. Fleury (Goodwin's private secretary), Milton B. Duffield (first U.S. marshal), Almon Gage (first district attorney); seated: Joseph P. Allyn (one of the first associate justices of the Supreme Court), John N. Goodwin (governor), Richard C. McCormick (first secretary of the Arizona Territory). Photo courtesy of the Arizona Historical Society/Tucson

1863·1912

Chapter 13

Territorial Politics

The Congress of the United States didn't fall all over itself welcoming Arizona into the Union in 1863. When Ohio congressman James Ashley introduced the Organic Act, he found strong opposition in both houses. The 1860 census counted less than twenty-five hundred non-Indians in the area, and the great majority of them were Hispanic. However, the Ohioan was convinced that Arizona's mineral wealth could help the Union cause in the war against the South. Two of the largest mining operations in Arizona were chartered in Ohio and Congressman Ashley had seen the ore specimens. During a House debate a rich chunk of silver was displayed. That demonstration won the day and the battle.

The first territorial governor appointed was a "lame duck" congressman from Ohio named John Gurley. He died before assuming office and was replaced by another ex-congressman, John Goodwin, of Maine. Among the other officials were three judges, who would form three judicial districts and sit on a supreme court; a district attorney, surveyor-general, U.S. marshal and a superintendent of Indian affairs. The latter office

was filled by Charles Poston, who'd played a key role in promoting the creation of a new territory.

It was assumed they'd establish the capital in Tucson since the old Pueblo was the only community that could actually claim to be a community. But it wasn't meant to be. Tucson had been a little too supportive of the Southern Cause. And besides, Gen. Jim Carleton had a vested interest in the new gold discoveries in the Bradshaw Mountains. He'd already sent troops out to establish a military post nearby. So a temporary capital was chosen somewhere near the mines. The party left Santa Fe's comfortable environs and headed West. On December 29, 1863, certain they had crossed the boundary into Arizona, they held a ceremony. At a waterhole called Navajo Springs, in a raging snowstorm, the solemn oaths of office were taken and the territory of Arizona was officially established.

On January 22, 1864, the party arrived in Chino Valley where a temporary military post had been located. A few weeks later the capital was moved to the banks of Granite Creek. On May 30, a meeting was held in a crude log cabin known somewhat affectionately as Fort Misery, and a name for the capital was chosen. Some wag suggested Gimletville but fortunately, Richard McCormick, secretary of the territory, later governor and delegate to Washington, had in his possession William Hickling Prescott's classic history of Mexico. McCormick, in a bit of stirring oratory for which he was known, suggested naming the town Prescott. And that's what it became. They did alter Mr. Prescott's name some. It's local pronunciation is "Prescut."

Arizona's "Capital on Wheels" would be on the move during the next few years. In 1867, Tucson garnered enough votes in the territorial assembly to claim the capital. Tucsonians clung

Estevan Ochóa, Tucson pioneer, politician and freighter, was a well-educated man of refined culture who championed the creation of public schools in the Arizona Territory. Courtesy of the Arizona Historical Foundation

tenaciously to it for a decade before the Prescottonians stole it back. The assembly met every other year and at each gathering the battle lines were drawn. In 1885, the citizens of Tucson raised a satchel full of money and told the delegates to bring home the capital, that nothing less would be accepted. Meanwhile, the other delegates were getting ready to play their cards. Pinal County wanted a bridge across the Gila, while the northern part of Cochise wanted to secede. In Maricopa, Tempe wanted a normal school while Phoenix wanted an insane asylum. Prescott, of course, wanted to keep the capital and Tucson had other plans for relocating it again.

Delegates were paid fifteen cents a mile per diem and Tucson's delegates turned the trip to the capital into a twenty-two hundred mile junket. They climbed on board the Southern Pacific and rode to Los Angeles, then boarded the Santa Fe and headed east to Ashfork, some fifty miles north of Prescott. Since Prescott and Ashfork weren't joined by rail, they boarded a stagecoach and headed for the capital. A snowstorm held up the stage at Hell's Canyon so one of the delegates took the satchel of money and climbed on a mule and rode to Prescott. By the time he arrived, all the horse trading was over and the prizes had been handed out. Prescott retained the capital, Cochise County remained intact, Florence got a bridge over the Gila River, Tempe got a normal school, and Phoenix an insane asylum. When the delegates realized that Tucson had been left out, they awarded the only thing left—a university. "Why do we need a university?" moaned one of the city fathers who, incidentally, owned a saloon, "Those students won't drink." When the downtrodden delegates returned to Tucson, angry citizens pelted them with rotten eggs and overripe vegetables. One sore loser beaned a delegate with a dead cat.

Four years after the so-called Thieving Thirteenth Legislature convened, the Fifteenth met and, once again, the capital was up for grabs. This time Phoenix, the upstart city on the banks of the Salt River, was making the play. To insure victory, the Maricopa County delegates made a deal with a certain lady of the evening named Kissin' Jenny to delay one of the Yavapai County delegates during the crucial vote. The man in question had the only glass eye in the territory (something he was quite proud of) and he was also just about the most vain man in Arizona, so the delegates from Phoenix decided to use his vanity to their advantage.

Each evening after the assembly convened, the Prescott man was known to spend some time in Kissin' Jenny's boudoir. On the evening before the vote the delegate had a few drinks on Whiskey Row, then headed for Jenny's place on Granite Creek. Later, after blowing out the light, he carefully placed his glass eye in a water glass next to the bed, then went to sleep. Sometime during the night, Jennie got thirsty and reached over, picked up the water glass and swallowed the contents, including the eye. When the delegate arose the next morning and found his glass eye missing, he refused to go out in public.

Meanwhile, the politician's allies noted his tardiness and headed for Jenny's place to roust him out. Upon discovering the reason for his absence, they pleaded with Jenny to give up the eye but she wouldn't or couldn't cooperate. The one-eyed delegate was absent from the assembly that day and Maricopa County won the capital by one vote. So, in 1889, the permanent capital was established at Phoenix where it remains.

When Maricopa County was created in 1871, three candidates threw their hats in the ring for sheriff. Since the office was the county's highest, competition was keen. J. A. Chenowth and "Whispering Jim" Favorite were the leading contenders while "Silent Tom" Barnum was a distant third. Barnum wasn't figured to make a serious challenge as the race between the other two grew hotter. In fact, he didn't even campaign. Chenowth and "Whispering Jim" stalked each other like alley cats, their shouting matches drawing large crowds. Then one day tempers got out of hand and both men went for their guns. "Whispering Jim" had barely cleared leather when a bullet from J. A.'s six-shooter cut him down. Favorite was no more and city fathers advised J. A. he'd better leave town. When the vote was taken, the dark horse, Tom Barnum, was the overwhelming (and only) choice for first elected sheriff of Maricopa County.

The selection of a county seat for newly-created Maricopa County was also hotly contested. Some wanted it located "way out east" of the new Phoenix townsite (where downtown Phoenix is today). Polling places were set up and supporters of both sites fought a no-holds-barred battle. Barrels of whiskey were dispensed and wagon loads of Indians were imported and given names like Murphy, Smith, and O'Leary and hauled to the various places to cast their votes—again and again.

This brand of rowdiness, along with the Graham-Tewksbury feud in Pleasant Valley; the Cochise County War involving the Earps, McLaurys, and Clantons; Geronimo and his band; and a host of other not-so-famous outlaws and renegades gave Arizona a reputation for lawlessness in the East. Though some of the reputation was well-earned, most of it was exaggerated by writers of pulp westerns. Most Arizonans were decent, hard working, honest folks with a burning ambition to see their adopted home become a state.

The fervor with which Arizonans wanted statehood is perhaps best illustrated in the Spanish-American war. When war came in 1898, Arizonans eager to show their patriotism volunteered in droves. Colorful, dashing William O. "Buckey" O'Neill, former sheriff, newspaperman, and politician, was a noted warrior in the fight for statehood. He was also one of the most popular men in the territory. Naturally, he was selected captain of Company A. The volunteers quickly became darlings of the press who dubbed them the "Rough Riders." Irrepressible Teddy Roosevelt rode with them and sung their praise. In Cuba, the Arizonans fought with courage and intrepidity. The bravest and most gallant of them all was "Buckey" O'Neill. He stubbornly refused to seek cover from the fierce gunfire of Spanish soldiers. "An officer should always set an example to his men," he explained, when warned of the dangers. Miraculously, the spanish bullets never touched him. At Las Guasimas he seemed immortal. Other Arizona officers, including Col. Alexander Brodie and Capt. Jim McClintock fell wounded. "Buckey" wasn't scratched. At San Juan Hill he resumed his post, oblivious to the defiant Spanish marksmen. Again, he was cautioned. "Who wouldn't gladly lay down his life to put another star on the flag?" he replied. A few seconds later a sniper's bullet cut down the young officer who was so willing to lay his life on the line to see Arizona achieve statehood.

The Arizonans returned from the war with high hopes for statehood only to be told they weren't ready yet. Most still considered the place an uninhabitable desert full of cactus, rattlesnakes, and scorpions. Eastern Republicans also feared sending a pair of Democrats to the U.S. Senate. New Mexico, its neighbor to the east, was also experiencing difficulty becoming a state.

In 1904, a joint statehood bill was passed in the House permitting Arizona and New Mexico to merge into one large state. The capital would be at Santa Fe but it would be called Arizona. The latter concession was to appease the unruly Arizonans. Fortunately, an amendment was added stating that both territories must approve or it wouldn't pass. The bill came to a vote in 1906. New Mexico voted in favor and Arizona voted against it 16,265 to 3,141. During the debate, President Teddy Roosevelt came out in support of joint statehood, something that caused Arizonans in Phoenix to temporarily change Roosevelt Street to Cleveland.

Finally, on June 20, 1910, President William Howard Taft signed the statehood bill authorizing Arizona to hold a constitutional convention. The convention was controlled by progressives and the constitution included such radical provisions as the initiative, referendum, and recall.

Conservatives warned that Taft, a former judge, would veto the constitution if the recall of judges was kept in. The stubborn Arizonans refused to back down and Taft vetoed it on August 11, 1911. "Take it out and then, when statehood is granted, put it back in," the Arizonans were advised. A few months later another vote was taken and the recall was removed. Finally, on February 12, 1912, the bill was ready to be signed. Since the twelfth was a holiday—Lincoln's Birthday—and the thirteenth was considered unlucky, Taft waited until the fourteenth, Valentine's Day to sign the bill.

Word reached Arizona by telegraph at 8:55 a.m. and all over the state, people took to the streets to celebrate. Church and school bells rang out, pistol shots were fired and Phoenix held a big parade. The biggest blast came in boisterous Bisbee where a charge of dynamite was set which nearly blew the top off a nearby mountain.

In Phoenix one young couple delayed their marriage ceremony until word officially arrived. They wanted to be the first couple married in the "state" of Arizona. Meanwhile, the ring bearer, a young, energetic three-year old, fidgeted impatiently. Finally a messenger brought the news and little Barry Goldwater stepped forward with the rings and the state's first marriage vows were solemnized. ◆

Anson P. K. Safford, governor of the Arizona Territory from 1869 to 1877, was the third territorial governor and founder of the public school system.

The town of Safford, shown here in 1904, was founded in 1872 and named after him by a group of farmers who settled the Upper Gila Valley.

Photos courtesy of the Arizona Historical Society/Tucson

William Zeckendorf, of the Eighth Legislature of the Arizona Territory in 1875, was also a prominent merchant in Tucson. He arrived in Tucson in 1869 and opened a mercantile business in partnership with his brother, Louis (right). Years later, a nephew, Albert Steinfield, bought the business and renamed it Steinfield's. Photo courtesy of the Arizona Historical Society/Tucson

In the declining or twilight years of his checkered career, the old "Pathfinder," John Charles Fremont, was appointed territorial governor of Arizona. He spent most of his time back east promoting various personal ventures. Fremont was a man with good vision but lacked the skills to carry them out. Under pressure, he resigned in 1882. Photo courtesy of the Arizona Historical Society/Tucson

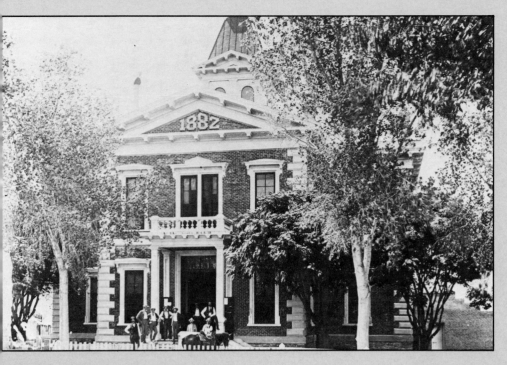

Tombstone-Cochise County Courthouse in Tombstone was built in 1882. Today it is a state park. Photo courtesy of the Arizona Historical Society/Tucson

Winfield Scott, Army chaplain, helped found the city of Scottsdale. In 1888, he rode horseback a few miles east of Phoenix to where the Arizona canal had just been completed. He homesteaded a piece of land and began growing crops. Eventually a town took shape around his farm and was named in his honor. Two other prominent men played a role in the development of Scottsdale—Albert Utley and William J. Murphy. Neither name, Utleyville or Murphyville, suited locals, so Scottsdale it became. Photo courtesy of the Scottsdale Historical Society

Pinal County Courthouse is pictured here in this 1895 photo. Built in 1890-91 for $29,000, the American-Victorian style buiding is still in use today. The "clock" never moves past nine o'clock. It is said that, upon completion of the building, there wasn't enough money left to install a real clock. Photo courtesy of the Arizona State Library

Arizona statehood proponent William "Buckey" O'Neill, third from left, was sheriff of Yavapai County in 1888 when this posse captured a gang of notorious train robbers. The desperados robbed the Santa Fe at Canyon Diablo, east of Flagstaff. O'Neill and his men chased them across the badlands of Arizona and Utah before finally bringing them to justice. The other members of the posse are, left to right, Ed St. Clair, Carl Holton and Jim Black. O'Neill was later a popular mayor of Prescott and a newspaperman. Photo courtesy of Maricopa Community Colleges, Southwest Studies

The Rough Riders, or First U.S. Volunteer Cavalry, go through drilling at San Antonio, Texas. At the right is Col. Leonard Wood; left front is Lt. Col. Theodore Roosevelt. The rider just over Wood's right shoulder is Capt. William "Buckey" O'Neill, the only Rough Rider officer from Arizona killed in the 1898 war with Spain. Photo courtesy of the Arizona Hall of Fame

Mike Goldwater, father of Morris and grand-father of Barry, arrived at La Paz on the Colorado River and opened a store. Later he ran a freighting business from the river to Prescott. Photo courtesy of the Arizona Historical Society/Tucson

Morris Goldwater, uncle to Senator Barry Goldwater, is considered the "Father of the Democratic Party" in Arizona. He spent most of his adult life in Prescott where he ran the family mercantile business. He served in the territorial assembly and, after statehood, the legislature. He was also vice-president of the Constitutional Convention in 1910. Photo courtesy of the Arizona Historical Society/Tucson

The Goldwater store in Prescott, across from the Courthouse Plaza, was built in 1879 and was the first brick building in Arizona. It was torn down a few years ago to build a parking lot. Photo courtesy of Maricopa Community Colleges, Southwest Studies

Carlos C. Jacome, a prominent business and professional man in Tucson, posed for this portrait around 1888-1889. At the Constitutional Convention in 1910, Jacome and four other Tucson Republicans refused to sign the liberal document. On Febraury 14, 1912, Statehood Day, Tucson was less than enthusiastic. While other communities cheered the event and newspapers throughout the new state wrote glowingly about statehood, the Tucson Citizen noted that the date marked the fiftieth anniversary of Arizona's admission to the Confederate States of America. Photo courtesy of the Arizona Historical Society/Tucson

Louisa Wetherill (1877-1945) spent most of her life among the Navajo. She and her husband John ran trading posts in northern Arizona. Among the guests at their home were such noted figures as Zane Grey and Teddy Roosevelt. An expert in Navajo history and culture, she traveled far and wide in later years as a lecturer. Photo courtesy of the Arizona Hall of Fame

The La Bonanza store in Tucson, is shown here on November 5, 1899. Out front are left to right, proprietor C. C. Jacome, (unknown), (unknown), proprietor L. E. Carrillo, and Alejandro Barreda. Photo courtesy of the Arizona Historical Society/Tucson

Statehood Day, February 14, 1912, in Mesa.
Photo courtesy of the Mesa Southwest
Museum

*February 14, 1912, Statehood Day celebrations
in Douglas, Arizona included the appointment
of Miss New Mexico, Margaret Latta-Wolf,
and Miss Arizona, Rowena Stillman, both of
Douglas.* Original postcard courtesy of Margaret Latta-Wolf McDonald of San Diego
through her daughter, Mary F. Weber; print
provided by Arizona Historical Society,
Phoenix

The streets of Bisbee were filled with citizens celebrating statehood in 1912. Photo courtesy of Maricopa Community Colleges, Southwest Studies

George W. P. Hunt, first governor of the new state, is inaugurated on February 14, 1912. Photo courtesy of the Arizona Historical Society/Tucson

Arizona's first capitol building and governor's mansion in Prescott today is part of the Sharlot Hall Museum. Photo courtesy of the Arizona Historical Society/Tucson

Mark Smith was a Tombstone lawyer during the heyday of the silver camp. Later he was territorial delegate to Washington. In 1912, he was elected one of the first two senators from the new state of Arizona. Courtesy of Maricopa Community Colleges, Southwest Studies

Sometimes the best respite from the Arizona sun is the local swimmin' hole. These girls bathe in a shallow river in Santa Cruz. Photo courtesy of the Arizona Historical Society/Tucson

The Territorial outing was another good way to escape the summer heat in southern Arizona around the turn of the century. Photo courtesy of the Arizona Historical Society/Tucson

Actors at the Dime Theater in Globe entertain audiences. Photo courtesy of Clara T. Woody Collection, courtesy of the Arizona Historical Society

Members of the Club Filarmonico band included well-known family names like Ronstadt, Carillo, Jacome, and Elias. Photo courtesy of the Arizona Historical Society/Tucson

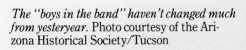

The "boys in the band" haven't changed much from yesteryear. Photo courtesy of the Arizona Historical Society/Tucson

The Bisbee Copper Queen Band. Photo courtesy of Maricopa Community Colleges, Southwest Studies

This open air coach hauled health seekers over fourteen miles of rough road to the resort at Agua Caliente Hot Springs. Photo courtesy of the Arizona Historical Society/Tucson

163

Courtesy of the Arizona Historical
Society/Tucson

*Back in those halcyon days before television,
locals had to create their own entertainment.
Groups like the "Horribles" of Prescott and the
"Don't Worry" club of Globe did much to
relieve the humdrum and inject a little humor
into life. The "Horribles" dressed up in out-
rageous costumes for the July 4, 1891 parade
in Prescott.*

Courtesy of the Arizona Hall of Fame

164

Anna Moore Shaw, dubbed "Dr. Shaw" by grateful Arizonians for all the babies she delivered, is honored in a parade in Globe, circa 1900. Shaw was the territory's best known mid-wife. (Note the stork poster above the cart.) Photo courtesy of the Arizona Hall of Fame

The Lowell Observatory in Flagstaff was designed and built by Godfrey Sykes. In this photo, taken in 1898, Sykes is standing at the opening in the dome. Below him on the ground are Emmie Sykes, Glenton and Stanley Sykes. Photo courtesy of the Arizona Historical Society/Tucson

The Carnival Parade winds through downtown Phoenix on December 7, 1900. Photo courtesy of the Arizona Hall of Fame

An archway welcomes visitors to this Yuma parade in 1904. Photo courtesy of the Arizona Hall of Fame

This float, sponsored by the Babbitt Brothers, was part of a July 4 parade in Flagstaff in 1907. The venerable Weatherford Hotel is in the background. Photo courtesy of Maricopa Community Colleges, Southwest Studies

A Sunday outing on a steamboat was a big social event for citizens of Yuma at the turn of the century. Dam construction beginning in 1907 put an end to the colorful era of paddle wheelers on the Colorado. Photo courtesy of Maricopa Community Colleges, Southwest Studies

Not all social events reflected times of celebration or relaxation. These Mexican mourners in Metcalf, circa 1910, gather to bury one of their own, the little girl in the lap of the woman seated. Photo by Risdon, courtesy of the Arizona Historical Society/Tucson

167

*The earliest known municipal swimming pool
in the state was located at Yuma, circa 1920.*
Photo courtesy of the Arizona Hall of Fame

*Some folks just have a knack for getting
around, such as these youngsters on an early
rendition of the soapbox derby in Bisbee in
1911.* Photo courtesy of Maricopa Community Colleges, Southwest Studies

Back in the days when ostrich feathers were the style and ostrich ranching was a going business in the Salt River Valley, these four young school teachers from Tempe are sitting down to breakfast with an ostrich egg, circa 1915. One of these eggs, scrambled, could easily feed six people. The teachers are, left to right, Jessie Belle Waterhouse, Mattie Agnes York, Emma French, and Gertrude York. Photo courtesy of Trudy Murphy

Long before sun bronzed skin was "in," the typical turn-of-the-century Arizona lady took great pains to protect her skin from the sun's harmful rays. Photo courtesy of Trudy Murphy

Arizona Rangers, *by Jack Graham*

Chapter  14

Dawning of a New Century

The dawning of the twentieth century brought little change to rural Arizona. Phoenix and Tucson were growing up and becoming "civilized" but the lack of good roads kept most of the territory isolated. Large gangs of rustlers still operated in eastern Arizona along the New Mexico line, having been driven into the Blue River country by lawmen from New Mexico. Cochise County was still pretty wild and wooly, too. The close proximity to the Mexican border made that area a fairly safe haven for obstreperous border riff raff.

Cattle rustling, along with a series of train robberies in southern Arizona, led to a cry for a ranger force that wouldn't be bound by county lines. In 1901, the territorial assembly responded by establishing the Arizona Rangers. Modeled after the famed Texas Rangers, these hard riding young men sought to bring law and order to the ranges. Burt Mossman, a rawhide-tough Scots-Irishman known as the "man who tamed the Hashknife" in northern Arizona, was picked as captain. The force was small, numbering only fourteen men, including a captain, sergeant and twelve privates. Mossman, an experienced cowman, had his men dress like cowboys, keeping their badge out of sight until they were ready to make an arrest. Each man was provided a six-shooter and a horse. Under Mossman's regime, the Rangers operated mostly in secrecy as undercover agents, hiring out for cattle outfits. During the first year, the Rangers put 125 major criminals behind bars, killing only one man in the process. Notorious gangs led by Bill Smith and George Musgrove were chased out of the territory. Only

one Ranger, Carlos Tafolla, lost his life during that period. Tafolla died game in a fierce gunfight when he and another officer took on an entire gang of rustlers over in eastern Arizona. (*See* "The Legend of the Bill Smith Gang.")

Mossman was as fearless as they came, never asking one of his men to do something he wouldn't. He climaxed his one-year appointment as captain with a daring capture of the notorious Augustine Chacon below the Mexican border. Prior to his arrest, Chacon had boasted of killing fifteen Americans and thirty-seven Mexicans.

Frank Stillwell was a part-time deputy for Cochise County Sheriff John Behan at the same time he was robbing stagecoaches. Locals around Tombstone claimed that Stillwell pulled so many heists that the horses pulling the stages were more familiar with his command to "halt" than they were to the drivers'. He was accused of murdering Morgan Earp in Tombstone in March 1882. Friends provided an alibi and Stillwell went free. A few days later Wyatt Earp avenged his brother's death by killing Stillwell in the train yard at Tucson. Photo courtesy of Maricopa Community Colleges, Southwest Studies

The Legend of the Bill Smith Gang

Everybody's heard of the James gang, the Younger brothers, and the Daltons. Their nefarious exploits have been the subject of many a sagebrush saga. What's in a name? Any hard riding hero who had the good fortune to have a natural born handle like Wyatt, Hickock, or Cody pinned on him had a big advantage on someone named Smith. Anyone who ever went out to Hollywood with a name like Marion Morrison or Leonard Slye knows the bodacious value of taking a pseudonym like John Wayne or Roy Rogers. Few gunslingers in the Old West were visionary enough to picture their name on a theater marquee forty years later; otherwise they might have done the same as Hollywood's shooting stars.

Butch Cassidy and the Sundance Kid are believed to be the only outlaws who actually saw themselves portrayed in a motion picture. It happened when they stopped off in New York City on their way to South America. They also had the dubious distinction of seeing themselves gunned down by a posse. It must have been rather disturbing to hear the audience cheer their demise. Incidentally, their real names were Robert Leroy Parker and Harry Longabaugh.

The Bill Smith Gang was one of the meanest bands of desperados who ever rode the owl-hoot trails of Arizona and New Mexico. Hollywood overlooked them and I reckon the name had something to do with it. So, I'd like to bend yer ear awhile and tell a story about Smith and his wild bunch.

Capt. Burt Mossman, of the Arizona Rangers, knew Smith about as well as anyone and according to him the outlaw chieftain had once been an honest cowpuncher who'd gone bad. According to Captain Mossman, nobody seemed to know why Smith turned his back on the law. Something he didn't spurn, as we shall see, was the chivalrous cowboy code of honor. He stood about six feet tall on a slender, muscular frame with dark eyes and thick, coarse hair. The only flaw in his handsome features was a gap between his two front teeth. He was about thirty-five years old when he decided to turn outlaw. The ex-cowpuncher gathered around him a band that included three brothers and four other fearless border hombres.

During the winter of 1900, the Bill Smith Gang terrorized most of southwestern New Mexico, holding up travelers and robbing stores. The brazen outlaws raided ranches and rustled livestock in broad daylight. Their fame spread far and wide, and before long they were being accused of every killing and foul deed that occurred in the territory.

Finally, in desperation, the citizens of southwest New Mexico grew weary of lawful efforts to apprehend the gang and formed a vigilance committee that numbered several hundred (New Mexico didn't have a territorial ranger force until 1905.) The manhunters were in the saddle constantly, scouring the rugged country along the Arizona-New Mexico line. Persistence paid off because the relentless pressure soon drove the lawless bunch into Arizona. A new base of operations was set up in the remote Blue River country along the eastern border.

When word spread that the Smith gang was now operating in eastern Arizona, Mossman dispatched four Rangers to the White Mountain area. In early October, members of the gang were seen around Springerville. According to informants, they had robbed a Union Pacific train in Utah. On the way back to their lair on the Blue River, they stole a bunch of horses.

Rangers Carlos Tafolla and Duane Hamblin of St. Johns, along with Apache county sheriff's deputy, Will Maxwell, and three others, went out in pursuit. Despite a raging snowstorm that buried the White Mountains under a thick white blanket, Tafolla and Maxwell picked up the outlaws' trail. Realizing they might lose the trail if they went back to get the rest of the posse, the two law men decided to take the band alone. They were attempting to sneak up on the camp when one of the gang's horses snorted and turned towards the pursuers. The surprised outlaws quickly reacted and dove for cover.

The two lawmen found themselves caught out in the open looking down the rifle barrels of seven desperate men not over forty feet away. Tafolla, a cool hombre under pressure if there ever was one, called out: "Bill Smith, we arrest you in the name of the law and the territory of Arizona, and call upon you and your companions to lay down your arms."

Those were brave words considering the odds and the advantage, but the Ranger was determined to play out his hand. Smith and Tafolla had known each other from the early days when they were both cowpunchers.

"Tafolla," he called, "we know each other pretty well. We've spent many an hour of weary toil and hardships together. I liked you then and I like you now. For your own sake, for the sake of your wife and your babies, I would spare you now. I would also spare your companion. Give me the benefit of one day and I will leave here and never trouble this country again. But do not try to take me, for by God I will never be taken, neither I nor any member of my party."

The fearless Ranger glared back at the outlaw chief: "Bill, this friendship between you and me is a thing of the past. As for sparing our lives, we may thank you for that and no more. For thirty days we've followed you, half starved and half frozen. Now we stand together or fall together. The only request I have to make of you—and I make that for old time's sake—is that if Maxwell and I shall forfeit our lives here you will send to Captain Mossman the news and manner of our death. Let him know that neither he nor the other members of the force need feel ashamed of the manner in which we laid down our lives on this spot this day."

The knightly parley was over. A furious fusillade of gunfire echoed through that snowy basin and when the smoke lifted, the two lawmen lay dead in the snow. Tafolla and Maxwell were game to the end. Each had emptied their Winchesters before cashing in. Smith and one other had gunshot wounds.

Captain Mossman was at Solomonville when word arrived of the deaths of the two brave lawmen. He quickly organized a posse and recruited two Apache trackers from San Carlos. They

picked up the trail and followed it until another blizzard obliterated the tracks.

Since the outlaws were the only survivors that day and they made a getaway, how did the Rangers learn the details of the fight and the chivalrous manner in which Carlos Tafolla and Will Maxwell died?

Well, it was like Captain Mossman said, Bill Smith turned his back on society and became one of the most ruthless desperados of his time. Yet, in spite of that, he maintained an honorable code that bonded men of the Old West.

True to his word, Bill Smith wrote a letter to the Arizona Rangers detailing those last brief moments in the lives of two brave men.

I reckon Hollywood let a good story get away. ◆

The Bill Smith Gang, *by Jack Graham*

Tom Rynning, a former Rough Rider and frontier soldier, took over the Rangers in 1902. Under Rynning the force was increased to twenty-six men. They pinned five-pointed silver stars on their chests and spent more time responding to corporate interests as strike breakers and less time chasing rustlers. Under Mossman, the Rangers had been the darlings of the press and heroes to the general public. These new duties tarnished their image in the eyes of many. Still they were colorful, tough and rode the hard country as if they realized they were a vanishing breed of law men.

The Rangers had an interesting working arrangement with the notorious *Rurales* of northern Mexico. Led by an almost-fictional ex-Russian naval cadet named Emilio Kosterlitzky, the Mexican soldier-police force dealt ruthlessly with the criminal element, rarely giving a prisoner the benefit of a trial. Cooperation between the Rangers and *Rurales* did much to rid the border of the lawless element. As an example, a man wanted by the Rangers might be sitting in a cantina in Cananea feeling secure. He'd have a few drinks with a pretty lady and next thing he knew, he was staring at four walls in a Bisbee jail. It seems the girl slipped him a mickey, then a couple of Rurales slipped a gunnysack over his head, threw him over the back of

a horse and delivered him to a Ranger waiting at the border.

The Rangers were supposed to headquarter in the roughest town in the territory. Under Mossman they worked out of Bisbee. When Rynning took over, they moved down the road to the new town of Douglas. With its gambling halls, saloons and dance halls, Douglas quickly became the gathering place for all nefarious scalawags in the southwestern United States and northern Mexico. Captain Rynning took a look at the place and noted: "I've been in many a rough town in my day, but from Deadwood to Tombstone I've never met up with a harder formation than Douglas was when we made the Arizona Rangers' home corral there in 1902."

Rynning cleverly broke up one family of rustlers near Douglas by an unorthodox manner of crime detection for which the Rangers were famous. The Taylor family had been branding their neighbor's cows and getting away with it for quite some time until the Ranger captain got into the act. He roped a bunch of their neighbor's calves, slit open their gullets and inserted a Mexican silver coin. He stitched up each incision and turned them loose. He waited about six months, then rode over to Taylor's spread and, sure enough, all thirteen calves had Taylor's brand. Taylor was arrested and the calves impounded in Dou-

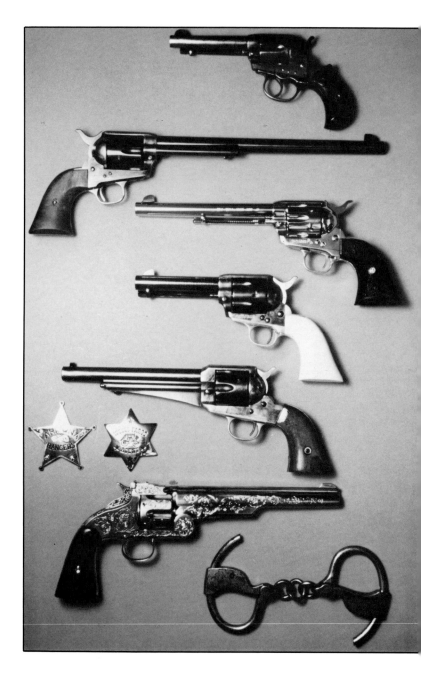

Guns such as these were used for both good and bad in Arizona's settlement. Top to bottom:

Colt .41 Caliber Thunder. Colt began selling the double-action revolver in 1877. This model was issued to the navy and was produced between 1877 and 1912.

Colt Single Action Army .45 caliber buntline 12-inch barrel. Ned Buntline, writer of the western legends and lore, was supposed to have presented one of these to Wyatt Earp. Only a few of these Buntline specials were made. Some had 16-inch barrels and were fitted for a shoulder stock.

Colt Single Action .45 Caliber, 7½-inch Barrell. This was the first large revolver for self-exploding metallic cartridges brought out by Colt. It was officially called the Single Action Army Revolver. The 5½-inch barrel Colt is best known as the "Peacemaker" and was the most famous pistol in the Old West. It is still made with only a few minor changes to its original construction.

Colt Single Action Army .45 Caliber 4½-inch Barrel Uberitti (Replica)

1875 Remington .44 Caliber, 7½-inch Barrel. This revolver never saw service in the regular army as it did not stand up well in dust and rust tests. Despite this, Frank James packed a Remington. Later, a .44-40 model fared much better.

Smith and Wesson .44 Caliber American. Wyatt Earp was reputedly packing a Smith and Wesson at the gunfight at OK Corral in 1881. This double-action six-shooter, introduced in 1881, could never overcome the immense popularity of the Colt single-action army.

Badges. At left is a replica of the badge worn by the Arizona Rangers 1901-1909. At right is a Wells Fargo Agents Star, a reproduction by Wells Fargo.

Handcuffs. This style was in use until well into the twentieth century. Photo by Gary Johnson

glas. During the trial a recess was called and the jury was led to the corral where Rynning explained what he'd done. Then he opened the gullets again and removed a coin from each. Needless to say, the verdict was guilty and the judge gave the Taylors just twenty-four hours to sell their ranch and get out of the territory.

The third and last captain of the Rangers was a fast-shooting young ex-soldier named Harry Wheeler. During his spectacular career, Wheeler had been involved in several heroic deeds, including a regular old wild west shootout in the Palace Saloon in Tucson. Late one night in 1904, a masked bandit named Joe Bostwick walked in through the back door and shouted, "hands up." The outlaw, wearing a long, faded coat and floppy old Panama hat, had his face covered with a red bandana with two slits for eye holes.

One of the victims slipped out the front door where he encountered Ranger Harry Wheeler. "Don't go in there," he warned, "there's a holdup going on."

"All right, that's what I'm here for," Wheeler replied.

Inside the customers were lined up against the wall with their arms fully extended, the nervous outlaw urging them to "hold 'em up higher" while he edged towards the crap table money.

Suddenly Wheeler stepped through the swinging doors. Both men fired. Bostwick's big Colt .45 missed its mark but the sure-shooting Ranger fired twice, hitting the outlaw both times. The holdup artist died the next day.

"I'm sorry that this happened," Wheeler told a reporter the next day, "but it was either his life or mine, and if I hadn't been a little quicker on the draw than he was, I might be in his position now...."

Typically, Wheeler's remarks were made matter-of-factly and without any bravado. The great Texas lawman Jeff Milton called young Wheeler the best he'd ever seen—and in his time, he'd seen the legendary John Wesley Hardin.

However, the old days were about over and the mostly-Democratic territorial assembly was getting tired of funding a Republican governor's police force. The Rangers were voted out of existence in February 1909, partly because the Old West was changing, and partly, as one historian put it, "because they were just too damn good and others were jealous of their accomplishments." ◆

"Black Jack" Ketchum was a hard-drinking cowboy who drifted into outlawry in the 1890s. A deadly gunman, he robbed stages, banks and trains in Arizona and New Mexico. Caught and sentenced to hang for killing four men in Arizona, he dashed up the steps of the gallows and shouted to the spectators, "I'll be in hell before you start breakfast, boys." When the hood was placed over his head, Black Jack said gamely, "Let her rip." The trap was sprung, but the weights were set improperly and the drop decapitated the outlaw. Photo courtesy of the Arizona Historical Society/Tucson

Burt Mossman, a top grade cowman and range boss, was hired as superintendent of the Hash-knife Outfit. In 1901, he was appointed first captain of the Arizona Rangers. Mossman's reputation as a lawman and cattleman earned him a place in the National Cowboy Hall of Fame. Photo courtesy of Maricopa Community Colleges, Southwest Studies

Col. Emilio Kosterlitzky was head of the Mexican Rurales, whose cooperation with the Arizona Rangers did much to rid the border of the lawless element. Photo courtesy of the Arizona Historical Society/Tucson

Capt. Thomas H. Rynning, of the Arizona Rangers, strikes a commanding pose in this 1903 photo. Photo courtesy of the Arizona Historical Society/Tucson

Augustine Chacón, a Mexican bandito, prepares to meet his maker at his hanging in Solomonville in 1902. In the photo (below), Chacón, right, and another fellow bandit model twin leg "bracelets" prior to the hanging. After each raid he made in the United States, Chacón retreated to his home across the border. He was finally caught by the Arizona Rangers but only after totaling as many as 20 killings. Photo courtesy of Maricopa Community Colleges, Southwest Studies

Arizona Rangers were armed with Winchesters at the Morenci strike in 1903. In 1962 the Winchester Arms Company ran an ad with the picture but called the lawmen Texas Rangers. Arizonans were indignant and pointed out the error, causing a few red faces at the Winchester Company. As recompense, they threw a big dinner for the Arizonans and all was forgiven. Photo courtesy of the Arizona Historical Society/Tucson

Johnny Brooks of Bisbee stands proud in the uniform of the Arizona Rangers. Photo courtesy of the Arizona Historical Society/Tucson

Marguerite Nunez, pictured in this 1895 photo, was apparently one of those anonymous citizens whose photo was taken at Markey's Studio in Bisbee. Photo courtesy of the Arizona Historical Society/Tucson

View of Flagstaff, circa 1900. Photo courtesy of the Sykes Collection, Arizona Historical Society/Tucson

Main Street Florence around 1900. The town was named for Florence Ruggles. Her father, Levi, arrived here in 1866 as Indian Agent and filed a claim on some land. In 1875, he transferred title to the town. Photo courtesy of the Arizona Historical Foundation

This view of Phoenix in 1900 shows Camelback Mountain in the background. In the center of the picture is the fabulous Adams Hotel built in 1895. It burned in 1910 in what is still the most spectacular fire in Phoenix history. Photo courtesy of the Arizona Historical Foundation

Tempe, circa 1900, was a sleepy farm community that was also the home of the small territorial normal school that grew up to become Arizona State University. Photo courtesy of the Arizona Historical Foundation

Prescott's Whiskey Row is a battleground after the fire in July 1900. During the fire, patrons in the Palace Bar carried the bar and its contents across the street where business resumed. A piano was also carried to safety and piano player banged out tunes throughout the night. The most requested song was "There'll be a Hot Time in the Old Town Tonight." Photo courtesy of Maricopa Community Colleges, Southwest Studies

The F. Ronstadt Company, founded by Frederick A. Ronstadt, was located on the southwest corner of Broaday and Sixth Avenue, in Tucson, circa 1905. Not only shrewd business leaders, the Ronstadt clan had an ear for music that continues to this day: one of their descendents is singer Linda Ronstadt. Photo courtesy of the Arizona Historical Society/Tucson

The Morenci Hotel, seen here in 1905, was demolished along with the rest of Morenci in the 1960s when the huge open pit mine absorbed the town. The Phelps Dodge Copper Company built a new town nearby and kept the name Morenci. Photo courtesy of Maricopa Community Colleges, Southwest Studies

Broad Street in 1903 Globe was the town's main drag, meandering along Pinal Creek. The street had more curves than an alley cat's tail. Old timers attribute this to the fact that the miners refused to move their shanties out of the right of way, forcing the surveyors to run the road around them. Photo courtesy of the Arizona Historical Foundation

Back in the days before electric trolleys, mules did the work. On this day, the Meyer Street trolley was delayed when one of the mules decided to go on strike. Photo courtesy of Maricopa Community Colleges, Southwest Studies

Bisbee dedicated its streetcar line in 1908.
Photo courtesy of

The year 1908 was a rough one for Bisbee, as these pictures show. In the summer of that year, a flood ravaged the town. Just a few months later, in October, the burning town cast an orange glow across the Arizona sky. Photos courtesy of the Bisbee Historical Mining Museum

❊GLENDALE❊

ATTENTION IS CALLED TO THE

Temperance Colony of Glendale.

The location is made upon the choicest fruit lands of the valley.   No more beautiful site could be selected. The town is well planned for convenience and beauty.

BROAD AVENUES, PUBLIC SQUARES, AND LARGE LOTS.

⊸ THE SALE OF INTOXICANTS ⊸

IS FOREVER FORBIDDEN

IN THE CONVEYANCE OF THE LAND.

School Houses and Churches,

But no saloons or gambling houses ! No drunken brawls ! No jails ! and no paupers !

The design is to furnish opportunities for **BEAUTI-FUL, PEACEFUL HOMES,** combining as fully as possible the advantages of the city with the security and quiet and charm of the country. This will be appreciated by a very large class of people.   It is the **First Colony** located in the territory, planned on this basis.

Address:—**GLENDALE COLONY CO.,**

PHŒNIX, A. T.

The brand new town of Glendale put a lot of emphasis on the high moral character of its prospective citizens. Photo courtesy of the Arizona Historical Foundation

The Arizona National Guard was represented at the National match rifle meet at Camp Perry, Ohio, in 1907. National shooting matches were held annually at Camp Perry. The Arizonans were newly organized and had no rifle range to practice marksmanship. Out of forty-eight entries, our boys finished a disappointing forty-third. Photo courtesy of the Arizona National Guard Collection

Aviatrix Katherine Stinson, at age 19, delivered the first air mail to Tucson in 1915, the first official air mail flight in Arizona. She also thrilled crowds at fairs with daring "loop-the-loops" and the "death dive." Photo courtesy of the Arizona Historical Society/Tucson

The last lynching in Phoenix was in 1918 and took the life of Starr Daley, who was arrested and confessed to rape and murder. The actual lynching took place at the scene of the crime in Pinal County. Photo courtesy of Maricopa Community Colleges, Southwest Studies

The earliest Chinese immigrants arrived in the Phoenix area during the building of the transcontinental railroad in the 1880s. They opened grocery stores, laundries, restaurants and other businesses but held steadfast to their time-honored culture. This handsome couple are Don Chun Wo and Lily Leung. Photo courtesy of Arizona Historical Society/Tuscon

Lee Tan Grocery was at the corner of Meyer and Ochoa in Tucson. Photo courtesy of the Arizona Historical Society/Tucson

rash, Hopi Indian reservation /
otheast of Flagstaff aris. Aug. 9. 6

Good roads were few and far between in turn-of-the-century Arizona. These hardy ladies on their way to the Hopi Mesas had to ford a stream the hard way. Photo courtesy of Trudy Murphy

Chapter 15

Guns Along the Border

The 1910 Mexican Revolution had a major impact on border states like Arizona. At times it created a special diversion for citizens in Douglas, Bisbee, Naco, and Nogales, while on the other hand it provided a training ground for green U.S. soldiers prior to entering the war in Europe.

In 1911, revolutionaries under Tucson-born Gen. Martín "Red" Lopez surrounded an army of *federales* at Agua Prieta, across the border from Douglas. The defenders fortified themselves along the U.S. border, forcing the revolutionaries to fire towards the American town. Stray bullets from the battle oftentimes sent Douglas residents scurrying for cover. One enterprising hotel owner nailed corrugated sheets of tin on the walls of his establishment and, with tongue-in-cheek humor, dubbed his business the "Bullet-proof Hotel." Spectators gathered eagerly atop railroad cars or any lofty vantage point to see the action.

In 1914, Gen. Francisco "Pancho" Villa attacked *federales* loyal to Venustiano Carranza at Naco, Sonora. Again the *Carranzistas* were entrenched with their backs to the U.S. border forcing residents of Naco, Arizona, to pile sandbags on their southern exposure. Black soldiers from the Ninth and Tenth Cavalry, stationed along the border, planted red flags along the unmarked border in hopes of keeping the battlers in Sonora. During the next two months, some fifty-four Americans were wounded, mostly by stray bullets.

On one occasion some *federales* were firing into the American side, prompting Cochise County Sheriff Harry Wheeler to ride between the warring factions carrying a white flag. The former Arizona Ranger captain persuaded both sides to relocate. The two armies apologized for any inconvenience they might have caused and moved their battle to another site.

During the siege of Naco, Sonora, Villa's men dragged a small cannon up a mountain overlooking the town and lobbed shells from on high. The damage was slight because, with each shot, the recoil caused the cannon to roll down the slope, causing long delays between firings.

Another time a band of revolutionaries loaded a railroad boxcar with explosives and tried to push it into the federales' lines. The boxcar jumped the tracks and exploded harmlessly. It did put on a spectacular fireworks display for the *touristas* gathered on the American side.

Pancho had a real propensity for commercializing the war. Once he persuaded a Hollywood film company to make a picture. He promised to stage his battles only during hours when the light exposure was good for the cameras. The film was shot but was a flop at the box office. Evidently the realism wasn't dramatic enough for moviegoers.

Pancho Villa was, in some ways, too wedded to nineteenth-century warfare to win twentieth-century battles. For example, he stubbornly insisted on sending his famed cavalry, the "Dorados," against the barbed wire and machine gun emplacements at Celaya. But at times he was also a visionary. Once he hired an American aviator to train his young pilot-recruits for aerial warfare. Since there weren't any air fields, the plane used a rocky cow pasture. During a demonstration landing, the pilot, Ed Parsons, touched down on the uncurried turf. The craft bounced violently before coming to a halt in a boiling cloud of dust. When the air cleared, Villa's fledgling young pilots had disappeared into the wild green yonder. Villa's "air force" never got off the ground, so to speak.

During the early years of the revolution, Villa had been friendly towards the United States. However, in October 1915,

Francisco "Pancho" Villa, was a legendary revolutionary leader during the 1910 Mexican Revolution. When a band of Villistas raided Columbus, New Mexico, in the early morning hours of March 9, 1916, the American Army was mobilized along the Mexican border. For nearly a year, U.S. troops searched in vain for the elusive guerrilla fighter. Photo courtesy of the Arizona Historical Society/Tucson

Harry Wheeler, a soldier in the Spanish-American War, worked his way up through the ranks of the Arizona Rangers to become the *third and final captain. Later he was sheriff of Cochise County.* Photo courtesy of the Arizona Historical Society/Tucson

President Woodrow Wilson, seeking stability in war-torn Mexico, threw his support behind Villa's arch-rival Carranza. When Villa attached Agua Prieta, Wilson allowed the *Carrancistas* to board American trains and travel inside the United States to intercept the *Villistas*. When Villa launched a night attack against Agua Prieta, huge searchlights were turned on, blinding his troops. Hundreds of *Villistas* were slaughtered by machine-gun fire. Supporters of Villa naturally blamed the *Americanos* for the severe defeat suffered at the border town.

That same year, Villa captured Nogales, Sonora, and had a shootout with American soldiers. Anticipating trouble, Col. William Sage deployed American sharpshooters along International Street. When Villa's hungry soldiers threatened to cross the border in search of food, a thirty-minute gunfight broke out. Several *Villistas* were killed before order was restored.

In 1918, Nogales became the scene of more violence when a Mexican arms smuggler was shot while sneaking across the border. Tempers flared and armed citizens from both sides of the border opened fire. Mexican and American troops arrived on the scene and they too began exchanging gunfire. The two sides battled for four days before Arizona Governor George Hunt and his Sonoran counterpart Plutarco Calles arranged a truce. More than thirty Americans were killed and some eighty Mexicans, including the mayor of Nogales, Sonora, died in the fighting.

Supporters of Pancho Villa, still smarting from his defeat at Agua Prieta and blaming the Americans for their setbacks, launched a bold raid into the United States at Columbus, New Mexico, in March 1916. In a surprise early morning raid, seventeen American soldiers were killed. U.S. troops rallied quickly, inflicting heavy casualties on the *Villistas* before chasing them back into Chihuahua. As a result of this action, President Wilson ordered a punitive expedition under Gen. John J. "Blackjack" Pershing into Mexico to capture Villa.

For nearly a year, Pershing's men kept Villa on the run but never succeeded in catching him. In Mexico the illusive revolutionary became something of a Robin Hood who made fools of the hated *gringos*. In Arizona he was more of a boogy man.

After the Arizona National Guard was mobilized and sent to the border at Douglas, rumors began to circulate that Villa was hiding in Arizona and was going to blow up Roosevelt Dam. Others claimed he was planning a bank-robbing spree in Phoenix. Mesa, Phoenix, and Tempe organized home guard units. A local bank furnished rifles and ammunition for training, while ladies prepared for the impending battle by taking Red Cross instruction.

If the problems along the Mexican border did nothing else, they prepared the citizens and soldiers for a much tougher war overseas. Revolutions in Mexico would continue right into the 1920s.

In 1929 the *federales* were battling yet another revolutionary army at Naco, Sonora. During the fighting, an American mercenary named Pat Murphy was hired to drop bombs on the *federales'* trenches. For reasons never explained, Murphy chose instead to bomb Naco, Arizona. He soared over the tiny border town and unloaded his bomb on the local Phelps Dodge store. Some irate citizen stepped out and shot Murphy's plane down with a rifle. He was locked up in a Nogales jail for a few days, then released. Murphy headed for parts unknown but his escapade will never be forgotten for it marked the only time a "foreign aircraft" has dropped a bomb on the continental United States.

Nogales, Sonora, Mexico is on the left—Nogales, Arizona is on the right in this 1897 photo. Photo courtesy of the Arizona Historical Society/Tucson

Casualties are carted away after the battle at Nogales, Sonora, Mexico. Photo courtesy of the Arizona Historical Society/Tucson

The federale trenches at Naco, Sonora, were located several miles from town. Photo courtesy of the Arizona Historical Society/Tucson

Mexican federal troops in trenches at Naco, Sonora, Mexico. Rebel cavalrymen (Yaqui Indians) who were unhorsed by federale machine guns fought from behind grave stones in the cemetery in the distance. Photo courtesy of the Arizona Historical Society/Tucson

Mexican insurrectionists pose with their cannon, Little Jerry *in this 1911 photo.* Photo courtesy of the Arizona Historical Society/Tucson

Villa poses with the casualties after the April 13, 1911 Agua Prieta battle. Photo courtesy of the Arizona Historical Society/Tucson

Gen. John J. Pershing meets Francisco "Pancho" Villa for the first time in 1914. On Villa's right is General Alvaro Obregon who would later be president of the Mexcian Republic. Photo courtesy of the Arizona Historical Society/Tucson

Venustiano Carranza tours Nogales, Sonora, Mexico in 1914. Carranza and Pancho Villa were at one time allies but became bitter enemies after the former refused to provide supplies to Villa's army. Carranza also attempted to get Villa and Zapata to disband their rebel armies in the summer of 1914. Within a few weeks, the Carranzistas and Villistas were battling at Naco, Sonora, just across the border from Arizona. Photo courtesy of the Arizona Historical Society/Tucson

Mexican Sharpshooters take aim in April 1915. Photo courtesy of the Arizona Historical Society/Tucson

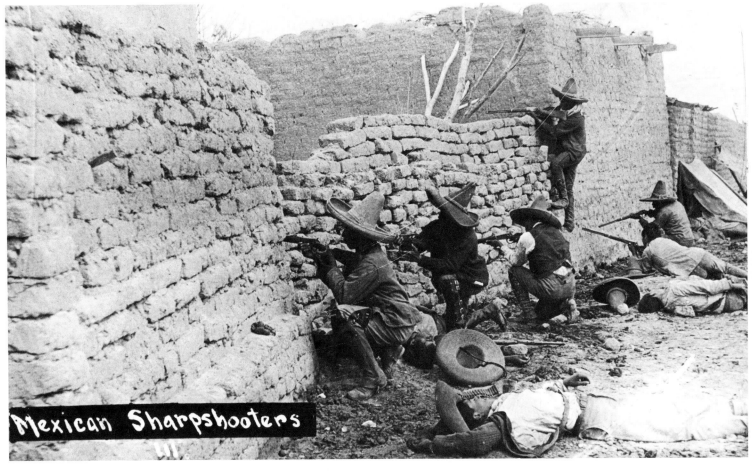

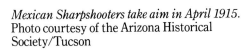

Touristas in 1914 get a closer look at this house in Naco that was riddled by Mexican bullets.
Photo courtesy of the Arizona Historical Society/Tucson

The town of Naco looked much like this when Patrick Murphy made his famous bombing raid. Naco, a border town near Bisbee, takes its name from local Indians who called the fruit of the barrel cactus "naco." The fruit is picked, cooked until tender, then left to dry in the sun.
Photo courtesy of the Arizona Historical Society/Tucson

While gunslingers stalked Allen Street in the 1880s, a few blocks away it was baseball as usual for Tombstone's home team. Photo courtesy of Maricopa Community Colleges, Southwest Studies

The batter at left, a member of the Tucson Baseball Club in 1883, seems unable to stop swinging even for a team photo. Photo courtesy of the Arizona Hall of Fame

This 1889 baseball team was sponsored by the DeMund Lumber Company of Phoenix. Photo courtesy of the Arizona Historical Foundation

The University of Arizona fielded its first football team in 1899. Photo courtesy of the University of Arizona Sports Information Office

The Douglas, Arizona Territory ball club, circa 1903-04: (not in order) J. H. Barrett, W. H. Warthington, R. B. Hatcher (holding put), George Hardgher, B. Allen, Dodge Hooper, Harry Overlock, Pete Martinez (pitcher, standing second from right) Ernest Hughes, Cebley Lucas (bat boy), R. Nelson, and Aaron (first base). Photo courtesy of the Arizona Historical Society/Tucson

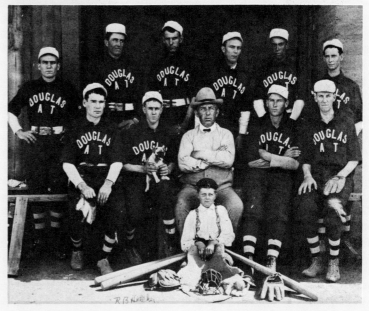

...owboy golfers at Russellville, Arizona, ...utt''-er around on a typical desert golf course ...cow country. These golfers were likely issued ...mpasses, maps, and canteens before embark-...g. Sand greens and horse-powered golf carts ...the Russellville ''country club'' were pretty ...pical around 1900 before someone got the idea ...damming the rivers and storing water to ...ant real grass. Photo courtesy of the Wien ...llection, the Arizona Historical Society/ ...ucson

University of Arizona Coach W. R. Ruthrauff lines up behind his 1905 football team. Photo courtesy of the Arizona Historical Society/Tucson

Hank Lieber, Phoenix, became a home-run hitter for the New York Giants and Chicago Cubs in the 1920s and 1930s. Photo courtesy of Maricopa Community Colleges, Southwest Studies

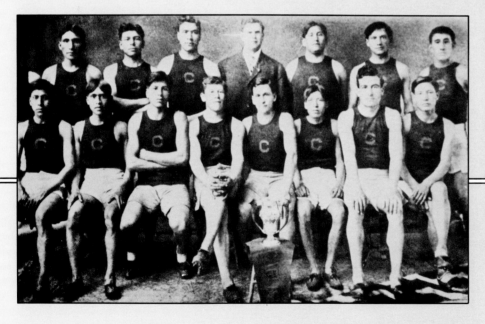

The Carlisle, Pennsylvania, Indian School track team in the early 1900s. The legendary Jim Thorpe is in the front row, fourth from left. Sixth from left is Louis Tewanima, a Hopi from Shungopavi. Both went on to win medals in the 1912 olympics.

The Williams Public School baseball team, circa 1924. A recent graduate of the Williams High School baseball team is slugger Billy Hatcher of the Houston Astros. Photo courtesy of the Arizona Historical Society/Tucson

The Ashfork 1928 girls' basketball team. Photo courtesy of Maricopa Community Colleges, Southwest Studies

The "pride of Ashfork" baseball team won the Route 66 baseball championship in the 1930s. Standing second from right is A. C. "Mac" McCoy who would later serve in the state legislature. Fourth from left is his younger brother, Roy. Photo courtesy of Maricopa Community Colleges, Southwest Studies

197

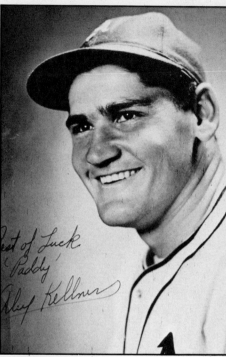

Women's professional softball was big in the 1940s. Photo courtesy of Maricopa Community Colleges, Southwest Studies

Alex Kellner of Tucson was a pitching star with Connie Mack's Philadelphia Athletes in the 1940s. Photo courtesy of Alex Kellner

Best of Luck
'Paddy'
Alex Kellner

The Tri-City All-Stars were the runners-up in the first Arizona State Little League Championship in Prescott in 1951. The team lost the state championship to the Prescott All-Stars, 2-0. The author, on the left in the middle row, was standing forlorn on second base with the tying run as the last out was made. The players on the Tri-City team represented the cities of Ashfork, Seligman, and Williams. They are, front row (left to right): Buddy Garcia, Ray McCoy (whose father, Roy M., played on an earlier Ashfork team), David Gardner, Ted Storms, Jerry Lee; middle row: Marshall Trimble, Fuzzy Brienas, Ed Torres, Doug Brown, Billy Herron, Bob Starr; back row: Coach Hank Martinez, Dale Payne, Tom Augustine, Louie Swanbeck, Alex Martinez, and Herman Schanbeck, Assistant Coach. Photo courtesy of the author

One of the teams in the Class C Arizona/Texas League were the 1951 Phoenix Senators. Photo courtesy of Maricopa Community Colleges, Southwest Studies

Wilford "Whizzer" White, "ol' number 33," was a star running back at Mesa High School and Arizona State College at Tempe (now Arizona State University) before going on to play for the Chicago Bears in the 1950s. He is the father of Dallas Cowboys quarterback, Danny White. Photo courtesy of the Arizona State University Sports Information Office

Stewart Udall (second from right), future secretary of the interior during the Kennedy and Johnson admistrations, starred on the University of Arizona basketball team during the post-World War II years. Photo courtesy of the University of Arizona Sports Information Office

199

Art Becker was a star hoopster at Arizona State University in the early 1960s, the golden years of A.S.U. sports. Becker's team wound up number three in the nation. He went on to star in professional basketball. In 1988 his son Mark is a star performer on the current Sun Devil basketball team. Photo courtesy of Art Becker

Ken Giovando of Globe played tackle at the University of Arizona. During the 1964 season, Giovando set an all-time university record for a lineman by intercepting two screen passes in one game, enabling the team to defeat Brigham Young 39 to 6. Photo courtesy of Ken Giovando

Modern-day amateur baseball has its "hammering heroes" too. Scottsdale Community College's 1987 team hit a hefty .358 average, including eighty home runs over a sixty-game schedule. They wound up the season at the Junior College World Series in Grand Junction, Colorado. Team members are, front row (left to right): Chris Foster, Kevin Long, Chris Dix, Dan Stenz, Wayne Klatt, Tyrone Gaines, Fudarrell Maggett; second row: Jim Campbell, Dave Brennan, Mario Moccia, Ed Beuerlein, Mark Norris, Joe Ortiz, Robert Word, Todd Unrein, Bill Kehoe; back row: Assistant Coach John Kazanas, Rick Miller, Rodney Eldridge, Dan Swatek, Reggie Leslie, Dale Moore, Vincent Makil, Mike Lewis, and Head Coach Jim Coveney. Photo courtesy of Scottsdale Community College

Rick Monday (left) and Coach Bobby Winkles cross bats. Monday was the first player taken in the first major league draft held in 1965. During his career, Monday played for the Athletics, Cubs, and Dodgers. Winkles came to Arizona State University in the late fifties and built a baseball program that led to several national championships. He left to manage in the major leagues. Photo courtesy of the Arizona State University Sports Information Office

Jim Palmer, an all-state baseball, basketball and football player at Scottsdale High, went on to a great career as a pitcher with the Baltimore Orioles. He won the coveted Cy Young Award three times. Photo courtesy of the *Baltimore Orioles*

Few people realize that Reggie Jackson came to Arizona State University to play football before embarking on his career as a professional baseball player. Photo courtesy of the Arizona State University Sports Information Office

Bob Horner was a baseball star at a Phoenix area high school before embarking on an outstanding college career at Arizona State University. He won first team All-America and All-College World Series in 1977-78, and Sporting News *Player of the year in 1978, along with the U.S. Baseball Federation Award as outstanding amateur player in 1978. He was the first player picked in the 1978 draft by the Atlanta Braves and was National League Rookie of the Year in 1978.*

Despite an injury-plagued career, Horner was a bona fide superstar for the Braves during the next eight years. In 1986 he hit four home runs in a single game. A contract dispute in 1987 caused Horner to take his talents to Japan for the season. He returned to the United States in 1988 to resume his career with the St. Louis Cardinals. Photo courtesy of the Arizona State University Sports Information Office

Danny White, now quarterback for the Dallas Cowboys, originally came to Arizona State University to play baseball. Photo courtesy of the Arizona State University Sports Information Office

An "American Sunday" parade was held in Tucson on April 1, 1917, just five days before America entered the "war to end all wars." Tucson's population was twenty-three thousand at the time, yet more than fifteen thousand American flags were sold. Photo courtesy of

Chapter  16

World War I

Arizonans went off to war with the patriotism that had come to characterize its frontier-bred citizens. The state contributed more soldiers, sailors, and marines per capita than any other. And fewer were rejected because of physical disabilities. The Arizona National Guard, the 158th Infantry Regiment, served with valor and after the war was chosen as President Wilson's special honor guard during the Paris Peace Conference.

Overseas, several Arizonans distinguished themselves in combat. Marine private John Henry Pruitt of Verde Valley singlehandedly captured forty German soldiers and killed several others. He was killed at Mont Blanc in 1918. Phoenix native Frank Luke, Jr., served in a combat zone for only seventeen days and flew just ten combat missions. In that short time Luke became a legend among aviators, shooting down fourteen German observation balloons and four aircraft. On September 18, 1918, in just ten minutes, he knocked down three balloons and two planes. Because they were so well guarded by antiaircraft guns and fighter planes, attacks on balloons were considered more dangerous than regular aerial combat missions. That same day, Luke's plane was shot down behind enemy lines. He crash-landed, then stepped out of the craft, drew his revolver and shot it out with German infantry troops. He died in a hail of gunfire and was given a hero's burial by the Germans. Both Pruitt and Luke were awarded the Congressional Medal of Honor for their bravery.

In other aerial combat, Lt. Ralph O'Neill of Nogales and Maj. Reed Chambers of Fort Huchuca shot down five and seven German planes, respectively. Both earned the coveted right to the title "ace" given to pilots with five or more kills. Mathew Juan, a Pima Indian from Sacaton, was the first of 321 Arizonans and also the first Native American to die in the War.

On the home front, the patriotic fever sent a four-man posse into the remote Galiuro Mountains to bring in a pair of suspected draft dodgers. Two brothers, Tom and John Power, allegedly refused to register for the draft. The posse surrounded their cabin on a foggy February morning in 1918 and supposedly without warning, opened fire, killing Jeff Power, the boys' father. In the ensuing gunfight, three posse men were killed and a fourth managed to escape with his life. Details of the gunfight are still debated today. The brothers, with the aid of a friend, Tom Sisson, fled towards Mexico with a posse of some three thousand men hot on their heels. It was the largest manhunt in Arizona history. They were captured by U.S. soldiers just below the Mexican border and turned over to a posse after being given assurances the three men would not be lynched. The young men had already been tried and convicted in the press. Long lines of curious spectators lined up to see the desperados, so local authorities put them on public display in cages. Their conviction at Clifton was a foregone conclusion and the three were locked up in the state prison at Florence. Despite the circumstances surrounding their gunfight and the

World War I volunteers parade through the streets of Bisbee. Photo courtesy of Arizona Historical Society/Tuscon

killing of their father, the two brothers served forty-two years in prison before they were released in 1960. Their accomplice, Sisson, died behind bars in the mid-1950s. Each time they came up for parole, relatives of the slain lawmen persuaded authorities to keep them in prison. A year prior to the gunfight, Arizona had outlawed the death penalty, otherwise the three men would have been executed. A year later, because of the incident, the death penalty was reinstated. Their forty-two-year term was by far the longest ever served in an Arizona prison.

The patriotic fever also attacked Bisbee in 1917 when members of the radical Industrial Workers of the World, the I.W.W. or "wobblies" as they were dubbed, called a strike. Copper prices were sky high because of the war and, although inflation was up, workers' salaries remained the same. The copper companies called upon the workers to stay on the job to help the war effort. However, many workers and other citizens felt the miners deserved a raise.

On the morning of July 12, 1917, two thousand armed vigilantes, deputized by Cochise County Sheriff Harry Wheeler, tied white handkerchiefs around their arms and took to the streets, rounding up some two thousand suspected wobblies and their sympathizers. They were herded to the ballpark at Warren and, by day's end, about twelve hundred were loaded in cattle cars and shipped by rail to Columbus, New Mexico. By some miracle, only two men, a vigilante and a suspected wobblie, were killed that day.

Another kind of fever also swept the country during World War I. The Great Spanish Flu Epidemic besieged the citizens of Arizona and the rest of the nation and before the virus ended in 1919, over a half a million people would succumb. During the height of the epidemic, social gatherings and sporting events were prohibited and even pool halls were closed to prevent folks from gathering unnecessarily. Schools around the state were converted into hospitals while citizens in Phoenix and Tucson were required to wear gauze "flu" masks in public. A special police unit arrested those going in public unmasked. Anyone offering a friendly handshake was looked on with apprehension or suspicion. In early 1919, the virus mysteriously changed its target and went after pigs and chickens, leaving a decimated human race in its destructive wake.

World War I brought much prosperity to Arizona. Prior to the war, the economy was in a downturn. At the outbreak of the war in 1914, business prospered again until the German U-boats closed the shipping lanes. America's entry into the war on April 6, 1917, had a dramatic, positive effect on the state's economy. Copper, cotton, cattle and lumber, along with the horse and mule business, boomed. In 1918 farmers around Scottsdale could earn enough on one cotton crop to pay off the mortgage. Pima, a long-staple high-grade cotton fiber developed on the Pima Indian Reservation, was used as fabric on airplanes and in the new balloon tires. Cotton quickly became the major crop in Arizona and today remains the king of agriculture in the state.

The cotton boom also brought significant sociological changes to Arizona during these years as many farmers converted semi-grazing lands previously used for dairy cattle to cotton fields. For the next several years, a large number of transient cotton pickers swarmed into the state and, when there wasn't any work, became a burden on welfare programs.

The "Great War to End all Wars" ended on November 11, 1918. The news reached Arizona in the middle of the night. Despite the late hour, citizens staged impromptu parades and pep rallys. Church and school bells rang, pistols were fired, and fireworks were set off. For those who hadn't suffered a personal loss in the war, these were the best of times. The economy was booming and employment was high. There was no reason to believe the good times weren't here to stay. ◆

Mathew Juan was the first Arizonan, as well as the first Native American do die in World War I. Photo courtesy of Maricopa Community Colleges, Southwest Studies

Women of the Tucson Canteen get ready to welcome a trainload of soldiers during World War I. Volunteers are, left to right, Ione Peas, Mrs. Otto Schoenky, Mrs. William Sawtell, Mrs. William F. Kitt, Mrs. Fred W. Brown, and Mrs. Frank L. Culin. Photo courtesy of the Arizona Historical Society/Tucson

These suspected I.W.W. Union sympathizers were marched into Warren Ball Park from Bisbee, July 12, 1917, for deportation. Photo courtesy of the Arizona Historical Society/ Tucson

Governor Thomas Campbell, far right, welcomes Arizona boys of the Fifty-eighth Infantry home from World War I at El Paso May 1, 1919. Photo courtesy of the Arizona Historical Society/Tucson

Gen. John J. Pershing addresses the people of Tucson January 31, 1920, at the dedication of Memorial Fountain at the University of Arizona, erected in honor of the university men who died in World War I. Photo courtesy of the Arizona Historical Society/Tucson

Corp. John Henry Pruitt, United States Marine Corps, of Verde Valley, received both the Army and Navy Medals of Honor for bravery in the Battle of Belleau Wood in 1918. He was killed in action separate from the heroic deeds that won the medals. Photo courtesy of the Arizona Hall of Fame.

Frank Luke was the first American aviator to win the Congressional Medal of Honor. Credited with shooting down eighteen German planes and observation balloons during World War I, he was himself shot down behind enemy lines and killed on September 29, 1918. Photo courtesy of Maricopa Community Colleges, Southwest Studies

The Civilian Conservation Corps (C.C.C.) was one of the most popular relief programs to come out of the Great Depression of the 1930s. It was designed to give jobs and job training to young men between the ages of eighteen and twenty-five. At the same time it promoted a nationwide program of conservation. Starting in 1933 and before the program ended, there were over forty C.C.C. camps in Arizona employing nearly fifty-three thousand young men. The semi-military life helped prepare young men for service in World War II, just around the corner. On August 5, 1933, Dr. Taylor spoke to this group of the C.C.C. camped at Rucker Canyon in the Chiricahua Mountains. Photo courtesy of the Arizona Historical Society Tucson

Chapter 17

The 1920s & 1930s: Boom and Bust

The bottom fell out of the copper market in post-war America. The red metal which had brought twenty-seven cents a pound in 1916, slipped to twelve cents a pound by 1921. A new social phenomenon, buying on the installment plan, came into vogue in the late 1920s, and folks loaded up on washing machines, radios, toasters, and cars, causing copper prices to rise again.

When the war ended, cotton prices also took a plunge because the government had a huge surplus on hand. Many cotton farmers went belly up when the 1920 cotton crop went unsold. By the late 1920s, however, sturdy, three-wheeled tractors were rapidly replacing mules on farms. The early models had spiked iron wheels which were soon replaced by rubber-tired "tricycles." Also, the nations's highways were filling with trucks and cars creating a brand new market for long staple cotton which was used to strengthen the rubber tires. As early

as 1928, Arizona was producing more than 40 percent of the cotton in the entire Southwest.

On June 23, 1920, a real estate ad appeared in the *Arizona Republican* (today's *Arizona Republic*) offering for sale a three-room frame house for $1,500. Another advertised a six-room, double-brick house with a garage and location near a streetcar line for the grand total of $3,000. Bargain hunters could pick up a two-room home for $800 with only $200 down. These halcyon days marked the beginning of Phoenix's first real estate boom.

Longtime Phoenix builder and developer John Sandige was the brainchild behind these "wonder homes." He called them shell houses. Sandige would subdivide parcels, then build small frame houses with just the bare essentials—roof, floor, walls, doors, windows, cupboards, plumbing and wiring—and also the kitchen sink. The concept was to build enough so that families could move in and do the finish work themselves.

Cotton pickers line up in the Roosevelt cotton growing area in Western Maricopa County during the winter of 1934. Photo by Rev. Albert C. Stewart, courtesy of the Arizona Historical Society/Tucson

The Day Santa Died

The Great Depression was in full bloom and hard times had fallen on the rural communities of Tempe and Mesa. It was the height of the Christmas shopping season and local merchants were feeling the pinch. Not only was business slack but it looked as if the annual Christmas parade was going to be a big flop.

John McPhee, colorful editor of the *Mesa Tribune,* looked upon the dismal scenario and was determined to inject some spirit into the holidays. The popular McPhee loved promotional schemes and he came up with an idea to save the Christmas parade that dazzled

times. For that matter, aviation was still in the realm of adventure. Lindbergh had crossed the Atlantic solo only three years earlier.

Well, the merchants loved the idea. Their eyes sparkled with gleeful anticipation. They could already hear jingle bells, or better yet, the jingle-jangle of change dropping into their cash registers.

McPhee persuaded an itinerant stunt pilot to make the jump in a rented Santa suit and all seemed well—that is until the morning of the big event when the stunt man failed to appear.

McPhee finally located his flying Santa

An ingenious idea, the merchants agreed.

On the day Santa was to take the plunge, a large crowd gathered near an open field on the outskirts of town, and the merchants waited anxiously on their cash registers. The sputtering of the tiny airplane's engine heralded Santa's arrival and the anxious crowd gazed skyward.

Suddenly there he was—Santa himself standing in the doorway of the aircraft. The people cheered enthusiastically.

Then Santa, with parachute attached, exited from the plane and began a free fall descent to earth.

Down, he fell.

Down, he tumbled, end over end.
Down, like the proverbial lead balloon, the limp, unopened chute streaming skyward.
Down came the dummy in the department store Santa suit.
Splat on the edge of a field in front of hundreds of horrified spectators.

The Day Santa Died,
by Jack Graham

Undaunted by the sudden turn of events, McPhee came out in his own Santa suit anyway and rode in the parade as if nothing had happened. But the public wasn't buying, literally or figuratively.

Children went about in a daze, and downtown merchants gazed around their empty stores in dismay. McPhee was about as welcome as a coyote in a hen house.

He left town for a few days, hoping all would be forgotten, but it wasn't. He would always be remembered around Mesa as the man who killed Santa Claus, a fact that was highlighted in his obituary a few years ago. ♦

the town merchants with its brilliance.
"Why not," he asked, "hire a parachutist to dress up in a Santa suit and jump from an airplane, then he can lead the annual Christmas Parade through town."

Never before had Santa dropped from the sky dangling beneath a billowing canopy.

Now remember, parachuting was considered a dangerous stunt in those

screwing up his courage in a local tavern. In fact, he had screwed it up so tight, he couldn't get off the barstool. The merchants were worried. "What now?" they asked.

"Fear not!" said the irrepressible editor. "I'll borrow a department store dummy Santa and have the pilot circle over the town, then push the dummy out the door. I will then appear in a Santa suit and lead the parade. No one will know the difference."

By the mid-1920s, Phoenix boasted a population of 42,500. Two railroads served the area, along with thirty miles of streetcar tracks, fifty miles of paved roads, eighty-five miles of sidewalks, 9,363 telephones and twelve public parks. The city limits were Sixteenth Street on the east, Nineteenth Avenue on the west, McDowell Road on the north and the Salt River on the south.

During the cotton boom when prices rose to $1.25 a pound, residents became part-time farmers as nearly every backyard and vacant lot in Phoenix became a cotton field.

The Depression years of the 1930s, like the rest of the nation, brought hard times to Arizonans. Its devestating effects took longer to be felt but it held on for a longer period. Government programs like the Civilian Conservation Corps (C.C.C.) helped by hiring unemployed young men to build bridges, roads, and recreational facilities around the state. The outfits were semi-military in structure and helped prepare the men for duty in the war that followed. By 1940, there were twenty-seven C.C.C. camps located throughout the state.

School districts suffered during these years as the number of transients and migrant families increased, placing a larger burden on the schools which were, at the same time, laying off teachers to cut back on costs.

Cotton was hit particularly hard by the Depression as prices dropped to as low as four cents a pound in 1938. Cattlemen and sheep men saw their markets drop from nine cents a pound in 1929 to three cents four years later. By 1939, the price had risen to only seven cents. The price of wool went from thirty-six cents to nine, then back up to twenty cents during those same years.

The population of Arizona decreased by some fifty thousand people between 1932 and 1936 as people packed their belongings and moved on. Many of these came from the copper towns. In 1929, national consumption dropped by 25 percent and, when a huge amount of Arizona copper was dumped on the market against foreign competition, the price dropped to six cents a pound. Nearly all the copper mines in the state were either closed or cutting way back on production between 1931 and 1934. The Clifton-Morenci mine didn't open again until 1937. Unable to produce by-products such as gold, silver, zinc, and lead, which paid much of the overhead in copper production, companies had to cut even more wages and jobs. The copper industry would never again see the glorious days of prosperity it had come to know during World War I. Nor would it ever again wield the mighty power and influence on politics and business in the state.

During these years, horseless carriages became affordable to the common man. When Arizona became a state in 1912, less than 2,000 vehicles were registered. By 1920, the number had increased to nearly 35,000. A decade later the figure was just under 125,000 vehicles.

Arizona's tradition of fine resorts began in Scottsdale in 1909 with the opening of the Ingleside Inn and the fabulous San Marcos in Chandler three years later. Wealthy socialites from back east came west by train and most stayed the entire winter, playing golf on desert courses, riding horseback and basking in the sun. Before long the valley was booming with resorts. Dude ranches sprung up around Wickenburg and Tucson. Thus the "unsung hero" of Arizona industry—tourism—was born. Among the best known in the Salt River Valley were Jokake Inn, which opened in 1925, the Westward Ho in 1928, the Arizona Biltmore in 1930, and the Camelback Inn in 1936. These resorts were the exclusive playgrounds of the rich and famous during the Depression years. However, the good times were coming and before long even ordinary folks would be able to afford to spend some time in the sun. ◆

Visitors had no room for doubt about Arizona's position on Prohibition. Photo courtesy of Maricopa Community Colleges, Southwest Studies

During Prohibition, moonshine stills sprung up all over Arizona, that is, except in Mexican border towns. Stills could be well hidden in the rugged central mountains. In the desert, bootleggers had to bury their stills in the sand. "Prohibs" in search of desert stills used rebar, a slender iron pole used to reinforce concrete, to poke around in suspicious places. Photo by Risdon, courtesy of the Arizona Historical Society/Tucson

These Sunday drivers tour Prescott's Thumb Butte. The front seat passenger seems to be trying to get the drop on the photographer. Photo courtesy of the Arizona Historical Foundation

Fixing a flat on the open road in 1926 was a three-man job. Service stations were few and far between. Photo courtesy of the Arizona Historical Society/Tucson

Hazards prevailed in the early days of travel on Arizona "highways." In 1929 there were less than three hundred miles of paved highway in Arizona. Horses were still the most reliable means of transportation. Photo courtesy of the Arizona Historical Society/Tucson

A car crosses the Gila River at Florence. Since many of Arizona's rivers are dry most of the time, citizens were reluctant to spend big bucks on bridges—"after all," they reasoned, "tomorrow, it'll be dry again." Photo courtesy of the Arizona Historical Foundation

School buses "ain't what they used to be," as these early students at Ashfork School could attest. Photo courtesy of Maricopa Community Colleges, Southwest Studies

The Remuda Ranch in Wickenburg was one of Arizona's first dude ranches. Photo courtesy of Dana Burden

As can be seen from the Sabino Canyon Trailer Campground, camping in the mountains in 1938 was a far cry from what it is today. Photo courtesy of the Winn Collection, Arizona Historical Society/Tucson

The National Geographic Society's 1923 Dodge, fresh from Pueblo Bonito, stops at John Wetherill and Clyde Colville's Trading Post at Kayenta that same year. Wetherill in white shirt, Mrs. Wetherill and an adopted Navajo child talk to a Navajo friend. Photo courtesy of the Arizona Historical Society/Tucson

Capt. John Hance was an early day trail guide at the Grand Canyon. While leading tourists in and out of the canyon, Hance acquired an international reputation as a yarn spinner. He is, perhaps, Arizona's greatest windjammer. Photo courtesy of the Northern Arizona Pioneer Historical Society

Ingleside Inn, built in 1909, was the Salt River Valley's first resort. In the back is Camelback Mountain. Photo courtesy of the Arizona Historical Foundation

216

Bill and Ann Neal opened the Mountain View Hotel in 1895 in the cool, scenic Santa Catalina Mountains north of Tucson. Tourists were hauled out from Tucson on the Neal's stage-coaches. Ann Neal organized parties and picnics. This was one of the first resorts in Arizona. Photo courtesy of the Arizona Historical Society/Tucson

The El Tovar Hotel, perched on the 7,100-foot high south rim of the world's grandest natural architectural masterpiece, the Grand Canyon, was dedicated in 1905. It is certainly Arizona's grandest hotel. Photo courtesy of the Arizona Historical Society/Tucson

Dr. A. J. Chandler opened the San Marcos Hotel in 1913 to promote his land development in the East Valley. Today the city of Chandler is one of the fastest growing communities in the state and the old San Marcos has undergone a complete facelift. Courtesy of the Arizona Historical Foundation

Jokake Inn, in Scottsdale, opened as a tea room before expanding into a resort in 1928. The mission-type towers were added in 1935. The resort closed and the property was sold in the 1970s. Today a new resort, the Phoenician is being constructed on the site. Fortunately the old towers seen in this photo were saved. Courtesy of the Arizona Historical Foundation

Mary Elizabeth Jane Colter (1869-1956) was an architect and designer of structures at the Grand Canyon that include Bright Angel Lodge, Phantom Ranch, Hermit's Rest, Lookout Studio, and Desert View. She worked as designer and decorator for Fred Harvey for forty-six years. Her other Southwest projects include the Painted Desert Inn and the famed La Fonda Hotel in Santa Fe. Photo courtesy of the Arizona Hall of Fame

The Westward Ho Hotel opened in Phoenix in 1928. During construction it was called the "Roosevelt" but the name was dropped in favor of Westward Ho. It was the largest hotel between El Paso and Los Angeles. Courtesy of the Arizona Historical Foundation

219

The Biltmore Hotel opened in 1929. It was built by the McArthur brothers and designed by Albert Chase McArthur. (Myth-makers claim that Frank Lloyd Wright was the designer.) William Wrigley, chewing gum magnate, was an investor and, during the Depression, took control. Wrigley built a mansion on a nearby hill. During the 1930s the Biltmore was way out in the boondocks. Courtesy of the Arizona Historical Foundation

The Carnegie Public Library in Phoenix was dedicated on February 14, 1908, four years before statehood. The library was closed in the 1950s and fell into disrepair. After the new Phoenix library was built in 1952, the old building declined, finally becoming a way station for vagrants and the homeless. In 1984 it was renovated. The original building, which cost $25,000, underwent a $1.3 million face lift and is today the home of the Arizona Hall of Fame Museum. Dedication ceremonies were held on February 14, 1987, seventy-nine years to the day from its opening. Photo courtesy of the Hall of Fame Museum

A 1920s road crew works to build the "new" Route 66. Photo courtesy of Maricopa Community Colleges, Southwest Studies

The circa 1920 staff at the Carnegie Library in Phoenix assemble for a photo. Steel magnate Andrew Carnegie was one of this nation's great philanthropists. Between 1898 and 1919, he gave millions of dollars for the construction of libraries throughout America. In addition to the Phoenix library, he funded three others in Arizona. Photo courtesy of the Arizona Hall of Fame

Ashfork looked like this in the mid-1920s, during the heyday of "Route 66." In 1979 Interstate 40 bypassed the town and the main drag, Lewis Avenue, looks today pretty much the same as it did years ago. Photo courtesy of Maricopa Community Colleges, Southwest Studies

221

The dedication of the Coronado Trail in Huachuca Meadow, Apache National Forest took place in June 1927. The road, U.S. 666, runs from Clifton to Alpine and passes through some of the most scenic country in the state. Photo courtesy of the Winn Collection, Arizona Historical Society/Tucson

These buildings on Santa Fe Avenue in downtown Flagstaff in the 1920s are still in use today. Courtesy of Maricopa Community Colleges, Southwest Studies

It was standing room only as customers filled the Chinese-owned Arizona Cafe on the day of its grand opening on November 27, 1935, in Ashfork. Photo courtesy of Maricopa Community Colleges, Southwest Studies

Lawyer, teacher, politician, airplane pilot and skipper of a riverboat on the Colorado, Nellie Bush (1888-1963) was one of Arizona's most colorful ladies. During the 1920s, she attended law school at the University of Arizona. Policy at the time required that women couldn't sit in a classroom when rape was being discussed. Nellie went to the dean and asked if they'd ever heard of a rape case where a woman wasn't involved. The policy was changed. Photo courtesy of the Arizona Hall of Fame

Touring buses stop for gas at Apache Junction in the 1930s. Courtesy of Maricopa Community Colleges, Southwest Studies

The first water sprinkler douses a street in Globe. Photo courtesy of the Woody Collection, Arizona Historical Society/Tucson

Chapter  18

The Thirsty Land

In the nineteenth century, James Addison Reavis, the self-styled "Baron of Arizona," almost pulled off one of the grandest real estate scams in Arizona history. For a short time, a fertile mind, coupled with a keen ability to forge old Spanish documents vaulted the former streetcar conductor from St. Louis into one of the territory's largest landowners—almost twelve million acres—including the agriculturally rich Salt River Valley. Eventually the scheme failed and Reavis went to prison for a couple of years.

After his internment, the "Baron" returned to the Phoenix area. A few years earlier he'd been one of the most hated and feared men in the territory by those who stood to lose their hard-earned land. Now he was just a pitiful, broken, harmless, and penniless old man. He walked the streets of downtown Phoenix telling anyone who'd listen of the wondrous potential for irrigating and farming the Salt River Valley.

His tired eyes sparkled as he described his newest scheme: that of building canals and ditches to water the thirsty land. But no one cared to listen and Reavis soon went away. In retrospect, had Reavis turned his visionary schemes and talent to honest endeavors, he might be an honored figure today instead of a phony baron.

The old "Baron" was right. The Salt River Valley was an agricultural paradise. It was nestled at the confluence of some thirteen thousand square miles of watershed. However, the Salt River, which meandered through the heart of the valley, was as fickle as a stud at a snortin' post. One year it'd run its banks and flood all the way into the center of Phoenix, and the next year would be so dry the cows were giving powdered milk.

In 1891, a flood spread the banks of the Salt River eight miles wide, washing out the railroad bridge at Tempe. Later in the decade, water was so scarce that folks were loading up their belongings and moving on to California. It was said a cactus wren wouldn't attempt to fly across it without packin' a sack lunch. Those who stayed patroled their irrigation ditches on horseback, armed with Winchesters. During the drought, brief but furious flash floods washed out dirt diversion dams, and farmers watched the precious water escape into the Sea of Cortez.

As early as 1889 a dam site at the junction of Tonto Creek and the Salt River had been chosen but nothing came of the venture. Two years earlier, the Arizona Canal began carrying water, opening up new lands for farming and leading to the founding of new communities like Scottsdale. Still, citizens were at the mercy of the temperamental Salt River. Events in the 1890s dramatized the need for a dam to store water and control flooding, but nothing much was done until 1902 when Congress passed the Newlands or National Reclamation Act. The act provided the federal monies to build irrigation projects in the West. The Salt River Valley was a natural choice because a community with canals and ditches was already in existence and was fed by a vast watershed.

Arizona's rich natural resources of gold, silver, copper, and other precious metals prompted many a gunfight in the early days. But the greediest prospector would surrender his stake for water after a brief time lost in the Arizona desert. This Arizona farmer guards his water as if it were gold. Photo courtesy of the Salt River Project Archives

Before the dam could be built, the federal government wanted a guaranteed repayment plan. Valley movers and shakers, like Dwight Heard, Ben Fowler, John Orme, and Bill Murphy, persuaded some four thousand landowners to put up their lands as security. Washington refused to deal with individual landowners, so it was necessary for local citizens to unite and form an association. Thus was born the Salt River Valley Water Users' Association, later shortened to Salt River Project, whose duties would include management of the massive operation.

Italian stonemasons were imported to construct what was to become the world's highest masonry dam. A five hundred-foot tunnel was dug to divert water, and a town named Roosevelt was established which allowed no gambling halls or saloons—a rarity in the wild and wooly West. Other businesses also located there with the understanding that their tenure would be brief since the town would eventually be buried beneath the waters of a huge lake. Apache road builders, under the supervision of famed scout Al Sieber, hacked out a road up to the dam site. Sieber had fought in the Civil War and survived many a shooting scrape during the Apache Wars only to die when a loose rock came tumbling down and crushed him. The road, called Roosevelt, was later changed to Apache Trail. In 1987, it was formally dedicated as the first State Historic Road.

Tonto Dam, later changed to Theodore Roosevelt Dam, was completed in 1911 at a cost of $10 million. The ol' Rough Rider himself, who'd led the Arizonans on the famous charge up San Juan Hill more than a decade earlier, traveled out to make the dedication. With the completion of Roosevelt Dam, the future of the Salt River Valley was assured. Incidentally, the federal debt was paid in full in 1955.

Over the next few years Horse Mesa, Mormon Flat, Stewart Mountain, and Granite Reef dams would be built on the Salt River and Bartlett and Horseshoe dams on the Verde River to provide water storage and electricity. They combined to turn this thirsty land into a desert oasis.

Although the harnessing of the Salt River relieved much of the water problems in central Arizona, most folks looked to the mighty Colorado River, "The West's last great waterhole," as the future source of water. Ninety-five percent of the state's area drained into the river, and it was felt that the river could return at least a part of it. The state made up about 45 percent of the river's drainage basin and contributed about a third of the river's water. Arizona wasn't the only state interested in taking a share of the mighty Colorado. Our gluttonous neighbor to the west, California, wanted a lion's share, although it contributed not a drop. Also, Colorado, New Mexico, Nevada, Utah,

Fish Creek Hill on the Apache Trail. Apache Indians did much of the road building on this twisting road built in 1905 for the construction of the Theodore Roosevelt Dam. In 1987, sixty-two miles of highway were dedicated as the state's first historic highway. Photo courtesy of the Salt River Project

Vyoming, and the Republic of Mexico all had a claim to the iver's annual 17.5 million acre feet of water.

In 1921 a commission was established to draw up a plan for arnessing the river. They met in Santa Fe and, by the end of 922, completed their work, which became known as the Santa 'e Compact. All the state's legislatures, except Arizona, ratified he agreement. Governor George W. P. Hunt opposed the bill)ecause it didn't specify how California, Nevada, and Arizona vould divide the 7.5 million acre feet allotment. At the same ime, Arizona's representatives in Congress bitterly opposed the 3oulder Dam Reclamation Act, claiming it was unfair to the tate. It passed anyway and was signed by President Calvin Coolidge in 1928. Arizona took its case to the Supreme Court nd lost, so President Herbert Hoover put the plan in motion in 930. It called for the constructon of what became Hoover, then 3oulder, then again Hoover Dam. What really rubbed the Arizonans the wrong way was also the plan calling for the)uilding of the All American Canal to deliver water into Cali-ornia's Imperial and Coachilla valleys.

Boulder Dam was located in eight hundred-foot-deep Black Canyon located between Arizona and Nevada, prompting critics o claim that although California profited from the project, "she lidn't give a dam site for it."

Chief engineer on the job was Frank Crowe whose goal in life vas to build the largest dam in the world. In 1931 he put three housand men on the job. The temperature in that canyon xceeded 120 degrees and the rocks were hot enough to fry eggs.)aring workers hung by cables hundreds of feet above the anyon floor drilling holes with jackhammers and clearing lebris before concrete could be poured.

For the next two years, workers dumped sixteen-ton buckets illed with concrete into forms every sixty seconds. When the)b was finished, the dam was higher than a sixty-story sky-craper. Crowe, nicknamed "Hurry up" by his hired hands, lesigned a complex lighting system so they could work around he clock. At its peak, five thousand men were employed. A total f ninety-six died on the hazardous job. Crowe, living up to his iickname, completed the job in 1935, two years ahead of chedule and for a time, he had his dam, the largest in the vorld. Today it ranks fifty-second. Lake Mead, which formed ehind the dam, is still the largest man-made reservoir in the Vestern Hemisphere.

The construction of Parker Dam in the early 1930s gave birth o one of Arizona's most embarrassing episodes in its long ivalry with California. Governor Ben Moeur, a crusty Tempe octor-turned-politician, became infuriated with California's ower-play politics. The dam was specifically designed to eliver water to California, so Governor Moeur sent the Arizona Iational Guard to the east bank of the river and prohibited the onstruction workers from "touching the sacred soil of old Arizona." The guardsmen eagerly set up machine gun em-lacements aimed at the dam site. The action got the attention f the wary workers, and Secretary of Interior Harold Ickes alled a halt to the project.

To add insult to injury, a few weeks earlier, some of these ame over-enthusiastic, part-time soldiers had borrowed a)uple of relic steamboats from a colorful river pilot named Iellie Bush and, under cover of darkness, had "invaded" 'alifornia. Unfortunately, the "Arizona Navy" got tangled in)me cables and had to be rescued by the "enemy." The icident made the nation's newspapers and caused a few red ices among some Arizonans. Shortly thereafter, the U.S. upreme Court got into the act and ordered Governor Moeur to ring his troops home.

The thirsty farmers along the Gila River thought their water problems were over in 1930 with the completion of Coolidge Dam. But it seems the surveyors had explored the site during an unusually wet year. The dam was built, but a lake failed to materialize behind it. A verdant field of weeds did manage to subsist rather comfortably. Cowboy-humorist Will Rogers looked it over and wryly remarked, "If that was my lake, I'd mow it."

The grand plan to bring water into central Arizona began back in the 1920s. The Santa Fe Compact alloted the state 2.8 million acre feet. (An acre foot would cover one acre a foot deep or a football field ten feet deep). However, canals such as the 390-mile All American channeled water, including Arizona's share, to California. During the years following construction of the canal, the Californians found many devious ways to obstruct the Central Arizona Project (C.A.P.) It was hinted that the project would create a huge financial and industrial complex that would compete with Eastern interests. Also, it was said that large utility companies resented the cheaper hydroelectric power that would be generated. Despite these tactics, severe droughts during the 1940s and the great increase in population due to World War II dramatized the need to bring the plan to fruition.

In 1963, the U.S. Supreme Court divided the water allotments between California, Nevada, and Arizona. California lawyers and politicians were defeated in their attempts to have the million-acre-foot flow from the Gila River count as part of Arizona's allotment. At last, the Supreme Court had approved the state's right to the water and the U.S. Senate approved the C.A.P. bill. Construction on the massive project began in 1968 above Parker Dam. Through a series of pumping stations, water was to be lifted and passed through a tunnel in the Buckskin Mountains, then carried through an aqueduct 190 miles to the Phoenix area, then another 143 miles to Tucson. The expected date of arrival at the Old Pueblo is 1991. The stretch to Phoenix was dedicated on November 15, 1986. During an average year, 1.5 million acre feet of water will be channeled into the interior of the state. The C.A.P., estimated at some $3.6 billion, is the costliest water project ever built. About three-fourths of the money will have to be repaid by Arizonans by such means as higher property taxes and increased water fees.

Today, Arizonans are consuming water at about twice the replenishment rate. This is being done by overdrafting or mining the underground water reserves. For example, in Tucson citizens are drinking water that fell to the earth ten thousand years ago. How extensive these reserves are is anybody's guess. Currently Arizona relies on groundwater for 60 percent of its consumption. The state's renewable water supply (rainfall, snow, etc.) is 2.8 million acre feet. The C.A.P. should provide another 1.5 million acre feet per year. Add 1.5 to 2.8 and you get 4.3. Presently, residents are consuming over five million acre feet annually. (A family of four uses about one acre foot annually.) Incidentally, the Columbia River dumps 280 million acre feet of water into the Pacific Ocean annually.

It'll take about fifty years at fifty-seven dollars a year for a typical Phoenix area homeowner to pay for the project. Along with the increased amount of water, the project carries with it provisions that require strict water conservation measures, encouraging citizens and businesses to use less water rather than more. The day of reckoning will come with the advent of a drought as serious as the one that parched the state in the 1950s.

Still, because of Eastern opposition, this could be the last major water project in the West. Regarding the artificial water-ing of this thirsty land, the old arguments remain: No price is too high. Or should we live within the limits of our environment? ◆

Fish Creek Canyon, Arizona. Photo courtesy of the Arizona Historical Society/Tucson

Roosevelt was a stage stop and post office for workers at the dam from 1903-1911. The town is now drowned beneath the waters of Roosevelt Lake. Well-known Arizona author Marguerite Noble was born at Roosevelt. Her other claim to fame is that she was born at the bottom of a lake.

Photo courtesy of the Arizona Historical Society/Tucson

Photo courtesy of Maricopa Community Colleges, Southwest Studies

228

President Theodore Roosevelt travels the Apache Trail to dedicate the Roosevelt Dam in 1911. Photo courtesy of Salt River Project

The dedication of Theodore Roosevelt Dam in 1911 is still regarded as the most significant event in the history of central Arizona. The water stored behind this dam and the others that followed insured the future growth of the Salt River Valley. The dam is still the tallest stone masonry dam in the world. It is 680 feet wide at the top and rises 284 feet above bedrock. Photo courtesy of the Arizona Historical Foundation

A look downstream in Black Canyon shows excavation work for the foundation of Boulder Dam. Photo courtesy of the Arizona Historical Society/Tucson

Boulder Dam. Bureau of Reclamation photo courtesy of the Arizona Historical Society/ Tucson

At the Havasu Pumping Plant, Colorado River water from Lake Havasu is lifted 824 feet to the tunnel inlet (visible in top center of photo). It flows seven miles through the tunnel and into the Central Arizona Project canal system before winding its way across the desert to Phoenix, some 190 miles away. Official Photograph, courtesy of the Bureau of Reclamation

The Central Arizona Project carries water through a system of concrete-lined canals, inverted siphons, tunnels, pumping plants, and pipelines approximately 335 miles long across Arizona. The first water arrived in Phoenix in late 1986. By 1991, the project should reach its final destination at Tucson. Upon completion, the C.A.P. will deliver an average of 1.5 million acre feet of water each year to cities and industries, Indian communities and farmers. The canal is built to follow the topography of the land, giving it its curvy appearance from the air. Photo courtesy of the Bureau of Reclamation

George Wylley Paul Hunt arrived in Globe in '81 leading a burro, owning nothing but the clothes he wore. He worked as a waiter, mucker, and rancher during those early years. In 1890 went to work for the Old Dominion Commercial Company. Eventually he became president of the firm. He served several terms in the territorial legislature and was president of the Constitutional Convention in 1910. In 1911 he was elected first governor of the State of Arizona, the first of seven terms. He was a strong supporter of labor and the common man. His political career was controversial and his battles with the legislature were legendary. His nicknames included "Old Walrus" and "George VII" (for his seven terms). Hunt weren't always consecutive and he served governor, off and on, from 1912 until 19 Will Rogers called him Arizona's "peren governor." Photo courtesy of the Arizon Historical Society/Tucson.

Chapter  19

The Political Scene

Throughout the territorial years and until post-World War II, politics in Arizona were controlled pretty much by the Democratic party. Several gubernatorial races were tight. The one in 1916 between Democrat incumbent George W. P. Hunt and Republican Tom Campbell was so close the courts had to finally decide the winner. At first Campbell seemed to have won by a mere thirty votes. But Hunt, dubbed by Will Rogers as "our perennial governor" and by others as "King George VII" because he occupied the office for seven terms, refused to concede.

Both men took the oath of office in separate ceremonies on January 1, 1917. Campbell operated from his home while Hunt remained in the capitol building. The state treasurer, a Democrat, refused to honor checks signed by Campbell. Hunt demanded a recount but it was ruled against by Supreme Court Judge Rawghlie Stanford (a fellow Democrat and later governor of the state). Stanford always believed Campbell had won fair and square. Still, Hunt stubbornly refused to surrender his beloved office. He was an old political warrior whose Horatio Algier-like career in Arizona began in the 1880s when he rode into Globe penniless and, by the turn of the century, was one of the wealthiest men in the territory. Hunt appealed to the State Supreme Court on grounds that many Arizonans had marked their ballots for a straight Democratic ticket, then voted for Campbell. That must have stuck in his craw because obviously his fellow Democrats were sending a message: they were voting for everyone in the party on the ballot except him. This time the high court ruled in favor of Hunt. Campbell had served in office a year without pay before "King George" came in officially and finished the term. Campbell later served two terms, 1919-1922, (governors served two-year terms in those days).

Only one other Republican won the governorship between 1912 and 1950. John C. Phillips was elected on the Hoover landslide in 1928. Phillips, ironically, once worked as a stone mason on the construction of the state capitol building. He served as chief of state for only one term. The stock market crash of 1929 made for a bad year for Republicans in 1930. George W. P. Hunt, now an old warhorse, returned for his seventh and last term. The vote was close, however; Hunt received 48,875 votes to 46,231 for Phillips.

Sidney P. Osborn was governor during World War II, one of the great transition periods in the state's history. Many historians consider him the best of the bunch since 1912. He is the only governor to be elected to four consecutive terms. Osborn, a native son, had deep roots in the history of Arizona. His grandfather, John Osborn, was one of the founders of Phoenix and his father, Neri, was a page in the first territorial legislature back in 1864 at Prescott. He was the youngest delegate to the Constitutional Convention in 1910 and, upon Arizona's admission to statehood, became the first secretary of state. In 1934 he ran for the U.S. Senate against Henry F. Ashhurst and lost. Osborn wasn't deterred by political defeat. He ran for governor three times and lost (1918, 1924 and 1938).

Tom Campbell, in his familiar cowboy hat, was a native Arizonan, born in Prescott. He lost a disputed election to George W. P. Hunt in 1918 but later served two terms as governor. Photo courtesy of the Arizona Historical Foundation

The fourth time was the charm. In 1940 he finally achieved a lifelong dream. His greatest achievement as governor was the ratification of the Colorado River Compact in 1944. Arizona had been the only one among the upper and lower basin states not to sign the 1922 Compact. He pointed out to the legislature that Arizona's right to the 2.8 million acre feet of water from the Colorado River would not be forthcoming until the state ratified the compact. The legislators agreed and the compact was approved, opening the way for the eventual construction of the Central Arizona Project.

The election of Howard Pyle in 1950 marked the beginning of the real bona fide two-party system in the state. The new industries brought on by World War II created a great influx of people from Republican midwestern states. The Republicans attracted popular candidates like Paul Fannin, Jack Williams, John Rhodes, and Pyle. Pyle, a popular radio personality, had as his campaign manager a venturesome young man named Barry Goldwater. Two years after helping Pyle win the governorship, Goldwater challenged Senator Ernest W. McFarland. McFarland was Senate Majority Leader at the time and was figured to be the odds-on favorite. Goldwater won in one of the most stunning upsets in Arizona history. Goldwater's open honesty and strong, charismatic personality, along with his conservative political views, made him a popular political figure throughout the nation. In 1964, he was the Republican party's nominee for president, the only Arizonan to ever reach such lofty political heights.

The Democratic party had been a powerful force in Arizona since the early days of the territory. However, most of the governors were Republican appointees from Washington. The legislature was elected by locals and, naturally, when the Arizonans drew up their constitution just prior to statehood, they weakened the governor's office considerably by taking away most of the executive appointive powers. Those restrictions kept the office mostly ceremonial until the 1970s under Jack Williams when many state government agencies were reorganized and grouped into "super" departments with directors appointed by the governor.

For the first half century following statehood, the Democrats controlled the legislature. This didn't help their fellow Democrats in the governor's office, however. Liberal governors such as Hunt battled continuously with conservative Democrats who frequently formed coalitions with Republicans, causing one political sage to comment that the state had "three parties—the Democrats, Democrats and Republicans." Facing little strong opposition from the Republicans, the Democrats frequently broke up into factions. Powerful business interests such as mining, cattle, agriculture, and the railroads had much greater influence with the legislature than the governor.

During the early years of statehood the Republicans, although a minority party, were fairly competitive in political races. However, the Republican party took the brunt of the blame for the Great Depression of the 1930s and, by 1942, nearly 90 percent of Arizonans were registered Democrats. In 1950, Howard Pyle had to overcome a nine-to-two registration disadvantage to win the governor's office. That same year the Democrats won all nineteen Senate seats and sixty-one of seventy-two House seats.

The rise of the Republican party from the early 1950s was dramatic to say the least. A mere thirty years later they had become the majority party in the state.

The 1966 "one-man, one vote" decision by the U.S. Supreme Court had, perhaps, the greatest impact on Arizona politics. State legislatures were required to reapportion districts to represent an equal number of people. In Arizona, the ruling apportioned fifteen senators and thirty representatives, or half the members to Maricopa County which had half the population. Pima County was given six senators and twelve representatives. The rest were divided among the rural counties. Prior to 1966 the rural counties could form formidable coalitions against Pima and especially Maricopa counties. A good example was in 1954 when the Senate was reapportioned to twenty-eight members, two from each county. Although Pima and Maricopa counties had over 70 percent of the population, the top three senate leadership positions were controlled by the rural counties.

Arizona has, by proud tradition, been well represented in Washington. In 1912, former Maricopa County Sheriff Carl Hayden was elected as the new state's only representative. Hayden was elected to the Senate in 1926 after seven terms in the House. He served another seven terms in the Senate before retiring in 1969. Hayden's fifty-seven years in Congress gave him the distinction of serving more years in that body than any other in American history. At the time of his retirement, Hayden was president *pro tempore* of the Senate and third in line for the presidency. He was a quiet man who accomplished great deeds for the state without much fanfare and hoopla. Colleagues referred to him as a "work horse" in contrast to the more visible "show horse" politicians. Hayden's crowning achievement and realization of a dream to his long service to the state was the approval of the Central Arizona Project in 1968. During the years of John F. Kennedy's presidency *Time* referred to the venerable senator as the "last link between the New Frontier and the real one." ◆

Gen. John Campbell Greenway is one of two Arizonans whose statues are in the Capitol Rotunda's Statuary Hall in Washington, D. C He rode with Teddy Roosevelt's Rough Riders in Cuba and was promoted for bravery at San Juan Hill. He came to Arizona in 1910 and wa involved in mining and railroading. He served in World War I and entered politics afterward. He might have become governor but died at the height of his career in 1926. Photo courtesy of the Arizona Historical Society/Tucson

Henry Fountain Ashurst was called in Washington, "the silver-tongued orator of the Colorado" or less respectfully "five Syllable Henry." He was a member of a northern Arizona ranching family and later served in the territorial Assembly. In 1911, Ashurst was elected one of the first senators from Arizona. He loved the classics and was an authority on Shakespeare. Ashurst, a dashing figure, was known in Washington as a "show-horse" while colleague Carl Hayden was the "work horse." Ashurst served in the senate until 1940. Photo courtesy of the Arizona Historical Society/Tucson

Lorna Lockwood (1903-1977) was the first woman to sit as chief justice of a state supreme court. Born in the Mexican border town of Douglas, Lorna graduated from high school at Tombstone in 1920. By 1925, she had graduated from law school at the University of Arizona. The only woman in her class, she was elected president of the Student Bar Association. Her father was on the state supreme court from 1925-1942 and was chief justice three times. When she was elected, she chose to occupy her father's old office and desk. Lorna was also a lawyer, legislator, and superior court judge for many years. Photo courtesy of the Arizona Hall of Fame

235

Gov. Franklin Roosevelt (hat in hand at left), Eleanor Roosevelt, Isabella Greenway, and Sen. Thomas Walsh, Sept. 28, 1932, at the Greenway ranch in Williams, Arizona. Isabella, the widow of Gen. John Greenway, was the only woman to represent Arizona in the U.S. Congress. Photo courtesy of the Arizona Historical Society/Tucson

Bob Jones won the governorship in 1938 with only 35 percent of the vote. That year, five Democrats vied in the primary. C. M. Zander, "the little general" and a member of Hunt's political machine was the favorite but was killed in a plane crash. Jones emerged the winner. At the time, there were more than 155,000 registered Democrats to some 20,000 Republicans. Winning the Democratic primary was tantamount to getting elected in those days. Jones served only one term before being defeated in the 1940 primary by Sidney P. Osborn. Photo courtesy of the Arizona Historical Foundation

Sidney P. Osborn is considered by many historians to be Arizona's best governor. He was the only one elected to four consecutive terms. He was at the helm during the turbulent World War II years that brought unprecedented change to the state. Photo courtesy of the Arizona State Library

Ana Frohmiller (1891-1971), a democrat, was the first woman to be nominated for governor but she lost a close race to Republican Howard Pyle in 1950. She had held public office since 1922, winning fourteen consecutive elections before running for governor. Ana was state auditor from 1927-1950 and was so popular with the public because of her reputation as a watchdog of the treasury that she didn't even campaign during her last six terms. Photo courtesy of the Arizona Hall of Fame

Howard Pyle was a popular radio personality before being elected governor in 1950. For years he broadcast on NBC the famous Easter sunrise service from the Grand Canyon. During World War II, Pyle was a war correspondent and was on the battleship Missouri *when the Japanese formally surrendered. Pyle, a Republican, was only the third governor from that party since statehood and his election marked the beginning of the two-party system in state politics. His campaign manager in 1950 was a young political novice named Barry Goldwater.* Courtesy of the Arizona Historical Foundation

Dan Garvey became governor upon the death of Sidney P. Osborn in 1948. A few months later, he was elected to the office. A mild-mannered, polite man, Garvey cared little for the political fighting that characterized many other Arizona governors and the legislatures. Photo courtesy of the Arizona Historical Foundation

Lewis W. Douglas was born in Bisbee in 1894. He was the scion of the illustrious Douglas family, prominent in banking and mining. In 1926, he was elected to Congress and in 1933 he resigned to become director of the budget bureau in Roosevelt's administration. In 1947, President Truman appointed him ambassador to England. Photo courtesy of the Arizona Historical Society/Tucson

Jacque Mercer became Arizona's first Miss America in 1949. Photo courtesy of Maricopa Community Colleges, Southwest Studies

This handsome river runner doing his laundry in the bottom of the Grand Canyon about 1939 is the future senator from Arizona, Barry M. Goldwater. Photo courtesy of the Arizona Historical Foundation

Goldwater served in the Army Air Force during World War II. After the war, he maintained an interest in flying and rose to the rank of major general in the Air Force Reserve. He loved to fly and logged flying time in every Air Force combat aircraft. While in the U.S. Senate, he founded the 9999th Air Force Reserve which included all Air Force reservists among congressmen, senators, and their staffs. Photo courtesy of the Arizona Historical Foundation

Ernest W. McFarland won a stunning upset victory over Henry F. Ashurst in 1940 for a Senate seat. From 1951-53 he was senate majority leader but was himself defeated by political newcomer Barry Goldwater in 1953. From 1955 to 1959, he was governor of Arizona and later served on the state supreme court. Mac is the only person to hold such lofty positions in the three branches of government. Photo courtesy of the Arizona Historical Society/Tucson

Republican John Rhodes was elected to Congress in 1953. He was elected to successive terms until his retirement in 1983. Rhodes was one of the most respected members of Congress during his career and in 1974 was elected house minority leader, replacing Gerald Ford. Photo courtesy of the Arizona Historical Foundation

A native of St. Johns, Morris (Mo) Udall grew up in the small Mormon community. He attended the University of Arizona where he starred in basketball. He later played professional basketball but opted for the practice of law. During World War II, he served three years in the South Pacific with the Army Air Corps. In 1961 he went to Washington as a member of Congress where he continues to serve. In 1976 he made a strong bid for the Democratic nomination for presidency before losing to Jimmy Carter. A popular speaker and master of the "mixed metaphor," he is one of Washington's most colorful politicians. Photo courtesy of the Arizona Historical Foundation

Jack Williams was born in Los Angeles, something he never forgave his parents for. "I was conceived in Arizona," he insists. A popular radio personality, his love for Arizona runs deep. In 1955 he was elected mayor of Phoenix. In 1966 he was elected to the first of three terms as governor. Jack lost his right eye to cancer when he was only six years old. Photo courtesy of Jack Williams

Paul Fannin's family owned a highly success-ful butane gas company. When the family sold the business in 1956, Paul, too young to retire, went into politics. He was elected in 1958 and went on to serve three terms. When Barry Goldwater ran for the presidency in 1964, Fannin was elected to Barry's Senate seat. He served in the U.S. Senate until his retirement in 1977. Photo courtesy of the Arizona Historical Foundation

Stewart Udall, brother of Mo, descended from a historic old Arizona family. Stewart served in Congress from 1955 to 1961. From 1961 to 1969 he was secretary of the interior, the first Arizonan to serve in a cabinet post. Photo courtesy of the Arizona Historical Foundation

Raul Castro and his bride, Patricia Morris, at San Augustine Cathedral, in Tucson, pose for a wedding picture. Castro was Arizona's only Hispanic governor. Born in Cananea, Sonora, Mexico, in 1916, the youngest of fourteen children, he came to Arizona as an infant. A lawyer and judge, in 1964 he was appointed ambassador to El Salvador. Four years later, he was moved to Bolivia.

As a youngster, he was raised in Pirtleville, a suburb of Douglas. He won honors at Douglas High School as a scholar and athlete. In college he was an undefeated middleweight boxer. After a distinguished career as county attorney, superior court judge, and foreign ambassador, he returned to Arizona. In 1974, he was elected as the state's first Hispanic governor. He resigned in 1977 to become ambassador to Argentina. Photo courtesy of the Arizona Historical Society/Tucson

Dennis DeConcini is a member of a family with a long history in government, law, and business. In 1972 he was elected Pima County attorney and quickly established himself as a crime fighter, especially against organized crime figures. In 1976 he was elected to the U.S. Senate following the retirement of Paul Fannin. Photo courtesy of Senator Dennis DeConcini

Sandra Day O'Conner sits atop Chico at the Lazy B Ranch near Duncan. Who would have guessed this little cowgirl would grow up to be the first woman on the United States Supreme Court? Incidentally, Sandra and the current Chief Justice, William Rehnquist, a fellow Arizonan, were also classmates at Stanford University. Photo courtesy of Sandra Day O'Conner

Polly Rosenbaum is one of the most respected members of the Arizona legislature. Her husband, William George Rosenbaum, served for many years as House Majority Leader and Speaker of the House. He died in 1950 and she was appointed to fill his unexpired term. She has been continuously elected since then. In 1982, the legislature honored her as "First Lady of the Arizona Legislature." Photo courtesy of Hon. Polly Rosenbaum

Gov. Bruce Babbitt, scion of the mercantile-ranching family, earned high marks during his nine year tenure and must be considered one of the best governors in the state's history. During Babbitt's administration the office of governor moved from mostly ceremonial to a high profile position. This was due to his adept leadership and prowess with the legislature.

Evan Mecham

by Marshall Trimble

The election of arch conservative Republican Evan Mecham to the office of governor initiated the most turbulent period in Arizona's political history. Mecham was a long-time political maverick, who'd gained most of his political notoriety by losing races. He'd unsuccessfully run for governor four times previously, and the U.S. Senate once. However, in 1986, he pulled off the state's most stunning political upset in the primary then went on to win a three-way race in the general election. To ardent Mecham supporters it looked like the dawning of a new era in Arizona government. Mecham's grass-roots, populist campaign of reform appealed to many. Once elected he would drive out the fat cats and return government to the people. He was one of them, he claimed, not another slick politician. The feisty, strong-willed governor-elect vowed to root out corruption and rid the state of the "ruling elite"—those he perceived as the few political and business nabobs who held tight control over state affairs. Mecham enthusiastically prepared to impose his program of reform on the state of Arizona. He declared war on drugs and organized crime. He claimed to owe no political debts, therefore, had no obligations to grant political favors. "Arizona is ready to get into the big time," he boldly declared.

Evan Mecham quickly learned, as others before him, there's more to running the statehouse than populist rhetoric. He and his administration came into office with an attitude of mistrust for government. They stubbornly refused to seek or accept help from state agencies, the legislature or the attorney general. Relations with the media quickly soured. In retrospect, it's not surprising his administration, with both feet firmly planted in mid-air, was in deep trouble early on. The Washington Street honeymoon was over before it even began. Within a few months Evan Mecham would find himself facing recall, impeachment from office and a criminal trial, something unprecedented in American history. Ironically, Arizona's most scandalous chief executive had campaigned on a platform of honesty, integrity, and lawfulness.

Evan Mecham was born and raised in a small rural Mormon community in Utah, where there were no blacks or homosexuals, and a woman's place was in the home rearing children. Deeply religious, he grew up espousing the time-honored conservative values of the Mormon church.

After World War II Mecham married and took up residence in Arizona, eventually opening an automobile agency in Glendale. In 1960 he was elected to the Arizona senate. Two years

Governor Evan Mecham on trial. In background is Judge Frank Gordon. This was the only time in United States history a state governor faced recall, impeachment, and criminal charges at the same time. Mecham was found guilty by the Arizona State Senate and removed from office. Photo courtesy of *Arizona Republic*

later he ran and lost in a race against the legendary Carl Hayden for the U.S. Senate. With the strong backing of ultra-right conservatives, he ran for governor in 1964. During the primary, Mecham's bitter personal attacks on members of his own party contributed to the Republican's loss in the general election to Democrat Sam Goddard. Mecham established himself as a maverick by continually lashing out at party leaders. Mecham ran again in 1974, 1978, and 1982 before finally pulling the brass ring in a three-way race in 1986. Although he garnered only 40 percent of the vote, Mecham was determined to impose his right-wing political philosophy upon all Arizonans. Had Mecham's personal style not gotten in the way he might have succeeded. He made himself readily available to the media but suffered from foot-in-mouth disease. For example, his first act as governor was to rescind the Martin Luther King Jr. holiday. The holiday may or may not have been created legally and Mecham could have declared it illegal on those grounds. However, he went on to say King didn't deserve a holiday, something that brought national attention to the state.

Eventually, his insensitive remarks managed to offend Hispanics, women, Jews, and Orientals.

Mecham's reluctance to work with the Republican-dominated legislature turned what should have been an amicable relationship to all-out war. He cut off lines of communication with all who disagreed with him, vetoed bills if the sponsor had done something to offend him, and failed to consult with GOP leaders on key decisions.

One of Mecham's greatest problems concerned the qualifications of a number of key appointees. Critics claimed many were chosen by cronyism or those of his ideological bent. Many didn't even meet the minimal requirements yet the governor stubbornly insisted they be hired.

In the months that followed, Mecham began to perceive his critics as part of a plot by organized crime and the "establishment" business and political leaders to derail him. Mecham entered office with an outsider's mistrust and as time went by the enemy list grew from a "few dissident Democrats and homosexuals" to include most of the legislature, the Department of Public Safety, the attorney general, the media, and anyone else bold enough to criticize him.

Mecham saw his "miracle" election as divinely inspired. He would save Arizona, and the nation from embracing socialism. His mission would be a "trial by fire." It was this strong faith that enabled him to resist criticism even from those who honestly sought to help him. His fellow-Mormons were divided on the issues. The church takes no official stand in politics, however, many members saw Mecham as chosen by God to lead. Mecham also claimed to be receiving guidance from the Almighty.

Other Mecham supporters embraced him as a downtrodden underdog. They represented an anti-media, anti-establishment, individualistic fringe who saw the monied cosmopolitan, progressive, "yuppie" society as the ultimate enemy.

Six months after taking office a recall movement was begun to remove Evan Mecham from office. The governor was his own worst enemy, adding fuel to the fire with careless, off-the-cuff remarks and controversial letters that sent throngs of citizens in search of petitions

Mecham trial in Arizona State Senate. Presiding judge, Frank Gordon, chief justice, Arizona Supreme Court. Defense attorneys: standing, facing camera, Jerris Leonard, sitting at table, Fred Craft. Photo courtesy of *Arizona Republic*

Rose Mofford of Globe was a star women's softball player in her younger days. In 1990 she will have completed a half century of public service to her native state. She was Secretary of State Wes Bolin's administrative assistant for many years. In the election following his death, she was elected secretary of state and is one of Arizona's most popular elected officials. Following the impeachment of Evan Mecham in early 1988, Rose Mofford assumed the role of governor of Arizona and is the first woman to serve in that position. Photo courtesy of Rose Mofford

to sign. By November 1987 enough signatures were declared valid that a recall election was called for the following May.

A recall by the voters turned out to be the least of Mecham's troubles after the story broke about a $350,000 illegal campaign loan under investigation by the attorney general. A few days later the House hired attorney William French to investigate the charges. In January, the attorney general indicted Mecham on six felony charges stemming from the loan. A week later, French reported his findings to the House. Included were two other charges: obstruction of justice and misuse of a protocol fund. After two weeks of hearings the House voted forty-six to fourteen to impeach the governor. The trial was moved over to the Senate and presided over by Frank Gordon, chief justice of the State Supreme Court.

On April 5, 1988, Mecham was found guilty on two of the three charges (a third was dropped). That same day Rose Mofford, secretary of state and acting governor since Mecham's impeachment on February 5, became governor, becoming the first woman in Arizona history to hold the office.

On June 16, a jury found Evan Mecham innocent on criminal charges of violating state campaign laws. However, the ex-governor continues to be a force to reckon with on the state political scene. ◆

Lupe Velez, center, and Earl Haley, assistant director, right, take a break at Castle Hot Springs, Arizona, where Cecil B. DeMille's third remake of Squaw Man *was on location in 1931. Haley is from Globe.* Photo courtesy of the Arizona Historical Society/Tucson

Andy Devine, native of Flagstaff, grew up in Kingman. He was one of Hollywood's most popular and enduring characters. Photo courtesy of the Mohave County Historical Museum

Luisa Ronstadt Espinel, great aunt of Linda Ronstadt, was quite a performer in her day, traveling around the country as a dancer, singer, and lecturer on music and dance. Circa 1920 photo courtesy of the Arizona Historical Society/Tucson

Hollywood "heavy" Jack Elam is a native of Globe and graduate of Phoenix Union High School. For some thirty-five years he has been one of Hollywood's best known character actors, playing every kind of character from bad man to comic westerner. Photo courtesy of Maricopa Community Colleges, Southwest Studies

Rex Allen of Willcox was the only one of Hollywood's legendary "singing cowboys" who was a real cowboy. Photo courtesy of Maricopa Community Colleges, Southwest Studies

Marty Robbins, native of Glendale, was one of country music's legends. His classic hit, "El Paso," was the first country song to win the coveted Grammy Award. Photo courtesy of Maricopa Community Colleges, Southwest Studies

Future Arizona historian and author Marshall Trimble, center, began his career as a folk singer in 1963 with a Kingston Trio clone group called "The Gin Mill Three." The other two group members are Tom Nelson, left, and Dan Nelson, both from California. Photo by G. K. Nelson, courtesy of the author

GIN MILL THREE

1963

Katie Lee of Tucson, one of the country's top folk music stars of the fifties, is also a river runner and author of a definitive book on cowboy songs called Ten Thousand Goddamn Cattle. Burl Ives once said of Katie: "The best cowboy singer I know is a girl—Katie Lee." Photo courtesy of the author

Travis Edmonson performs in 1963. Travis, a native of Nogales, was one half of the popular folk duo Bud and Travis. Photo courtesy of Travis Edmonson

Gail (right) and Delia Gardner of Prescott pose on the front porch of their home in the mid-1980s. Gail, Arizona's "poet laureate," was born in this same house in 1892. The former brush country cowboy has written hundreds of cowboy poems, including "Tyin' Knots in the Devil's Tail," "Dude Wrangler" and "Moonshine Steer." Delia is an "eastern girl" (born in New Mexico) who "wested" to Prescott. She was a pretty good cowlady in her day, too. Photo by the author

Storyteller and trail guide Bud Brown came to Arizona in the 1920s and over the past sixty-five years has gotten to know, first hand, every horse trail in Arizona. Bud and his wife, Isabelle, owned and operated Friendly Pines, a popular summer camp for youngsters in the mountains above Prescott. During the nation's bicentennial, he drove a Wagon team cross-country from Arizona to Washington, D.C., to participate in festivities at the Capital. Photo courtesy of Dave Darby

Cliff Garrett's first aircraft was a single-engine Spartan that he often personally piloted. It was the beginning of the corporate fleet and Airesearch Aviation Service, which became a major business for Garrett in the post-World War II years. The young entrepreneur ventured out on his own to form, on May 21, 1936, the Aircraft Tool and Supply. In 1988 the Garrett Companies merged with Allied-Signal Aerospace. Photo courtesy of the Garrett Corporation

Chapter 20

The Recent Years

Someday historians will divide Arizona's history into two parts: prior to World War II and after. The unprecedented growth that overwhelmed the state after World War II went far beyond the most optimistic (depending on one's point of view) predictions. Back in 1920, one far-sighted banker predicted that, if Phoenix kept growing at such a phenomenal rate, it would surely have a population of a hundred thousand by the year A.D. 2000.

The advent of air conditioning certainly made a remarkable difference in the quality of life in the desert regions. Earlier, folks beat the hot summer nights by moving their beds outside and wrapping themselves in a wet sheet. Lazy summer days were spent swimming in canals, irrigation ditches, or in public pools like Riverside Park in south Phoenix. People often ask long-time natives how they stood the searing summer heat before air conditioning. The stock reply is "We didn't know any better."

¿*Quien sabe?* A hundred years from now a giant dome may cover the entire Salt River Valley, keeping the temperature at a constant seventy-two degrees. Every Wednesday at 4:00 p.m. it will rain for twenty-five minutes, so plan your life accordingly. Then some wag will wonder how people stood it back in 1988. "Imagine," they'll ask, "how anyone could have lived back then." Any of us unlucky enough to still be around can stick our thumbs in our belts and proudly proclaim, "I reckon we just didn't know any better." In honor of that projected occasion, we might today consider erecting a monument to all the ladies who have climbed into an automobile on a hot summer day, in the parking lot of a shopping center, wearing a short skirt and have had to sit down on black vinyl seat covers. A century from now folks will be awed by such formidable courage.

Speaking of monuments, one should be built for Sam Lount who established the first ice plant in Phoenix back in 1879. The sight of an ice wagon meandering through the neighborhood meant immediate respite from the heat for generations of youngsters. They trailed along behind the ice wagon eagerly snatching small chunks of ice to chew on. There's no way of telling how much happiness and comfort Mr. Lount provided.

Those who could afford it went to California for the summer. Others sought a refuge from the heat in the cool climes around Prescott. The Santa Fe Railroad made a stop at Iron Springs, a small community nestled in the granite rocks west of Prescott. The place became a veritable "little Phoenix" in the summertime. Working husbands commuted, spending weekends with the family, then catching the Monday morning train for Phoenix.

A story is told by tattling old-timers that each August, Phoenix night spots like the bar at the Adams Hotel filled with husbands on the make. It was quite a windfall for indiscreet secretaries and grass widows desiring to be wined and dined. This hot time in the old town cooled considerably when air conditioners and swimming pools came on the scene and families began spending the summers at home. Summer nights in Phoenix became noticeably quieter.

World War II brought tens of thousands of soldiers and airmen into Arizona to train for combat overseas. The year-round mild weather was a prime factor, and bases were located from Kingman to Douglas. Between 1939 and 1945, nearly 150,000 Americans trained in Arizona. In addition, some 3,000 Chinese and nearly 150 British pilots earned their wings over the Arizona deserts.

Governor Evan Mecham received pilot training at both Luke and Williams Air Force bases before shipping out to Europe to fly P-38s in combat. He was shot down over Germany and held in a P.O.W. camp until U.S. troops entered Germany in the last days of the war. Like thousands of other servicemen, Mecham returned after the war to make his home in Arizona. Other military aviators were destined to play a major role in contemporary Arizona history. Along with Governor Mecham are such illustrious community and business leaders as Dr. Lincoln Ragsdale, Burton Barr, Milt Graham, Hugh and Frank Knoell, and the most famous flier of 'em all, Barry Goldwater.

Arizona's greatest hero in World War II was Army Pfc. Sylvestre Herrera of Phoenix. On March 15, 1945, his outfit was pinned down by German machine-gun fire. The guns were protected by minefields but that didn't stop young Herrera. Twice he mounted one-man assaults on the machine-gun nests. On the first assault, he captured eight enemy soldiers. In the second assault, a mine exploded and blew off both his feet. Herrera continued to fight, pinning down the German troops until his comrades were able to mount an attack. For his bravery, Herrera was awarded the Congressional Medal of Honor. He was the only Arizonan to win that coveted medal in the Second World War.

War-related industries poured into Arizona during the 1940s as manufacturing came in to help balance the state's economy which, up to that time, was primarily cattle, copper, and cotton. The Garrett Corporation located in Phoenix became one of the leaders in manufacturing parts for B-17 bombers. Today, Garrett still builds components for the government and commercial aerospace applications, employing thousands at the Garrett Turbine Engine Company, Garrett Airline Services, Garrett General Aviation Services, and Garrett Fluid Systems Company plants. In 1988 these companies merged with Allied-Signal Aerospace.

In 1941, Goodyear Aircraft Corporation established a large plant west of Phoenix to build main assemblies for combat aircraft. The company evolved into Goodyear Aerospace Corporation as a part of Goodyear Tire and Rubber. In 1987, the Aerospace Corporation was purchased by Loral Corporation and became Defense Systems Division—Arizona of Loral Systems Group. The plant, located at Litchfield Park, employs nearly two thousand people. During the war, Alcoa also built a plant in west Phoenix which was later sold to Reynolds Aluminum.

When the war ended, most of these corporations continued their operations in Arizona. Thousands of servicemen, sent here to train, returned after the war with their families to make their home. In 1949, Dan Noble opened the first of several Motorola plants in the Phoenix area, offering the state an even more balanced and diversified economy. Other corporations like General Electric, Hughes Aircraft, Sperry, Honeywell, and IBM followed and, by the 1960s, manufacturing had become the state's number one income-producing industry. Phoenix is today the nation's third largest high-tech area.

Another major reason for the state's population and economic growth was the adaptation of the great natural resources to the nation's changing needs and interests. Americans in the post-war era had more leisure time and more money to spend. Arizona possessed one of the country's three distinctive winter resorts and playgrounds. Tourism today pumps billions of dollars annually into the state's economy. It also provides more jobs than any other industry. Hard times seem to have less effect on tourism. One of the Salt River Valley's greatest resorts, the Camelback Inn, was built during the height of the Great Depression when tourism continued to flourish.

With the new industries came more people. In 1940, Scottsdale was a quaint little farm village of some 400 residents "way out east" of Phoenix. By 1950, it had grown to 2,000. Ten years later the census reported a population of over 10,000. A special count taken in 1965 gave a figure of over 55,000. By the later 1980s, well over 100,000 residents called Scottsdale home.

Company H, 158th Infantry of the Arizona National Guard carry on with a homemade facsimile of the new 81 mm. high angle mortar at a drill in Armory Park, Tucson, July 28, 1940. Photo courtesy of the Arizona Historical Society/Tucson

Soldiers drill at Fort Huachuca. Photo by J. Robert Burns, courtesy of the Arizona Historical Society/Tucson

The same story can be told on Glendale, Peoria, Tempe, Mesa, Chandler, and Gilbert. Communities like Sun City, Green Valley, Carefree, and Awatukee didn't even exist thirty years ago. Arizona's population has doubled every twenty years since 1920.

Why do they come? Most say it's for the lifestyle. Not long ago, the desert was perceived as a forbidding place with desiccating heat inhabited by uncurried cowboys, Indians, cactus, coyotes, rattlesnakes, and scorpions. Today, it means a laid-back lifestyle, wide open spaces, year-round sports and recreation, and spectacular scenery. The great majority of newcomers, contrary to popular belief, are well-educated, goal-oriented young people. They have much to contribute. One has every reason to be optimistic about the future of Arizona. Problems such as transportation and water and air pollution do exist along with social problems associated with a highly mobile and transient society. But these same problems also exist in other major metropolitan areas and they can be dealt with.

Arizona is, contrary to popular myth, an urban state. Over 85 percent of the people live in the greater Phoenix or Tucson areas. Take away Yuma, Sierra Vista, Prescott, and Flagstaff and you have a lot of wide-open space.

What makes the state so special is that, although most of the citizens live in cities, one can easily venture into pristine wilderness areas a short distance from where futuristic architecture merges with the broad southwestern sky. One can walk across lands that belong to everybody and nobody. Naturalist John C. Van Dyke gave a poetic defense of these precious sanctuaries in 1901 when he wrote, "The deserts should never be reclaimed, they are breathing spaces of the West and should be preserved forever." ◆

Mrs. Kenneth Andreson distributes "doughnuts for doughboys" to National Guardsmen on their way to training at Fort Sill, Oklahoma. Photo courtesy of the Arizona Historical Society/Tucson

Nearly five thousand Tucsonans crowded local streets and the railroad station September 25, 1940, to bid farewell to three hundred National Guardsmen of the 158th Infantry off for training at Fort Sill, Oklahoma. Photo courtesy of the Arizona Historical Society/Tucson

Future Arizona historian Marshall Trimble stands ready to defend the homefront at the tender age of three in 1942. Photo courtesy of the author

Offering their services on December 10, 1941, to the U.S. Army Air Corps at the University of Arizona are Jim Benedict, Myron Mershon, Bill Breckam, Sam Benedict, Bill Smetana, John Root, Ray Rainville, and Master Sergeant James Nosvody. Photo courtesy of the Arizona Historical Society/Tucson

Scrap destined for recycling to aid the war effort spills over this vacant lot in Tucson during a scrap drive in October 1942. Photo courtesy of the Arizona Historical Society/Tucson

Girls of the Veterans Hospital of the A.W.V.S. in Tucson roll in the last of the scrap rubber to be collected by them. Photo courtesy of the Arizona Historical Society/Tucson

The Tucson Pilot club devised a creative campaign to aid the war effort. Photo courtesy of the Buehman collection, Arizona Historical Society/Tucson

Ira Hays became a U.S. Marine hero during World War II. This Pima Indian from Bapchule was one of those who raised the flag at Iwo Jima on February 23, 1945. The famous photograph brought both fame and misfortune to Hays.

After the war Hays returned home a hero, for reasons he never quite understood. He turned to alcohol and his drinking escapades were always front-page copy in the newspaper. One morning in January 1955, his body was found in an irrigation ditch near his reservation home. Hay's tragic life has been memorialized both in song, "The Ballad of Ira Hays," and movie, The Outsider. Photo courtesy of Maricopa Community Colleges, Southwest Studies

At Papago Park German P.O.W. Camp on a cold and rainy Christmas Eve in 1944, twenty-five German prisoners escaped through a 400-foot tunnel that had taken three months to dig. They scattered into various parts of southern Arizona. Several made it to downtown Phoenix Union High School and holed up in the furnace room to stay warm. Three quickly surrendered to escape the inclement weather. Another pair surrendered to a Tempe housewife. Others were rounded up in the desert as they tried to make their way to Mexico. Capt. Jurgen Wattenberg, the leader, was the last to be captured thirty-five days after the "great escape," the largest

P.O.W. escape in the United States during World War II. Wattenberg hid in a cave near Squaw Peak in North Phoenix. He was captured on January 28, 1945, when he walked into downtown Phoenix and asked for directions (to Mexico?). His German accent aroused suspicion and the captain was returned to Papago Park. In 1984 a reunion was held at the prison camp, and many of the ex-P.O.W.s, including Captain Wattenberg, returned to Arizona for the ceremonies. Photo courtesy of Maricopa Community Colleges, Southwest Studies

These Navajo Code Talkers, part of the U.S. Marines, saved countless American lives during the intense jungle island-hopping campaigns in the South Pacific. They were escorted by white marines lest other U.S. troops mistake them for infiltrators in American uniforms. The Japanese were never able to break the code designed by the Navajo to transmit battle plans. U.S.M.C. photo

Ida Redbird (1892-1971) was a famous Maricopa Indian potter. Most of her life was spent on the Gila River Reservation. Her distinctive pottery was coveted by museums and private collectors alike. Other Maricopa potters followed her example and today this beautiful pottery is known throughout the world. Photo courtesy of the Arizona Hall of Fame

His success as a Phoenix businessman was still in the future when Lincoln Ragsdale was stationed at Luke Field during World War II. He came to Arizona in 1945 to train as a young Army Air Corps fighter pilot. After the war, he returned to make his home in Arizona. Dr. Ragsdale is president of Valley Life and Casualty Insurance Company, International Investment Company, and Universal Memorial Centers of Phoenix. Since 1981 Ragsdale has been one of ten advisors to President Ronald Reagan on small and minority businesses. Photo courtesy of Dr. Lincoln Ragsdale

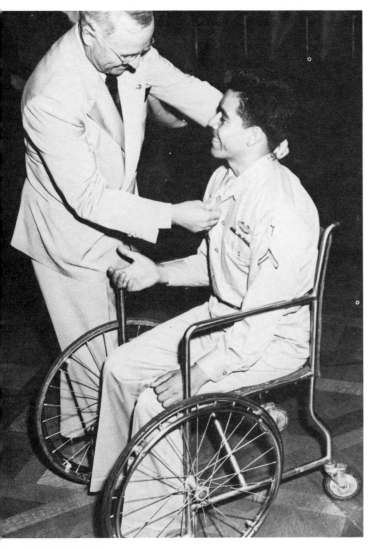

President Harry S. Truman congratulates Army Pfc. Sylvestre Herrera in ceremonies at the nation's capital. Herrera was the only Arizonan to win the Medal of Honor in World War II. Photo courtesy of the Arizona Hall of Fame

Carl Gorman of Chinle keeps a lookout on Saipan. Today he is a well-known artist and the father of artist R. C. Gorman. U.S.M.C. photo

Airplanes motor down the street in Safford, Arizona, in what has to be one of the most unusual parades in "cow country." Photo by Charles W. Herbert, courtesy of the Arizona Historical Society/Tucson

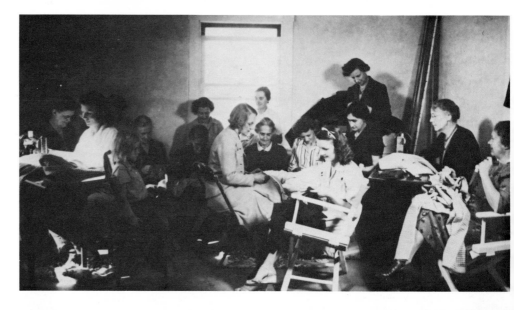

Volunteers in Tucson work on "bundles for Britain." Photo courtesy of the Arizona Historical Society/Tucson

Six Tucson women are sworn in to the Women's Army Air Corps by Lt. Roberta House. They are (left to right) Dorothy Freeman, Elsie Spieden, Mary Samoyoa, Janette Arbie, Hope Gotham, and Shirley Angel. Photo courtesy of the Arizona Historical Society/Tucson

The Green Guards of America drill in Tucson on March 16, 1941, with tools lent by W.P.A. workers. Their hope was to eventually drill with real rifles. The Works Projects Administration was created during the Great Depression to provide jobs on public projects. Photo courtesy of the Arizona Historical Society/Tucson

Lake Havasu City

Robert F. McCulloch, Sr., was a twentieth-century visionary and entrepreneur reminiscent of those enterprising men of a century ago who developed mining ventures and irrigational oases in the arid wilderness.

Back in the late 1950s, McCulloch was flying above the Colorado River in western Arizona looking for a place to test the outboard motors his company produced. Perched on a small desert peninsula jutting out into Lake Havasu was an old World War II emergency air strip. McCulloch liked the site and through some smart wheeling and dealing was able to purchase the piece of land for about seventy-five dollars an acre. He later claimed to have envisioned a new city at the foot of the picturesque Mohave Mountains the moment he first laid eyes on the site.

Next, he teamed up with a Texan named C. V. Wood, whose major claim to fame was being the creative genius who developed the original Disneyland. The dynamic duo were a perfect match to create this new jewel in the desert. "Lake Havasu is McCulloch's baby," someone noted, "but Wood is the guy who spanked it and made it breathe." The dream started to become reality in the fall of 1960 when McCulloch flew Wood over the site and said, "Let's build a city." The rest is history. In 1980, the *Los Angeles Times* wrote: "This city of 16,000 on the 'West Coast' of Arizona is arguably the most successful free-standing new town in the United States...."

What really put Lake Havasu City on the map was the acquisition of a London Bridge in 1968. It is only fitting that, in this land of startling contrasts, the strangest of all should occur.

Legend has it that McCulloch went to France and tried to buy the Eiffel Tower. Predictably, the French told him where to go. So he went to Italy and offered to purchase the Leaning Tower of Pisa. He got the same response from the Italians. He tried the same thing in England. "Boy, have we got a deal for you," the British exclaimed enthusiastically. The venerable bridge on the Thames with bullet-riddled piers from Luftwaffe gunners in World War II was unable to stand up under modern day traffic and had to be replaced. McCulloch offered $2,460,000, "a thousand dollars for each year of your age," and the British accepted.

The bridge was dismantled, the bricks numbered and hauled by sea to Los Angeles and then by truck to Lake Havasu City. The bridge was reconstructed, brick by brick, and a mile-long channel was cut through the peninsula creating a flow beneath the bridge for boat traffic. On October 10, 1971, the bridge was formally dedicated in the Arizona desert. Appropriately, the Lord Mayor of London, Sir Peter Studd, was in attendance.

Today, the spectacular London Bridge in Lake Havasu City is second only to the Grand Canyon as a tourist attraction in Arizona. ◆

Lake Havasu is spanned by a London Bridge. During the 1960s a new city rose in the desert country along the Colorado River in western Arizona. Robert McCulloch, developer of Lake Havasu City, purchased a London Bridge for $2,460,000 *in the 1960s and had it shipped more than ten thousand miles to Arizona where it was reconstructed and dedicated on October 10, 1971.* Photo courtesy of Lake Havasu City Chamber of Commerce

One World War II "Rosie the Riveter" was Elene Wiltbank of Phoenix who, prior to the war, had been a cowhand on an Arizona cattle ranch. Photo courtesy of the Garrett Corporation

Anna Moore Shaw (1898-1976) was born on the Gila Indian Reservation and was educated at Phoenix Indian School and Phoenix Union High School. She married Ross Shaw, a Pima-Maricopa, and although the couple made their home in Phoenix, she never forgot her Pima heritage. In 1968, she wrote Pima Indian Legends, *a classic work on her people.* Photo courtesy of the Arizona Hall of Fame

Pfc. Oscar Austin, U.S. Marine Corps, was awarded the Congressional medal of Honor posthumously for heroism in the Vietnam War. Photo courtesy of the Arizona Hall of Fame

Lance Cpl. José F. Jiminez, U.S. Marine Corps, was awarded the Congressional Medal of Honor posthumously for heroism in the Vietnam War. Jiminez was born in Mexico and raised in Arizona. Photo courtesy of the Arizona Hall of Fame

Army Pfc. Billy Lauffler was awarded the Congressional Medal of Honor posthumously for heroism in the Vietnam War. Photo courtesy of the Arizona Hall of Fame

Marine Lt. Jay Vargas of Winslow and his family met with President Richard Nixon during the presentation of his Congressional Medal of Honor. Photo courtesy of the Arizona Hall of Fame

Staff Sgt. Nicky Bacon receives congratulations from President Richard Nixon following ceremonies at which he was awarded the Congressional Medal of Honor. Photo courtesy of the Arizona Hall of Fame

CWO Fred Ferguson points out the bullet hole in his helicopter near the cockpit. Ferguson won the Medal of Honor during the Vietnam Tet Offensive in 1968 when, despite heavy enemy fire, he made a daring rescue of a downed crew. Photo courtesy of the Arizona Hall of Fame

These Arizona ranch brands were found carved in an abandoned adobe ranch house. Photo by the author

Joe Beeler, Charlie Dye, John Hampton, George Phippen, and Robert McLeod, left to right, meet at Sedona's Oak Creek Tavern in 1966 to formally organize the Cowboy Artists of America. Photo by Elizabeth Rigby.

At the CO Bar Ranch, cowboys can still be found "ropin' and draggin' 'em to the fire." Photo by the author

Pioneer, Arizona, is a living museum outside Phoenix. Photo by the author

The Cedar Mesa Ranch north of Flagstaff boasts the oldest barn still in use in northern Arizona. Photo by the author

Old Route 66, east of Flagstaff. Photo by the author

The grave of gunslinger Johnny Ringo stands beside tree-shaded Turkey Creek. This is also the spot where his body was found in 1882. Photo by the author

Old Tucson. Photo by the author

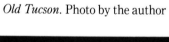

The Hubbell Trading Post. Photo by the author

Winter blankets the White Mountains of Pindale, site of the only covered carriage bridge in the state Photo by Gary M. Johnson

The cavalry stables at old Fort Rucker in the Chiricahua Mountains, still stand. Photo by the author

The grave of Mollie Williams in the Swisshelm Mountains of Cochise County. She was the girlfriend of gunfighter Buckskin Frank Leslie. In a jealous rage, he shot her to death and spent several years in the Yuma Territorial Prison for the crime. Photo by the author

Canyon Diablo at sundown. Photo by the author

Old Tombstone. Photo by the author

Dan Trimble's unique two-story house made of railroad ties at the Golden Reef Mine north of Cave Creek. It was over a century old the day it was completed. Photo by the author

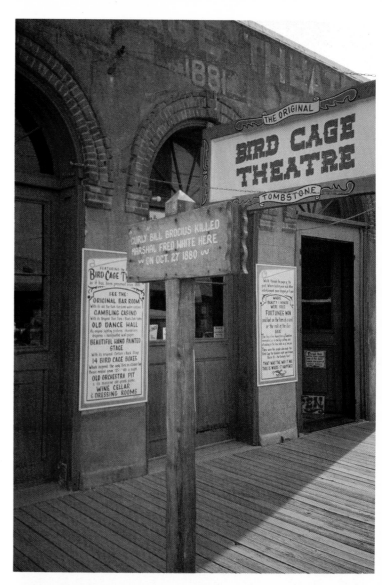

The Lost Dutchman Monument at Apache Junction. Photo by the author

This statue, near the Prescott courthouse, pays tribute to Rough Rider "Buckey" O'Neill. The names of all the Rough Riders are engraved on a plaque at the base of the statue by artist Solon Borglum, one of the finest examples of equestrian statuary in America. Photo by Gary M. Johnson

The assayer's office at the Jerome State Mining Museum displays some of the tools of his trade. Photo by Gary M. Johnson

A rodeo clown is part of the show at the Parada del Sol Rodeo. Photo by Gary M. Johnson

The flag bearer at the Parada del Sol signals the beginning of festivities. Photo by Gary M. Johnson

The Sawdust Festival in Payson features lumberjack competition events which include ax throwing, tree topping, and log rolling. Pictured are the Ponderosa pine poles set in place for the pole climb. Photo by Gary M. Johnson

A saddle bronc rider tries his luck. Photo by
Gary M. Johnson

*The House of Joy Restaurant in the ghost town
of Jerome was once a bordello and bawdy house.
It is now a gourmet restaurant. This picture,
taken at dusk, captures a tourist petting the
ghost of a cat.* Photo by Gary M. Johnson

*The Orange Tree Resort was built in the style of
traditional Spanish architecture.* Photo by
Gary M. Johnson

*Jeff Hengesbaugh is one of the nation's most
respected modern day mountain men. He made
up his mind to become one as a youngster after
seeing the movie, Davy Crockett. In the early
1970s, he led a three-man expedition from
southern Arizona to Calgary, Alberta, Canada.
The trio rode horseback and lived off the land
on a journey of several hundred miles. Since
then Hengesbaugh has led larger groups along
historic trails of the mountain men throughout
the West.* Photo courtesy of Jeff Hengesbaugh

Bessie Mike, a Yavapai basket maker, is among a vanishing breed of artists at old Fort McDowell, northeast of Scottsdale. Courtesy of Maricopa Community Colleges, Southwest Studies

The Jokake Inn is a renowned Arizona resort. Photo by Gary M. Johnson

Lightning illuminates the Papago Buttes in Phoenix. Photo by Gary M. Johnson

Dolan Ellis is the official balladeer of Arizona. Photo by Gary M. Johnson

The Western Savings Building in Mesa is a well-known landmark. Photo by Gary M. Johnson

The Hyatt Regency in Phoenix. Photo by Gary M. Johnson

A sunset in Phoenix paints the town. Photo by Gary M. Johnson

"Mama, don't let yer babies grow up to be cowboys." Photo by the author

Index